The Image-Interface

Digital Tools and Uses Set

coordinated by
Imad Saleh

Volume 3

The Image-Interface

*Graphical Supports for
Visual Information*

Everardo Reyes-Garcia

WILEY

First published 2017 in Great Britain and the United States by ISTE Ltd and John Wiley & Sons, Inc.

ISTE Ltd
27-37 St George's Road
London SW19 4EU
UK

www.iste.co.uk

John Wiley & Sons, Inc.
111 River Street
Hoboken, NJ 07030
USA

www.wiley.com

Library of Congress Control Number: 2017952099

British Library Cataloguing-in-Publication Data
A CIP record for this book is available from the British Library
ISBN 978-1-78630-062-1

MIX
Paper from
responsible sources
FSC
www.fsc.org   FSC® C013604

Contents

Preface

This book studies interfaces as images and images as interfaces. By interfaces, I mean specifically graphical user interfaces; the systems which we use to interact with information displayed on an electronic support.

My interest on this topic has grown over the years and it reflects both personal motivations and professional work as a teacher and researcher. As someone who has always been fascinated with technological objects (I remember as a child programming a VCR, discovering how to change the time in an LCD watch and climbing to the rooftop to redirect the TV antenna), I think one of the best ways to approach a domain is to "touch it", to do things with it, either under special supervision or under our own risks. I hope this book will provide inspiration to the reader in producing his/her own examples and prototypes, either by hand or with software applications or with computer code.

I have had the opportunity to discuss many of the topics included in this book with colleagues and students. I learned a lot about computer graphics and 3D software while serving as a program director of the BA in Animation and Digital Art at Tecnológico de Monterrey in Toluca, Mexico. Later, I could appreciate the intricacies of web design and human–computer interaction for the web when I was appointed as a program director of the MA Interface Design at Université Paris 13. More recently, data culture, data visualization, digital humanities, semiotics, cultural analytics and software studies appear on a daily basis at the heart of my current professional family at Université Paris 8.

I want to extend my thankfulness to colleagues and students around the world who have kindly invited me or deposited their trust in me to collaborate somehow. Friends in Mexico at Tecnológico de Monterrey, UAEMex, Centro Multimedia, CENART, UAM Xochimilco; in USA at Cultural Analytics Lab and UCLA; in Belgium at Université de Liège; in Italy at Università di Torino; in UK at King's College and Winchester School of Arts; in Sweden at Lund University; in France at médialab Sciences Po Paris, ENS Paris, ENSAD, MSH Paris Nord, IEA Paris, MESHS Lille, Université Paris 3 Sorbonne Nouvelle; in Brazil at UFRJ; in Spain at Universidad de Castilla La Mancha; in Argentina at Universidad Nacional de La Plata and Universidad de Buenos Aires. I hope we all meet together at the same space and time one of these days.

Everardo REYES-GARCIA
August 2017

Introduction

This book is situated within the period of time that has been influenced by the information age. The time span has developed from the invention of digital computers to the contemporary scene of massive generation and storage of data. From the standpoint of information and communication studies, this period of time is deeply related to electronic media. In this book, we understand *data* as digital information and *electronic media* as the means to access and make sense of it.

In our present study, we are interested in a particular modality of electronic media: the graphical mode. Although most of the physical world perceptible to human senses has been simulated and described with electronic media (sounds, smells and tastes can all be quantified and stored as bits and bytes for a latter representation), the vast majority of developments in electronic media have taken place in visual form. We look at the computer screen as the main material support where digital information is represented in order to convey meaning. Nowadays, screens have become pervasive. We see and interact with them in laptop and smartphone displays, in desktop monitors, as beamer projections, in LED displays in elevators, city signage, museum exhibitions, park attractions, airports and public transportation. Screens can be public or private and shared or intimate (such as head-mounted displays).

The kinds of images depicted in computer screens are closely related to the display technologies that underlie them. As computing power increases, for instance, supporting more complex and multiple tasks, larger files or higher resolutions, the look and style of images reflect on those advances. Consider the differences between a 1980s videogame graphics and today's consoles. Or let us evoke the first computer animations that were used in music video clips to compare them with today's amateur and blockbuster films. The World Wide Web has also witnessed this evolution. The first images supported by web browsers are not the same in quality and resolution if we consider recent developments in technologies such as CSS3 and WebGL. What we can observe in all these cases is foremost a quest for realism and hyperrealism. Technicians and artists have devoted great efforts to make images look "more real", i.e. to represent the physical world with more detail, with the highest possible similarity.

But at the same time, there is another kind of image in electronic media. In order to produce those realistic images, creators use the same computer screen in a different manner. They use graphical interfaces. Whether the authoring software is based on user interface elements such as windows, icons, menus, pointers, or uses a command-line console, it is the same rectangular space of the screen that is redrawn to allow the interaction between data and meaning.

We are interested in studying the computer graphical interface as an image. For that matter, we have to take a step back from the representation of "realistic" images. Graphical interfaces are visual supports of information and we look at the way in which the interfaces are constructed to convey meaning. Throughout the history of computing, the community of researchers in human–computer interaction (HCI) has developed models based on cognitive and linguistic capacities in order to describe efficient ways to create graphical interfaces. Our study intends to contribute to the domain by relating interfaces to images. In other words, it is about regarding the visual constituents of interfaces before and at the moment they are identified as interfaces.

To illustrate our purpose, it is possible to list some visual constituents that exist not only in interfaces but also in any other visual form of image. Following the theoretical tradition of visual semiotics, we can talk about plastic categories: colors, forms and textures. For each category, there are smaller units of analysis (colors can be described according to numerical values of saturation, brightness, "redness", "greenness" and "blueness"). It is interesting to note that, when we describe a picture or an interface, we can establish the relationships between units at the same granularity level or we can reassemble them in other semantic units. Imagine, for this case, that the position of forms in an image motivates the perception of vectors of direction, by means of graphical abstraction and Gestalt principles. Hence, we could now examine "vector" patterns in different images, for example.

Studying interfaces as images means that there is a visual meaning behind the construction of any authoring and exploring environment. Whereas one of the main influences of HCI in everyday interfaces can be perceived through the WIMP paradigm (Windows Icons Menus Pointers), it is necessary to broaden this perspective. Authoring software has a long tradition that builds on reading–writing schemes. The pioneering research on hypertext systems during the 1960s – long before the invention of the World Wide Web – introduced models for nonlinear writing and reading. Among such models, we may cite the relational, the taxonomical and the spatial.

While the first authoring environments were mainly conceived for textual content, the introduction of different types of media came with an explosion of paradigms and visions. With the support for images, video and audio, creators could now explore storytelling in different ways. However, it was necessary to think about new metaphors to signify actions on abstract objects: to link, to import, to animate, to copy, to delete and to paste. Closely related to graphical interfaces, there is also the development of programming languages and programming paradigms. Starting from declarative and functional languages, we then saw the emergence of generative and object-oriented languages. The syntax is, of course, a visual matter. The kind of programming marks, such as dots, commas, brackets and curly brackets, is a way to represent dependencies, inheritances and encapsulations of data. It is not surprising that more recent graphical programming languages were introduced: boxes connected to other objects by means of links and edges.

As it occurs with photographs and paintings, an interface as image can be approached as a diagram, symbol, index or other category of sign. The image of an interface conveys in itself the traces of its production. It is possible to relate the operative system, the authoring software and the complexity or simplicity of functionalities. It is also a symbol of its time: the visions foreseen to be accomplished with electronic media; the ideologies associated with such productions. Interfaces, through language and affordances, are meta-images of enunciation that speak to their users, in a similar instance as mirrors, reflections, windows and depictions of the painter inside the painting.

Today, any user of electronic devices can take photographs, add visual effects, edit them, share them and comment on them. The new user has become a sort of media producer. Graphical interfaces have become easier to use, at least at their basic level. While we can study the evolution and the effect of portable devices in the esthetics of social images, we are more interested in: how do designers produce and distribute data and images? Which functionalities are integrated and which ones are left behind? How are our new images and interfaces shaping the emerging post-digital culture?

Designers in the information age are expected to invent new ways to explore information and to make sense of data in environments that change constantly. As it happened to pioneers of authoring systems, designers need to investigate new metaphors, new platforms, new actions that are possible with digital and networked technologies. In this context, designers and developers have embraced the World Wide Web as a privileged environment to create and distribute their creations. The technological possibilities of the contemporary web, along with the development of computing devices, allow experimenting with and dreaming about such new models. The tradition of multimedia authoring systems converges today with massive quantities of social and historical data. The kind of interfaces that designers produce is related to reading–writing software in the sense that they are interactive, they support explorations, discoveries and insights that might have passed unattended otherwise. Designers are like image craftsmen because they take decisions about visual composition, arrangements and metaphors. Moreover, they must reflect on the potential outcomes of the interface: the kind of data, format and media, the parameters that can be modified, the series of actions that a user can perform, the pertinent vocabulary, language and syntax, etc.

While common users have increasing access to cameras and image editing software, designers have a wide variety of production tools at their hands. Some research is necessary to investigate the kind of software available (desktop, mobile apps and web apps) as well as programming languages, APIs and libraries that handle data and communicate with the ever-changing environments. Although many software and production tools are developed with a particular objective in mind, it is interesting to see that tools can be mixed and remixed. While the material support remains constant (the screen), it is when we pay attention to its configurations that innovations take place.

Thus, where we position our study design will be neither a specific discipline nor a bunch of recipes and ready-made toolkits to add visual effects or improve the visual style of a project. Design will be understood as a way of life. It is more like a reflective thinking posture about our practices in order to produce new kinds of explorations and actions. It is about questioning defined models to propose unexpected schemes. It is about producing meaningful tools that communicate aptly in the context in which they function. It is about going beyond the pre-defined figure of a "user" and to consider her/him/them as "visitors", "wanderers", "researchers", "learners" and "meaning-makers". It is about taking seriously and responsively the work of tool-making; to remember that through our work, we are also shaping ways of being (as it was suggested by Winograd and Flores [WIN 86, p. ix]).

As we said, screens have become pervasive; they are material supports of representations. But at the same time, the screen is alive; it reconfigures itself as formal support. The computer screen is today's canvas of painters, designers, researchers and students in information and communication. Interfaces are the pervasive kind of images of the information age.

Contents of the book

Chapter 1 compiles relevant insights forged within the tradition of sciences, humanities and media studies about the study of images. Although this book is not about interpreting cultural images, it does take into account research that pays attention to material and technological descriptions of images. This is important because we will identify levels of analysis and methodologies that in other chapters will be used as strategies to design and produce visual interfaces. In this respect, a brief discussion regarding the notion of interface is also contemplated.

Chapter 2 is devoted to the foundations of graphical information. In this part, we consider images as data and digital information. We look at the technical aspects that define a digital image: from data types and data structures required to render an image on the computer screen to seminal algorithms and image processing techniques.

Chapter 3 adopts a pragmatic perspective towards image-interfaces; it studies how image-interfaces are practiced, observing the different manners in which those elements are put together, notably through software applications. This chapter is organized into different categories according to practices of imaging, for example, image editing, parametric design, and also writing and web environments. As long as we talk about image-interfaces, we are not only concerned with the results of some software manipulation, but also with the graphical elements that accompany the user to achieve such transformations.

Chapter 4 pays special attention to those cases where the image being manipulated acts as the graphical interface. It deals with multidisciplinary fields at the crossroad of several disciplines, such as graphic design, data science, computer science and humanities. The kinds of results that are produced from these perspectives include data visualization, networks, graphs, infographics, cultural analytics and data art.

Chapter 5 presents our own productions and experiments created within the context of image-interface and data visualization. It covers a range of prototypes, screen shots and sample codes for scripting software applications, integrating data and media visualization, and extending the generated images beyond the screen, to "data physicalization" via 3D printing.

The conclusion points to perspectives that still have little or recent exposition to information sciences. The term "visual hacking" is used to make reference to speculative advances in image-interfaces inspired by the non-visible electromagnetic spectrum, non-Euclidean geometry, obfuscated code and exotic data structures, and critical and radical design. Finally, the appendix section summarizes the software applications in the form of tables, which are discussed in Chapter 3. It also includes the tables of JavaScript libraries, web links to data visualizations and tools.

1

Describing Images

This chapter explores relevant insights about the study of images that have been forged within the sciences, humanities, and media studies traditions. Although this book is not about interpreting images, it does take into account research that focuses on material and technological descriptions of images. This is important because we will identify levels of analysis and methodology which in other chapters will be used as strategies to design and produce visual interfaces. In this respect, a brief discussion regarding the notion of interface is also contemplated.

1.1. Light, visual perception and visual imagery

Where do images come from? Where do they take place? Before images are printed or displayed on a computer screen, they are physical and psychological phenomena. A brief account of the processes underlying the formation of images will illuminate the perceptual and cognitive approaches that will inform further sections of this book.

On the one hand, visual perception puts attention on the physical and material aspect of vision. It occurs in the eye and its organic layers. The physical explanation of vision starts when light stimulates the retina. From there, different photoreceptor cells, mainly rods and cones, process signals and send information to the region of the brain called the primary visual cortex. On the other hand, visual imagery is related to mental experiences of representation and simulation; it occurs in the brain. Henceforth, the explanation moves to the domain of cognitive sciences. The cortex identifies basic visual features and redirects information according to two pathways:

visual properties (shape, color) and spatial movement properties (location and motion).

Vision and imagery cooperate whenever we interact with images depicted on the computer screen. As we will note, we do not only perceive and explore visual constituents of images but also think about different things at the same time: maybe a mental scheme of the interface, a subjective critique of design decisions, a memory evoked by a picture, or even our grocery list or plans for the next weekend.

1.1.1. *Physical light*

Light is what allows visible sensation. It is worth starting our account on visual media by considering some physical conditions of light as they have been postulated by sciences. This section will be useful to review basic concepts, properties, units of measure, and applications derived from the study of light.

Optics is the branch of physics concerned with the phenomena of light, particularly its propagation and image formation [TAI 13, p. 485]. Broadly speaking, optics has three subdomains, each one describing light differently: geometrical, wave, and quantum optics.

For geometrical optics, light is understood as a series of rays or beams. Here, the object of interest is not really the physical properties of light, but rather the "controlled manipulations of rays by means of refracting and reflecting surfaces" [HEC 05, p. 156]. The light that arrives from the Sun, for example, crosses the atmosphere, which is composed of air molecules that conform the density of the medium. Light particles interact with these molecules at different moments and angles, varying its diffusion: lateral diffusion produces the blue of sky; low diffusion, when the Sun is closer to the horizon, the red-orange of dusk; and, after 18 degrees below the horizon line, the black of night. This optical phenomenon is also referred to as Rayleigh scattering.

When the light hits more solid substances than air, it is said to be refracted and/or reflected. The former specifies the change of direction as the light traverses a substance. The latter occurs when the light is returned or bounced off the surface. More precisely, reflection can be of two kinds: specular (when the reflecting surface is smooth, creating a mirror image) and diffuse (when light bounces off in all directions). In the natural world, both phenomena rarely occur in pure manner; the correct behavior lies somewhere between the two [HEC 05, p. 103].

For our purposes, geometrical optics will be further evoked regarding its applications: it has been an integral part of the development and understanding of optical systems (human's eye, glasses, magnifying glasses, binoculars, microscopes, camera lenses, and telescopes); it also provides explanations for peculiar optical phenomena in nature (mirages, rainbows, halos, shadows, etc.)[1], and it has informed the development of software for computer graphics (such as 3D projection techniques like ray tracing).

For wave optics, light is studied as radiation, that is, as energy transmitted in the form of waves. In this respect, signals can be described as a spectrum consisting of frequencies (times per occurrence measured in Hertz, where 1 Hz equals one oscillation per second) and wavelengths (distance between repetitions of the shape measured in meters). From this perspective, light waves are part of the larger electromagnetic spectrum, which includes other types of radiation: gamma, X-ray, ultraviolet, visible light, infrared, T-ray, microwaves, and radio waves.

Visible radiation can be perceived by the human eye and analyzed according to the visible spectrum. It identifies approximate wavelengths for spectrum colors, going from violet (400–450 nm), blue (450–500 nm), green (500–580 nm), yellow (580–590 nm), orange (590–620 nm) and red (620–700 nm) [TAI 13, p. 635]. The other types of radiation can be detected or generated with special instruments, although they are not always of an optical nature.

Wave optics investigates the superposition of waves mainly through polarization, interference and diffraction. The first takes advantage of the fact that natural light waves oscillate in multiple directions, and therefore it is possible to filter and change the direction of the electromagnetic field. Famous cases where we see applications and types of polarized images are in stereoscopy using 3D glasses, photography lens filters, and liquid crystal displays (LCD). Interference and diffraction use barriers and slits of different shapes (rectangular, circular, single and multiple) to describe how waves move around or change when crossing an opening space in the obstacle.

---

1 You can find a socially updated list of optical phenomena on Wikipedia: https://en. wikipedia.org/wiki/Optical_phenomena.

Even though it is not always appropriate, interference considers small number of waves, whereas diffraction deals with a big number [HEC 05, p. 459]. Among the applications, we see some effects in fringes of light, interferograms, speckle textures, and Airy rings.

Finally, for quantum optics, light is studied at the subatomic level where the fundamental particle is the photon. It describes the minimal amount of all electromagnetic radiation and is part of the boson classification, together with the gluon, the Z boson and the W boson. The whole picture of elementary particles includes fermions (quarks and leptons that correspond to matter and anti-matter particles)[2]. Among the applications of photons in optical technologies and imagery, we cite the diverse varieties of lasers (acronym of Light Amplification by Stimulated Emission of Radiation, introduced in 1958), the multiple techniques used in holography (holograms by reflection, transmission, volume holograms, interferometry holograms, etc.) [HEC 05, p. 640], and ongoing advances in quantum computing.

1.1.2. *Visual perception: Gibson's ecological approach*

The ecological approach to visual perception differs from physical studies of light by focusing on the perception of the environment. The approach was initiated by the renowned psychologist James J. Gibson [GIB 86] during the second half of the last century. For him, environment is the physical terrestrial world constituted by substances and surfaces. The latter are the visible faces of the former, inasmuch as substances keep a more or less solid state of matter. In other words, surfaces separate substances. For example, consider your field of view right now. You see different objects, perhaps a chair, a table and a wall. Before calling them by their names, you discern their boundaries and contours because some parts are more or less illuminated; they also have some kind of texture, and they are placed at different positions from your angle of perspective (up, down, in front, behind, aside, etc.).

According to Gibson, what we really put attention to when we perceive the environment are not the properties of the surfaces, objects and places (e.g. their shape, color, composition, size) but their "affordances", that is, what the object permits one, or not, to do with them. If we come back to the

---

2 At the date of mid-2016, other particles exist in a theoretical form. A comprehensive list with updates and references can be revised at: https://en.wikipedia.org/wiki/List_of_particles.

chair, table and wall, the chair affords sitting (but also standing on it, or even grabbing, lifting, pushing, pulling if it is not too heavy or attached to the ground). The table affords placing other objects on top of it, and the wall affords separating spaces, hanging objects, painting or covering with tapestry. An important aspect of affordances is that they are properties taken in reference to the observer; they are not physical or phenomenal [GIB 86, p. 143]. In this respect, the chair, table and wall afford differently to a child, a cat or a fly.

As we can infer, Gibson was really occupied by perception in the natural world. He introduced notions such as "ecological optics", "ecological information" and "ecological events" that helped him re-contextualize traditional understandings of psychology. The importance of his approach was to study visual images as a kind of knowledge. Because in nature we do not have descriptors, visual perception is an implicit and direct knowledge that coexists with others: metric knowledge (by means of optical instruments that allow one to change scale), explicit knowledge (by means of languages that define and categorize objects and places) and mediated or indirect knowledge (by means of pictures, images and written-on surfaces).

The work of Gibson inspired the development of computational solutions to capture and record visual information. We will come back to this question in the following chapter. For now, let's review what images are from the ecological approach to visual perception.

In Gibson's terms, images and pictures are surfaces, which means they exist as part of the world, within the context of other objects and surfaces. They have the property of specifying something other than what they are [GIB 86, p. 273], in the same line as "displays", which are surfaces shaped to show information for more than just the surface itself (e.g. the surface of porcelain, which could be molded as a figure or as a traditional lithophane from Limoges). In the words of Gibson, images and pictures are "surfaces so treated that they make available an optic array of arrested structures with underlying invariants of structure" [GIB 86, p. 272].

From this standpoint, drawings, paintings and photographs record a moment from the real world experience. The ambient light is divided into component parts, which are then organized into an optic array made of visual angles. Such angles may vary according to the point of view of the observer, but they form relations of inclusion: smaller parts or details can be seen within a larger structure (to illustrate, imagine the hierarchy leafs-trees-forest). The so-called "invariants of structure" are elements common to all points of observation. Furthermore, in the specific case of drawings and paintings, where the artist can add imaginary objects, they are also depicted as surfaces. Although previously visualized and abstracted by information processed by the perceptual system, imaginary objects need to be presented in a visual form, with the available material possibilities.

1.1.3. *Visual imagery and cognitive sciences*

We said earlier that visual imagery is related to mental experiences of perception and action in the absence of their external expression. Visual imagery is also referred to in literature as mental imagery, imagination, or seeing with our mind's eye. In this section, we move from the natural world to the realm of the brain and mind. The intention is twofold. First, we want to revise how both dimensions could converge and provide helpful insights regarding creativity and innovation. Second, it is crucial to evoke notions of "representation", "description" and "simulation" within the context of cognitive sciences because they have played a central role in the development of digital images.

In contrast to the ecological approach to visual perception, the concept of "representation" becomes central to cognition. For Gibson, representation is misleading because it would imply recreating a whole natural scene. From this point of view, it is of course impossible to represent exactly the same physical conditions in space and time of an event, and that is why invariants record some of its characteristics.

However, in cognitive sciences, "representation" is a form of mental imagery. The notion is associated with interpretation and meaning making. In the case of images, we say that they are "iconic representations" [AND 04, p. 37], and this already suggests that there exist other types of representation systems: language, words, music, mathematics, logics, etc.

Following the cognitive science approach called "connectionism", the information stored in the brain is not in the form of explicit packages. It is rather distributed and loosely connected. Hence, mental images imply being reassembled and connected, instead of loaded directly from the memory [HOF 85, p. 410]. Moreover, the structure seems to be rather dynamic, since the elements of a representation system trigger modifications in different parts or processes of the mind (this is what Marvin Minsky refers to as "agents" [MIN 85, p. 196]).

One of the important aspects of regarding mental imagery for our study will be to consider it as a source of creative thinking. This will be decisive when we will talk about designing innovative graphical interfaces. To take a glance at imagination and simulation is also to think reflectively about our experiences. It is a way to visualize new virtual features that could be later implemented in projects and interactive interfaces.

Minsky has noted that "there is an intimate relationship between how we 'represent' what we already know and the generalizations that will seem most plausible" [MIN 85, p. 303]. In another strand, Douglas Hofstadter, when relating the work of artists and scientists, mentioned the example of a musical interpreter who establishes a multidimensional cognitive structure that is a mental representation of the song, fed by many other different mental structures related to previous experiences [HOF 85, p. 653]. The meaning of the song emerges in the process. Once again we observe the dynamic and complex situation of elements of the representation system, acting both as triggers and substantial supports of signification.

In more recent studies, Benjamin Bergen has introduced the term "embodied simulation". He proposes that "maybe we understand language by simulating in our minds what it would be like to experience the things that the language describes" [BER 12, p. 13]. The neurophysiological fact behind this idea is that we use the same parts and mechanisms of the brain for visual perception and for visual imagery. Therefore, whenever we simulate an event in our mind, we activate the same regions of the brain that we use in the physical world. Furthermore, Bergen points out that both kinds of images are indeed integrated. Visual imagery might interfere or enhance actual vision [BER 12, p. 28].

The other aspect that interests our study regarding mental images is the way in which they are understood as representation system. The earlier mentioned "connectionism approach" has found profound applications in computer science, particularly in digital imagery among other domains.

First of all, by the late 1930s, the basic components of computing were already invented (i.e. electrical circuitry, Boolean processing, propositional logics), and cybernetics established the umbrella field to explore relations soliciting the brain, the mind and the machine. As we can suspect, those different ingredients also constitute different levels of analysis and description. The question was: how to pass or move from one to another?

A simple way to understand a "description" is to think about a different language to describe something. What the computer central unit does can be described in machine language, but this is very difficult for humans because we do not think in binary terms. Thus, we go a step further to think in assembly language, which is easier and can be described in the decimal system. However, we know that, even today, assembly language is hardly taught in any "data visualization" workshop. What we do is go several steps higher. We describe in terms of another language what assembly does (and in consequence, what the machine language does at lower levels). We can now imagine the complexity of imbricated layers required for us to write a document in a word processor or to type a line of code in JavaScript.

Neuroscientist David Marr has defined "description" as "the result of using a representation to describe a given entity" [MAR 10, p. 20]. But then, what is a "representation"? Marr continues: "is a formal system for making explicit certain entities or types of information, together with a specification of how the system does this" [MAR 10, p. 20]. These definitions were formulated with visual information in mind, and we will come back to the work of Marr in the following chapter. For the moment, let's say that Marr was very aware of the importance of representation mainly because it determines how easy or complicated it is to do things with information: "any particular representation makes certain information explicit at the expense of information that is pushed into the background and may be quite hard to recover" [MAR 10, p. 21].

At the moment of writing these words, the influence of the connectionism or "network approach" is latent in recent advances in machine learning, most notably "neural networks" and "deep learning". The logic behind this approach remains anchored on the idea that the machine is expected to resemble the brain in the sense that small constituents act in parallel, without any hierarchical control and interconnected by links where the efficiency is modulated by experience, thus "representing" the knowledge or learning of the machine [AND 04, p. 43].

To conclude this section, let's come back to those "small constituents" or formal rules of the system. Given the fact that a computer is a very complex system and that we do not interact with it except at higher levels, it is necessary that the transmissions of information between layers avoid as many errors as possible. This is achieved through formal structures with no ambiguity at all. While natural language is polysemic (i.e. words or images may have several meanings), the machine needs a clear input in the form of 1 or 0. Other examples of formal rules are cardinal numbers, which require a specific syntax and combinatory rules different from Roman numbers.

1.2. Visual media

Visual media will be for us the means to make sense of visual information. Following the precedent sections, where we have tried to describe levels of incidence of visual information, it is obvious to say that visual media are types of mediated images. If direct perception consists of discerning surfaces, textures, objects, places and other visual information within the natural world, then any kind of image is indirect and mediated because it already contains a pre-figured point of view, disposition of elements, and choices of illumination.

While the digital screen is the preferred material support in our study, it is convenient to distinguish between different forms of expression that we encounter. First, we have the *screen as object*: it has sizes, weight, resolutions, electronic components, technologies, mechanics of functions, etc. Second, we have the *image that appears on the screen*. This image is determined by the technical possibilities of the screen as object and, in general terms, it is the image that simulates an existing media: digital photographs, digital cinema, digital magazines. Third, the images that we see on the screen are created with other kinds of images: digital graphical interfaces (or, as we call them, *image interfaces*). Here we are thinking about buttons, sliders, menus, boxes and other elements that facilitate interacting with software. In this section, we explore the latter two forms; the third is be the opening section of Chapter 2.

1.2.1. *Visual media as mediation*

Visual media consists of what is depicted as image and the material support on which it appears. This first approximation is of course too vast and vague, but it has the advantage of not confining visual media exclusively to digital technologies. Mediation, as a process that connects a message to a cultural form, exists at the level of the depicted image, but also when the material support is used as image. This is the case when drawing pictures on the sand or forming figures with peddles on the ground or, rather differently, constructing a golem-like sculpture out of TV sets. Furthermore, material supports will continue to develop and different kinds of surfaces are likely to be exploited: projections on physical objects and holograms, to mention a couple of examples.

Literature in visual media is abundant in media studies, media art history, media archaeology, sociology of media, and other related areas. We learn that media often get their names from the relation of techniques and supports. Photography associates the Greek words "photos" (light) with "graphé" (drawing with lines) to stand for "drawing with lines". The word television puts together "tele" (far) and "visio" (sight). More recently, electronic terms derive from acronyms pointing to technical components: "pixel" stands for "picture element", "codec" means "coder-decoder" and "modem" refers to "modulator-demulator".

Although it is not our purpose to elaborate a theory or classification of visual media, it will be useful to consider some of them as entry points. Among many classifications, instances of visual media commonly include: painting, photography, graphic design, comics, magazines, cinema, television, video clips, advertising, video games, virtual/augmented reality and websites. These media first come to mind as they are also the most popular. Three kinds of material supports are observed: canvas, paper and screen. However, a different list can be created if we consider media that remained at the state of visual artifact and technology, that were not produced massively or that became obsolete and forgotten. Oliver Grau, an important media art historian, recalls: peep show, panorama, anamorphosis, myriorama, cyclorama, magic lantern, eidophusikon, diorama, phantasmagoria, silent movies, films with scents, cinéorama [GRA 07, p. 11]. For these instances, the supports explored are not always solid and rigid: smoke, fog, glass, water, etc.

In a similar ecological approach as visual perception, media theorist Marshall McLuhan understood media as environments, as technologies, and as extensions of man [MCL 03]. For him, media are not only about communication, like our lists before, but also about changing effects in culture. Thus, for him, media was also money, clothing, transportation, weapons and clocks. Gibson's idea of medium relates to McLuhan's inasmuch as both are imperceptible to us because we are immersed in them. A medium is like an environment that allows doing and thinking according to its own conditions. The perceptible traits accessible to us are other media that act as content of the former, for example, one of McLuhan's favorite cases was that movies are the content of TV; literature and theater are the content of movies; and speech is the content of writing.

For McLuhan, we are only aware of the content and not the medium itself. Furthermore, what happens to the medium that acts as content is a "cultural upgrade", from an ordinary form to an art form. By making explicit a previous environment or technology, a medium gets studied, explained and refashioned. In other words, we abstract its properties and components for their comprehension and use. When TV started transmitting moving pictures, cinema left its technological phase and gave birth to TV shows, TV series, advertising, and televisual culture.

Following McLuhan, the arts act as "anti-environments" since they allow us to perceive the environment itself [MCL 03, p. 14]. In the electronic age, technologies move so fast that they also perform as arts. This is true in our context of study: constant innovations in digital imaging make us aware of different constituents and their relationships regarding digital images (new algorithms, new filters, new procedures, new visual designs, new applications). Since old media can be simulated and depicted as digital image, and because different communities tackle similar problems from diverse perspectives, it occurs that digital images advance, evolve and mediate as small fragments distributed along the ecology of software, formats, codecs, domains, disciplines, intentions and experiments. This is to say that an image mediates another one in different manners: it could be that it mediates the depicted image or that it mediates the technique or algorithm used. What we have to do, following McLuhan, is to discover, recognize and re-orchestrate patterns in those small fragments, which are residues of the mechanized environment of the machine revolution.

Therefore we can ask, how does the electronic environment upgrade mechanized parts and processes as art? According to media theorist Friedrich Kittler, who situated digital images in the long tradition of optical media, it is about opening up the total programmability of Turing machines to the users [KIT 10, p. 227]. The main thing to remember about digital images, contends Kittler, is that they are no longer optics. They are part of a sequence of dimension reductions, going from the 4D space-time of the natural world to 3D sculptures, to 2D paintings, to 1D text, and finally, to 0D bits. At each reduction, the possibilities augment via abstraction and description of the precedent level, that is, there are more possibilities by representing the upper dimension instead of actually working with it (it would be easier to draw a golem made of TV sets than actually constructing it). However, digital images restart the process from the bottom, operating a dimensional growth: from 0D bit to 1D command lines to 2D graphical interfaces to 3D virtual reality interfaces to forthcoming 4D holograms, quantum computing, and non-Euclidean speculative data visualizations.

In their digital form, visual media are mediated by the computer, which is the environment that precisely allows this total programmability. In order to create or manipulate images, we use the language of hardware and software, that is, their conventions and modes of existence. Media theorist Lev Manovich has defined media in the era of software according to the formula "*Medium = algorithms + a data structure*" [MAN 13, p. 207]. For him, data structures are the digital representations of physical materials, while the algorithms relate to tools, techniques, operations and actions on such data structures; examples of data structures are bitmap and vector images, polygonal and NURBS 3D models, and text files.

The relationship between data structures and physical materials is of course not straightforward. Manovich observes that all different material supports that exist (or have existed) to create images (all the types of canvas, papers, celluloid films) are reduced to two data structures: bitmap and vector images. Moreover, the same data structures can be used to simulate different media: photographs, maps, software icons, and, we should add, the whole graphical interface.

As we can see, when visual information enters a process of signification, its understanding broadens in complexity. We encode and decode messages according to our particular experiences, which are framed by social structures (profession, country, religion, institutions). To say it differently, visual media are forms of expressing our thoughts and feelings. Moreover, visual media combines different meanings, styles and codes (not only pictures, but also texts and symbolic elements). Perhaps the difficulty and complexity of describing and defining digital visual media resides in the fact that it is ourselves who are the medium. If mechanized culture was the medium whose content was agrarian life, and the electronic world is the medium whose content is the machine revolution, we might suspect that humanity and its representation models are the media whose content is the digital life. With software, algorithms and data structures, we are slowly shaping ourselves and changing our culture.

1.2.2. Metaphors of visual media

In the last section, we used the notion of "mediation" in a broad sense, as it fits media artifacts: how they function as forms or placeholders when a message needs to be constructed. In this part, however, we present briefly other contemporary views of mediation that, in general, ask to go beyond the material part and to focus on effects and processes. This observation will lead us to open up the kind of metaphors through which we usually understand visual media.

Through a critical reading of Kittler, McLuhan and Manovich, and informed by thinkers such as Louis Althousser, Gilles Deleuze, Alain Badiou and Jacques Rancière, media theorist Alexander Galloway contemplates new media, and particularly computers, not as objects but as processes, techniques, practices, actions and sets of executions. His endeavor is to leave media in favor of investigating modes of mediation. In philosophical terms, his theory invites one to move from the domain of ontology and metaphysics – which describe what media are – towards ethics, pragmatics and politics. Because computers define general principles for action, Galloway suggests studying digital media politically: reading the contemporary world as the actually existing social and historical reality. An example of putting this approach into practice could link formal structures and their realities, that is, what he calls centers and edges: image to frames; representation to metrics; realism to function; text to paratext. As Galloway puts it, "the edges of the work are the politics of the work" [GAL 12a, p. 42].

The political stakes of media and software take into account the institutional, economical, governmental and military origins of computers at the time of the Cold War, economical crisis, and labor organization. Media theorist Matthew Fuller asks in the same strand about the kind of user that is being imagined by software. Which "models of work" have informed a software application like Microsoft Word, for instance? As we have noted, Word cannot order lists alphabetically or produce combinatorial poetry

[FUL 03, pp. 137–165]. In association with the same principle of identifying "edges", we can consider how the graphical space of Word is organized: it follows an idea of what is most important to have at hand in order to get work done. To think about the interface as edge means to forget for a moment that we are writing a document or a letter; instead, we are using a software dispositive.

Fuller points out that multiple working teams collaborate behind the design of tools available throughout graphical interfaces. To a large extent, this is made possible thanks to the programming paradigm implemented in development and production. As we will see in more detail in the next chapter, object-oriented programming constitutes a synthesis of procedural structurability and functional logic design [HAG 06]. Examples of OOP languages are SMALLTALK, EIFFEL, C++, Java and Ruby. Today, the great majority of software applications are produced and maintained with the latter three, and almost every aspect of industry has been restructured to cope and adapt to "the potentials and vicissitudes of software" [GAL 12b, p. 97].

From a similar perspective, media theorist Wendy Chun situates computers as neoliberal governmental technology and names them "mediums of power", not only because they simulate to empower users (through easier to use interfaces and the impression of mastering the system) but, more importantly, because their interfaces embody ways to navigate the world: conceptually, metaphorically and virtually. Among such metaphors, we find software as mind, as culture, as society, as the body, as ideology, as biology, as economy and, in fact, as metaphor for metaphor. Software as power has to do with combining something visible (such as images and software on the screen) with something invisible (operations of computation). The result is an "invisible system of visibility, a system of casual pleasure" [CHU 11, p. 18] that we vaguely understand due to its technical layers of complexity, thus carrying sometimes unexpected effects. For us, it will be important to pay attention to those unattended situations that really do not exist in old media and that recall the human construction behind technological innovations: glitches, crashes and "creative bugs" (which refer to noticing behaviors through an error or chance, as is the case with serendipity).

Visibility and invisibility: political questions are closely related to esthetics. Media theorist Warren Sack has shown, in a very informed manner, how we can trace the origin of computers to the division of labor, as originally introduced by Adam Smith and accurately identified by Herbert Simon [SAC 14a]. Sack retraces a history of computing in order to understand how computers are language machines before they are numerical: it was through the translations from "work language" into "machine language", from the machine diagrams of labor depicted by Charles Babbage, to their arithmetical description by Ada Lovelace, to their implementation as the language of computers by Goldstein and von Neumann.

Mediated as it is through the screen, computer code is also commonly understood as image and number [SAC 14b, p. 123]. Besides "visual programming languages", which will be explored in the next chapter, this is precisely the case in web graphics and data visualizations: we can verify the data URI of a PNG image at the location bar of the browser, or check the X and Y positions of graphical elements in the SVG file. Following Sack, his take on data visualization is to avoid worrying about beautiful or culturally pleasant criteria; it is about asking whether it is aligned to bureaucratic or democratic principles. In short, he calls for an "aesthetics of governance" (where works interpret, organize, articulate subjects and things woven together), which is in tune with the principles and traditions of conceptual art [SAC 06].

In sum, this section intends to serve as a brief account of digital images from a standpoint beyond their material support. Specifically, the relation with social and historical contexts was established through political and ethical mediations, both in a sense more related to Jacques Rancière's philosophical elaborations [RAN 00, RAN 03]. We observe the importance that is given to effects on the individual subject, the society and the community. Furthermore, these views consider seriously the mediated power and ideologies conveyed by software, artifacts and *dispositifs*, in the sense of Michel Foucault and Gilles Deleuze [DEL 86]. In the second part, we established a link with esthetics not only as a door that opens to material concretizations but also as a pathway towards artistic practices and positions.

Throughout this book, this section will be repeatedly evoked. This is even more important if we accept that more forms of mediation and metaphor can be invited into reflection. For example, what happens with ephemeral data art and data visualizations? Can we archive them when every instance of an image is an original, in the sense of [GRO 16]? What if we consider software, images and interfaces as a spatial and ecological flux that we and other species inhabit, acclimate and alter during certain moments [SPU 16, ALE 77]? Or, can we approach a phenomenology of other species and object operations in a similar terrain of "flat ontologies" [BOG 12]? In any case, our point of view will be to intend so by making and reflecting on things, to couple theory and practice or, rather, making theory out of our practices.

1.3. Visual interfaces

Visual interfaces are a type of visual media with their own specific characteristics: they convey action and they establish a dynamic space where multiple actors interact at the same time and level (human users, computational procedures, digital media, computer devices). In this section, we explore some characteristics of visual interfaces from the tradition of computer science, history of technology, and media studies.

Media theorists Jay Bolter and Richard Grusin aptly imported what McLuhan called content and medium in terms of new media [BOL 99]. They introduced the notion of "remediation" to indicate the manner in which media, old and new, refashion constantly through two distinct yet interrelated logics. On the one hand, the logic of "immediacy" tends to make us forget the medium: it describes the state where the individual is immersed into the imaginary of the film, the novel, the news, etc. On the other hand, the logic of "hypermediacy" brings forward the medium: it makes us aware that we are immersed in content through the multiplicity and heterogeneity of material supports and configurations of a medium [BOL 99, p. 33]. Besides the examples they provide in their book, hypermediacy can easily be seen through breakouts that happen when we are using or watching a medium: we remember we are reading a book when we suddenly loose the page (so we come back to the page interface); we remember we are using a web browser when we have to locate the back and forth buttons to get out of a web page.

This section is then precisely about the visible, multiple and heterogeneous frames inside media. Visual interfaces organize content in space and also provide help for effectuating operations on it. Moreover, it seems that designing visual interfaces is also about designing momentary lapses of invisibility. We can think about buttons in media players as an example of small interfaces that disappear when we are not using them, but we know they are there. Something alike happens to our experience within a whole web page: its entire spatial organization is also an interface, a large interface space where we spend some time. Finally, we consider an interface as the place that materializes deeper levels of abstractions: actions, behaviors, algorithms, objects and techniques.

1.3.1. *Remediation of machines and media*

The origin of the term "interface" has been traced back by cultural theorist Branden Hookway to the domain of fluid dynamics [HOO 14]. In 1869, engineer and physicist James Thomson used the term to "define and separate areas of unequal energy distribution within a fluid in motion" [HOO 14, p. 59]. If we imagine two water currents flowing in different directions, the interface is the form that originates when both currents meet. This creates fluidity. Since fluids (liquids and gases) are studied in motion, it might be difficult to perceive their changes; therefore, the interface also defines the potential forms that might emerge. Examples of complex and remarkable forms are found in a vortex or turbulence.

Among the technological developments based on fluid flows, there are windmills, water mills, and, more recently, turbines designed specifically to transform energy into work. We might observe how technical components such as blades and sails act as interfaces. They are shaped and produced to capture, in the most efficient manner, the flow.

Historian Sigfried Giedion stresses that the method that forms the basis of all mechanization is the human hand. "It can seize, hold, press, pull, mold with ease" [GIE 13, p. 46]. What the hand cannot do is to move permanently, and this is where mechanization becomes determinant. For Giedion, its first phase consisted of transforming into continuous rotation the pushing, pressing and pulling of the hand. The second phase was about the procedures by which mechanical components would be produced. For him, stamping, pressing, embossing, casting, all relied on dies and molds and facilitated standardization and interchangeability of parts.

This brief account is important because the history of inventions and technologies is also a history of interfaces. Through illustrative works such as [GIE 13, LER 73, ECO 61, GLE 17], we have a glance at those moments and situations where innovations took place. These can also be seen as abstractions or virtualizations. It is about extracting the essence of an act that can be achieved with an object by which we can later communicate its function, even in the absence of the object. Consider the act of hammering. It might have been discovered with a rock, but it certainly can be realized with another object.

For philosopher Pierre Lévy, who identified media as virtualizations of actions, organs and things, inspired by Gilles Deleuze and Henri Bergson [LEV 98], there is, throughout the history of inventions, a small number of virtualizations, but a large number of realizations: how many times has the act of hammering been discovered in contrast to the amount of times people have performed the act of hammering?

When something is made or created, it can be done either creatively or in a more standardized form. This is not to say that there is no creativity in the standard, but only that its focus is on the practical achievement of something. Of course, innovation may rise from standards and, when the standard was first invented, it was once a creative type, but as it is widely adopted, it is more of a repetition and not a difference [DEL 68]. However, when something is created in a creative manner, it explores and approaches a solution in a different manner. This is the actualization. The creative thinking implies refashioning, modifying, remixing and combining elements. And when this creative solution is questioned and re-articulated, it is being virtualized.

To describe stable innovations, philosopher Gilbert Simondon uses the notion of "technical object", which refers to a seamless communication of the human actor with the technicity: this "is specified by the convergence of structural functions because there is not, at a given epoch or time, an infinite plurality of possible functional systems. Human needs diversify to infinity, but the directions of convergence of technical species are of a limited number" [SIM 69, p. 23].

Giedion points to the fact that the quest of progress and perfection in mechanized societies is related to "rationalism". It has always been necessary to analyze, describe and represent the endless movement put in practice by the machines, and Giedion retraces the history of the representation and capture of movement: from Nicolas Oresme, who first created a graphical representation of movement (a kind of proto-bar chart or histogram), to Franck Gilbreth's physical wire models.

From the representation of movement to the capture of movement, Giedion shows us the work of Étienne-Jules Marey, who in the 19th Century invented devices like the spygmograph and the myograph to record movement in a graphical form. Later, Marey used photography to register the trajectories and transformations of movement that the naked eye could not perceive. The "chronophotographs", as he called them, traced the movement at the rate of 12 frames per second in the same image. In complement to the work of Eadweard Muybridge, who depicted phases of movement in separated frames, Marey was interested in showing these states in a single frame. Besides his chronophotographs, he also experimented with capturing the movement of an object from different angles (by using three cameras: front, left, top), and he even crafted 3D sculptures of the successive attitudes of a seagull in movement.

These examples of remediation make evident a passage that goes from abstract geometrical figures to figurative images. It was in the late work of Marey and most prominently in the works of Frank Gilbreth that the passage comes back to abstract lines. Gilbreth invented the cyclograph around 1912 with the intention of recording the movement of workers at their posts. The resulting image was also called light curves because they were mainly white lines over black background. Later, Gilbreth also created a physical 3D model of those lines, but this time using wires. Contrary to Marey, whose interest was especially in scientific experimentation and the production of graphical forms, Gilbreth was interested in assisting workers to improve their efficiency. His graphs can also be considered mechanizations of human motion, and its abstraction could then be implemented as a model for a machine.

1.3.2. Conventions and standards in human–computer interaction

Regarding computer-based models of interaction, the kind of interfaces that we will revise are those that came after the era of punched card computers which flourished between the introduction of the ENIAC in 1946 and the 1970s.

In computer sciences, interfaces are not only visual or projected on a screen. A broad typology can be listed as follows [FUL 08, p. 149]:

– users to hardware (input/output devices, etc.);

– hardware to hardware (such as bus systems);

– hardware to software (for instance, device drivers);

– software to software (application programming interfaces or APIs);

– software to users (graphical user interface or GUI).

A more refined and detailed typology of interfaces can also be evoked: command line, WIMP/GUI, multimedia, virtual reality, information visualization, web, consumer appliances, mobile, speech, pen, touch, air-based gesture, haptic, multimodal, shareable, tangible, augmented reality, wearable, robotics and drones, brain computer interaction (BCI) [PRE 15, p. 159].

Although in this part of our study, we mainly focus on graphical and visual interfaces, we can identify a commonality to all those interfaces if we describe them one layer above: they require being created and programmed in a graphical developing environment (also called SDK, or software development kits). We are talking about software to create software. Such environments, we will see in further sections, use a combination of graphical interfaces and programming languages adapted to specific purposes and domains.

After the era of punched card computers, several command-based or command line interfaces (CLI) appeared in the 1980s. At that time, some computer systems had already used a CRT (cathode ray tube) display, as exemplified in the famous demo of the "NLS" system by Douglas Engelbart in 1968. Moreover, virtual reality was being pioneered in that decade as well: the "Sensorama Simulator" by Morton Heiling in 1960 and the "Ultimate Display" by Ivan Sutherland in 1965.

Examples of CLI are DOS/UNIX shells that allow accessing the operating system of a computer. Today, we still use CLI when we manage files or launch batch operations from the Terminal application in OSX, which is based on Bash as Unix shell, or with programming languages that include a CLI mode: Python, R, MATLAB, LISP. Among the issues of interest in CLI, the syntax of commands has been paramount. Should we use an abbreviation or full name to invoke a command? How can we combine different commands? One of the principles that prevailed is that of consistency: using the first letters of word to abbreviate or adopt a noun-verb/verb-noun logic [RAS 00].

CLI were rapidly challenged by graphical user interfaces (GUI). In 1970, Xerox Corporation established the Xerox Palo Alto Research Center (PARC), and by 1972 they created the Xerox Alto, the first personal computer with a bitmap screen, a pointing device, and a graphical interface. It was their second landmark, the Xerox Star in 1981, in which visual interfaces benefited from extensive research on visible mechanisms, design principles, user-oriented methodology, and empirical testing [WIN 96, pp. 32–36].

Computer scientist Ben Schneiderman explains some aspects that made it easier to understand relations in a visual rather than linguistic form through GUI. With the concept of "direct manipulation", he states the importance of presenting continuously the object of interest and being able to simulate physical actions on it, which would also immediately inform the user about the result. Direct manipulation can be seen in WYSIWYG (what you see is what you get) interfaces, visual programming, and GUI. One of the important tasks is to build an appropriate representation or model of reality and to keep in mind the simple syntactic/semantic model of human cognition [SHN 83].

On the one hand, syntactic knowledge is ephemeral. It demands that the same operations be constantly reproduced, otherwise they are forgotten. On the other hand, semantic knowledge can be imagined as layers. At the lower level, there are actions similar to command language: copy, paste, insert, delete, etc. These are commonly software agnostic. Subsequent layers would add combinations of series of actions: correct spelling, moving paragraphs among sections of a text, etc.

The basic GUI visual elements that were introduced by the Star were later refined by the Apple Macintosh in 1984 and consolidated by Microsoft Windows in 1995. The elements are windows, scroll bars, checkboxes, panels, palettes, dialog boxes (confirmations, error messages, checklists, forms), buttons; icons depicting tools, applications, and low-level semantic operations (e.g. cut, copy, paste); and different styles of menus: flat lists, drop-down, pop-up, contextual and expanding menus.

Those visual elements have also been the subject of graphic design explorations in style: B&W, color, shadowing, photorealistic images, 3D rendering, animations, flat design [PRE 07, p. 236]. Besides that, inside the space of an interface, they are arranged in visual frameworks [MUR 12, p. 79]: table, columns, flow charts, hierarchy charts, taxonomies, networks, maps, timelines, bubble diagrams, or any other arbitrary form (such as infographics, which might use visual metaphors [BOL 01, p. 52]).

As we know, all those basic elements from the 1980s are still in use today. They have become conventions, in the sense of media theorist Janet Murray: "social practices and communication formats shared by members of a culture or subculture, as well as media formats shared by artifacts within the same genre" [MUR 12, p. 415]. For her, the move towards conventions must follow a direction in which digital media is exploited according to four affordances, each one of them related to concepts and knowledge from special disciplines: encyclopedic (information science), spatial (visual design), procedural (computer science) and participatory (human–computer interaction) [MUR 12].

Perhaps the most advanced efforts to standardize digital media come from guidelines and specifications, best practices, international recommendations, consortiums and, more recently, design patterns. Among the most acclaimed software guidelines, we may cite the Macintosh Human Interface Guidelines, later changed to Apple's Human Interface Guidelines, and the more recently available iOS Human Interface Guidelines. In those documents, Apple describes its vision of WYSIWYG, metaphors, direct manipulation, and how to use the interface elements (i.e. menus, windows, dialog boxes, controls, icons, colors, behaviors and language) [APP 85a]. Regarding specifications, around the same years, in 1993, the International Organization for Standardization released the ISO 9241 titled "Ergonomic requirements for office work with visual display" starting with requirements for visual displays and keyboards. Today, ISO 9241 covers ergonomics of human–computer interaction on eight levels, going from software ergonomics to environment ergonomics and tactile and haptic interactions [ISO 14]. Another example of standardization is the World Wide Web Consortium (W3C), initiated by Tim Berners-Lee in 1994. Its focus is on the standards for the web: languages, technologies, protocols and guidelines (W3C 2014).

One of the underlying principles that has allowed media software to flourish and expand is the potentiality to interchange files and data between applications and operating systems. This is possible because data structures and data formats are common in several environments. For example, although the Graphics Interchange Format (GIF) started as a proprietary technology developed and owned by CompuServe in 1987, it can be used for free today, that is to say that the technique of compressing data with the algorithm LZW and its packaging in a GIF file can be freely used by developers. As we know, GIF animated images have gained popularity with the explosion of web-based social networks; hence, they can be opened, distributed, embedded and produced with many different software.

1.3.3. *Visual space of image interfaces*

We have seen that visual interfaces are particular types of visual media that exist on the electronic screen. We understand display devices as material supports that delimit the potential kinds of images to be depicted. Visual interfaces act by organizing commands and operations as representations of such potentialities. For instance, when we use application software, most of them have low-level operations that allow us to copy and paste but, in some cases, the software itself allows us to regroup in a macro, or through a script module or plugins, a bunch of operations that we might use recurrently: crop, adjust levels, and add filters for a series of images. These are abstractions or descriptions of a higher level.

A fundamental critique of standardization has been that it constrains creative and original alternatives. This happens when we want to do something different to what the software confines us to. But why would we be willing to do something different? A possible answer has already been noted with Simondon: because human needs tend to evolve continuously and technical objects have to be rethought, experienced, tested. In short, they have to be used by the society.

Hookway has noted that an interface theory is also a theory of culture. An interface describes a cultural moment: "to use an interface is to participate in culture" [HOO 14, p. 16]. Furthermore, the interface comes into being when it is actively used. The cultural relation between interfaces and human users is a critical part that motivates its creative developments and uses. Of course, today screens are pervasive. They are everywhere, with different sizes and technical specifications. We use them for different aspects of our life, from work to leisure. As such they are cultural objects that mediate and simulate our physical interactions. Media theorist Lev Manovich named software interfaces as "cultural interfaces", integrated in "cultural objects" (websites, games, mobile apps) that allow us to access "cultural data" (images, texts, videos, etc.) [MAN 01, p. 70].

The fact that the screen is a visual machine makes us aware that everything projected on it is a digital image. More precisely, this means that multiple visual media cohabit the same space, but also that they can exchange visual properties between them. The text written in a text editor can be, for example, resized, colored, stylized. While the text conserves its linear properties in order to be read, it can also be animated, fragmented, turned over or around, and it might also be deleted, replaced or shaped into another form. More interestingly, as we will see, visual media can also exchange operations.

The interest in challenging predisposed organizations or relations between media is not new. We recall experiments in text by poet Stéphane Mallarmé (*Un coup de dés*, 1914); writer Filippo Marinetti (*Zang tumb tuum*, 1914 or *Mots en liberté*, 1919); and poet Guillaume Apollinaire (*Pablo Picasso SIC*, 1916 or *La cravate et la montre*, 1916 or *Lettre Océan*, 1916). Later, with the advent of video technologies, text was conceived as motion graphics: *Catalog* (1961) by artist John Whitney and movie title sequences such as designer Maurice Binder's 007 James Bond movies from 1962–1989 or graphic designer Saul Bass' in *Vertigo* (Hitchcock, 1958). More recently, with classical net art pieces such as *Jodi.org*[3] by Joan Heemskerk and Dirk Paesmans in the mid-1990s, or recent exhibitions like *Chercher le texte*[4] (curated by Philippe Bootz in 2013), text has also become an animated web element. From this point, design of visual interfaces has been influenced by graphic design and modern and contemporary art. One of the motivations behind those explorations is, as digital art pioneer Frieder Nake says, that "aesthetic computing deliberately introduces subjectivism into computing" [NAK 08].

In the academic world, we can also see innovations in the field of digital humanities. Media theorist Johanna Drucker calls on us to rethink our

---

3 http://wwwwwwwww.jodi.org/

4 http://gallery.dddl.eu/en/home/

interfaces under the sight of a humanistic design which is subject-oriented [DRU 14]. Her approach consists in taking into account the "subject positions in relation to the act of engagement with media" [DRU 14, p. 151]. By redefining the user as a subject, instead of having pre-defined "needs", she can also wander around or discover a corpus of data by applying scholarly methodologies (e.g. comparison, interpretation, discussion, suspended conclusions). In this respect, visual interfaces and their graphical organizations might function as provocations to cognition and esthetics.

Some examples of developments created in the digital humanities domain take advantage of the web as a platform. For a person, it is possible to use a website as a web app. That means the design of web pages becomes also a matter of interface design. Consider the popular Wordle[5], which generates text visualizations in the form of a cloud, where the size of text is not an arbitrary decision but is rather related to the number of frequencies of that word. Another example is the more robust Voyant[6], which not only has traditional graphical representations of text analysis, but also includes some experimental representations such as Lava and Bubbles.

With this brief description, we learn that the visual space of an interface can be questioned by practice. In order to go beyond a certain model of action or user, it is sometimes necessary to dig down a level below the visual interface, that is, the programming code, data structures, data types and algorithms. However, once we have manipulated and constructed a prototype, we come to the surface by means of standard elements of the interface. However, the new object has the novelty that it has been thought from a different angle, perhaps artistic, experimental, technical, or as a new tool for digital humanities or cultural analytics. In any case, interface designers should be aware of such levels as well as the cultural and structuring regimes in which they takes place.

Graphical organizations are abstractions of "structuring spaces whose relations create value through position, hierarchy, juxtaposition, and other features in an act of interpretation" [DRU 14, p. 177], in a similar manner in which menus, windows, and frames abstract operations and sequences of commands. As we have seen, an abstraction is a model that extracts a mode of operation; therefore, it can also be used in different contexts. Interfaces

---

5 http://www.wordle.net/
6 http://voyant-tools.org/

abstract actions, tools and components. What we will put attention on in further parts of this book is how graphical supports of visual information (mainly in digital art and digital humanities) impersonate interchange operations that were dedicated to interface elements before. If translations from one language to another are called intra-linguistic, and if the combination of multiple types of images into the same context (such as collages or websites) is called inter-pictorial, then we will call interface exchanges as inter- and intra-interfacial.

1.4. Visual methods

In this last section of the first chapter, we will deal with the general question: which methods exist to analyze images and how can they help us in the design of graphical information? The intention is to explore existing frameworks that put in practice the description of images through a defined model with its values and components. This section is more focused on research from humanities and social sciences before we study in more detail methods from computer science in the following chapters. The overall objective will be to think about the problem of elaborating and envisioning new methods suited for graphical information and interfaces.

The first observation to make at this point is that the analysis of images depends on the context of use and the type of actors that intervene in the process. Examples of context of use are disciplines and fields. They generally ask the question: why do we need to analyze images? What are the goals and outcomes? It is obvious that analyzing images implies different objectives for a computer scientist specialized in computer vision, whose techniques might include image segmentation and image recognition of objects, than for an art historian who specializes in styles, connotations and themes from one epoch to another. The types of actors that intervene in such examples may be human and technological: an artist, a scholar but maybe also a series of algorithms that extract information, recognize shapes, and take decisions. However, although contexts and actors may differ, the object of study remains the same: it is about studying images and creating models to understand them. We believe that creative forms of graphical information might be found if we adopt a larger point of view regarding the variety of visual methods across different domains.

In the following sections, we cover four main areas where visual methods can be found: 1) the so-called field of visual studies; 2) visual semiotics; 3) diagrams and graphics; and 4) visual analytics and interface design.

1.4.1. *Visual studies*

A large amount of literature that deals with images falls within the domain of visual studies. The area of study has been described in the works of David Mitchell, Nicholas Mirzoeff, James Elkins or Gunalan Nadarajan. A common trait of visual studies is the recognition of the differentiated power of images in several states: when it is being constructed (how the producer imprints desires and messages); when it is already constructed (how it coexists with the ecosystem of images); and when it is consumed (how it talks to the viewer and how it might have an influence).

The largest field that has attracted researchers of visual studies is the history and theory of arts. Traditional types of images that serve as objects of study include paintings and drawings. More recently, with the development of mass media, researchers have diversified these types to include photographs, advertisements, comics, film, television and fashion. The case of scientific imagery, although less prominent in visual studies literature, has also been evoked in some works [ELK 08].

Broadly speaking, the description of images from the standpoint of visual studies represents efforts to adopt a more systematic mode of seeing pictures. They try to structure the gaze of the observer in front of a picture and to relate her insights with the context of the production of the image. The result of an analysis informs about the tools and techniques used, its visual construction, and the social practices that it raises. Such methodologies seem more suited for students and young researchers interested in understanding and interpreting images, documenting and cataloging corpora of images, and collecting qualitative data with techniques such as photo-elicitation: "using photographs to invoke comments, memory and discussion" [BAN 07, p. 65].

Scholars like Gillian Rose or art historians like Laurent Gervereau have defined similar methods that distinguish between the description of the image itself, its context of production, and its context of reception or interpretation. They promote the use of a grid of analysis that helps structure the observations: name of producer, date, type of support, format, localization, main colors, main objects, theme, what was the purpose of producing the image, how does it fit in its historical context, how was it received, which meaning does it evoke, and the personal appreciations of the observer.

Regarding the gaze of the observer and the image itself, visual studies often use terminology from other disciplines in order to provide strategies of seeing. From the description of the format and dimensions of the image, they identify golden proportions, the movement of the gaze in the surface (linear or circular depending on how figures, colors and tones drive the attention of the eye), symmetrical or asymmetrical compositions (in the form of triangular or diagonal), horizon lines, vantage points, golden sections, and chiaroscuro relationships. It is worth noticing how some authors modify the image analyzed to depict their findings: they often make diagrams or trace marks on top of the image or create simplified models of the main objects of interest in the form of contours (see Figure 1.1).

Taken together, we can ask where the producer, the image itself and its reception come from. It might seem straightforward to relate these kinds of image analysis to the basic model of communication: sender (the producer of the image) – message (the image itself) – receiver (the public or the observer). If we would like to elaborate or construct methods in the same line, we could recall, for example, the work of linguist Roman Jakobson, who extended the communication model into six elements and identified communicative functions for each element:

– *Sender*: the attention is placed on the producer, that is, the actor(s) who create the image or any other message. Jakobson describes the function of the sender as expressive.

– *Receiver*: the public or the observer are seen as performing a conative function as they have to engage in the process of understanding and modifying their behavior based on the expression of the sender.

– *Message*: the message itself is regarded as a poetic function based on the many ways to enunciate and express something. Esthetic and rhetorical values are considered when the focus is placed on this element.

– *Code*: the material expression by which a message is realized. The function is metalinguistic in the sense that both the sender and the receiver are expected to understand the expressive form and substance. Examples of code can be language, pictures or sounds.

– *Channel*: the attention is put on verifying that the distribution channel works properly. It ensures contact or can also inform about the general atmosphere and conditions for communication. The function is called phatic.

– *Context*: the reference ground in which the communication exists. When attention is given to this element, it can point to historical epochs, themes, places or circuits of distribution, and background environments. Its function is referential.

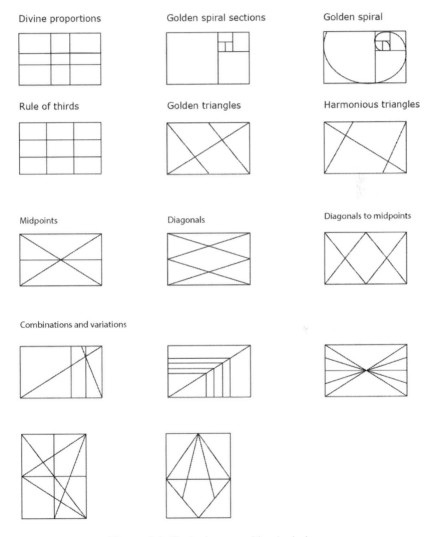

Figure 1.1. *Typical composition techniques*

The hierarchy of Jakobson's model of communication does not intend to be exhaustive or discriminatory; it is rather a formalism that aims to direct attention. In practice, the situations are more complex than the examples because all the elements can be present in a communicative process or can behave in a dynamic fashion, varying and modulating their position within the hierarchy.

As we have said earlier, this book is not strictly about interpreting images, but rather about discovering strategies to design and implement graphical information. We will refrain from making interpretations or talk about the styles and esthetic effects of images. Visual studies often have the intention of explaining meanings, from symbolisms attached to objects to the historical momentum in which non-figurative images such as abstract art can be understood. In the next section, we turn to models from visual semiotics, which have studied more rigorously the visual aspects of images and tried to describe the mechanisms underlying meaning production.

1.4.2. *Visual semiotics*

Linguistics has influenced in several ways the description of images. Besides Roman Jakobson, major exponents such as Louis Hjelmslev, Algirdas Greimas or Émile Benveniste have drawn on the work of Ferdinand de Saussure, who initiated the field of semiology within the theory of language at the beginning of the 20th Century. However, around the same time as Saussure, the field of semiotics was also conceived by philosopher Charles Peirce with the intention of situating a doctrine of signs within the boundaries of pragmatism. Today, semiotics benefits from both its philosophical and linguistic heritage, and it strives to extend to experimental methods informed by cognitive sciences – a branch known as cognitive semiotics.

The study of images has been widely associated with Peirce's most famous triad that identifies a sign in relation to its object. First, an icon is a sign that keeps a relationship of similarity with its object. Paintings, photographs and drawings can be icons if they resemble the depicted object. Second, an index is a sign that relates to its object by perceptible or perceived directness. Popular examples are footprints in the sand (produced at a moment before perception) and arrows (perceived as direction). All images have indexical properties: they relate to their mode of production (made by hand or using technological means), the material support used (paper, screen, etc.), the title given by the author, and may have internal directions, such as vectors that direct the movement of the eye. Third, signs are symbols by cultural convention to their object. Here, the observer adds cultural categories to images: a figure of a man with ornaments and accessories can be seen in its social role (a warrior, a sorcerer, a worker, etc.) and, ultimately, it can symbolize an ideology or a greater category (Christianity, capitalism, socialism, etc.).

A more systematic description of images came from the distinction between figurative and plastic signs, which was first observed by Algirdas Greimas and further elaborated by Jean-Marie Floch, Félix Thürlemann and the Groupe Mu. On the one hand, figurative signs constitute the layer of the image that simulates the world as it appears to human perception, also called iconic signs and developed as pictorial signs by semiotician Göran Sonesson [SON 89]. The plastic layer, on the other hand, has emerged from studies of proto-iconical and non-figurative signs, such as abstract art. The Groupe Mu categorizes three main components that exist in this layer: colors, forms and textures. Extensively, in a similar way of linguistics, they decompose each category into basic units of meaning: colorèmes have variations of hue, saturation and brightness; formèmes can be arranged in direction, position and dimension; and texturèmes observe single patterns and their laws of repetition and distribution.

In general, methods for analyzing images have been configured according to two planes: the expression plane and the content plane, which developed from the linguist separation of signifier and signified. Louis Hjelmselv refined each part into planes and proposed that each one has two further dimensions: form and substance. In this respect, there are substance and form of expression on one side, and form and substance of content on the other side. Following this theory, meaning or semiosis arises from the collaboration of both the planes. The importance of such a distinction establishes a systematic focus either on the material or on the interpretative part of a sign. Algirdas Greimas, for example, developed a generative trajectory of content associated with narrative and discursive instances. More recently, semiotician Jacques Fontanille elucidated a possible generative trajectory of expression: going from signs to texts to objects to practices and then to strategies and life forms [FON 08]. The scheme has been useful to determine formal supports that give ground to substance supports. In this view, forms are like syntax vocabularies and rules that delimit how the substance will be manifested. Accordingly, the substance of one level becomes the form of its upper level (see section 2.1 for a more detailed discussion).

Seminal examples of image analysis in the semiotic field that put in practice plastic and figurative signs, as well as content and expression planes, can be found in Thürlemann and Floch, who have pushed forward historical analyses by semioticians Roland Barthes and Umberto Eco. In his own strand, Sonesson has criticized and studied the possibility of different models that can also be used: the narrative model, the rhetorical model (in its taxonomic and systematic modes), the Laokoon model and experimental models [SON 89, SON 94]. The investigations in pictorial semiotics by Sonesson announce that its goal is not really to analyze images or producers of images, but rather to identify general rules that might apply to particular types of images. His emphasis is on finding the specificities that make an image a kind of visual sign, in all its possible varieties of signification.

An image is then considered as a way to distribute marks on a surface; it is a surface treated in some manner. As an object of study, the image must possess signification for someone and should participate in different pictorial kinds (the picture type, the picture function or the picture circulation channel). Sonesson's concept of sign is taken from phenomenologist Edmund Husserl and psychologist Jean Piaget: a sign is a complex entity that is perceived directly as non-thematic (the expression), while the theme is given indirectly (the content); and the sign must comply with a principle of discontinuity between the signifier and the signified (this is the case with objects represented only by some of their parts, mainly because the rest might be hidden or because the frame of a picture interrupts them). Throughout the exemplary image analysis made by Sonesson in different publications, he makes recourse to structural and textual analysis traditions in order to describe properly the elements of an image. Then, for each observation of figurative and plastic signs, there are series of attributes and values that elaborate meaning when viewed as oppositions and factorialities (relationships between the whole and its parts). Experimental studies in psychology such as Gestalt theory and prototypical (and anti-prototypical) structures also find their place in tackling internal composition and human expectancies in perception where shapes, colors, symbols and picture types conform or do not conform to universal structures.

We believe that visual semiotics can be broadened by taking into account research from different fields and domains. Just as in psychology and cognitive sciences, advances in computer science can contribute to the description of images. The objective would not precisely be to automatize methods, but would rather be to offer the possibility of new and different descriptions, configurations and terminology for the expression plane. We will refer to this section in further parts of this book, especially when we discuss practices of image interfaces in Chapters 4 and 5.

1.4.3. *Diagrams and graphics*

Let's come back to Peirce, as briefly mentioned in the previous part. As is known, much of his reasoning used triads to explain categories. A sign for him is conceived as a relationship of three parts: an object, a sign vehicle, and an interpretant (the latter should not be identified as a person, but rather with interpretative or meaning making mechanisms that provoke an action or reaction in the light of the object). Then for each category, there are special kinds of signs. We have already talked about the types of signs in relation to their object: icons, indexes and symbols. In this section, we want to consider his further typology of icons: images, diagrams and metaphors.

For Peirce, images, in their restricted sense, are icons that share similarity with their objects by means of simple qualities: color, size, tonality, shape. Diagrams are icons that represent "the relations (…) of the parts of one thing by analogous relations in their own parts" [PEI 98, p. 274], for example, mathematical diagrams, maps, statistical diagrams, and certainly different forms of data visualization. Finally, metaphors refer to their object by the intermediary of a third object that relies upon the general understanding of different types of diagram schemas.

In a study devoted to icons and diagrams, semiotician Frederik Stjernfelt shows how diagrammatic reasoning can be used in the analysis of pictorial images. Because diagrams are skeleton-like sketches of their objects (and the author indeed creates sketch versions of art paintings), the relations between their parts follow a rational form of seeing and thinking that allows for obtaining more knowledge about their objects. Moreover, natural perception, explains Stjernfelt, possesses diagrammatic abilities that permit one to perform ideal manipulations on the object. Consider how, for instance, in front of a picture, it is possible to imaginarily simulate being inside of it, or how we can mentally rotate or scale depicted objects. From this standpoint, all images are also diagrams: "what is gained by realizing the diagrammatical character of picture viewing is not least the close relation between picture and thought" [STJ 07, p. 288].

Of course, diagrams are not only derived from visual phenomena; they can also emerge to chart ideal relationships. In mathematics, different diagrams are used to support proofs or demonstrate relationships between parts of geometric figures: from diagrams in Euclid's Elements to algebra diagrams by René Descartes to complex higher dimensional abstractions such as in Riemann and Klein models. In other sections of this book, we also evoke logic diagrams that represent states of a machine and diagrammatic attributes of the visual programming paradigm, where computing code written in environments such as Max/MSP, Pure Data or NodeBox specify variations of a generative digital image while making the code a diagram as well.

Further cases of diagrams can be found in social sciences and humanities. A prominent example is of "sociograms", introduced by Jacob Moreno in 1932 to depict social relationships among groups. Sociograms have developed through the work of scientists like Albert Barabási and many more working in the field of network sciences. Artists have extensively used diagrams too, not only as primary sketches of paintings but also as a way of making notes, organizing thinking, or even as pedagogical resource, as was the case for Johann von Goethe, Filippo Marinetti, Wassily Kandisnky and Paul Klee, to mention only a small sample. Although subjective and arbitrary, personal diagrams reflect on the thinking processes and potential knowledge that can be gained from the study of their parts.

One of the differences between functional diagrams and pictures as diagrams are the explicit symbolic set of rules necessary to complete the meaning of relationships. Here, we are thinking about legends, numbers and other symbolic forms which, in their absence, would make diagrams closer to proto-iconical images, such as visual jokes (see Figure 1.2).

In his seminal work on the semiology of graphics, cartographer Jacques Bertin [BER 05] deals precisely with the study of rational images where the meaning of each sign appearing in a graphical form is conceived before it is observed by its public, that is, elements are previously and carefully arranged according to visual variables and levels of organization. The goal of Bertin is to provide a method based on visual syntax and combination rules in order to produce meaningful ways of conveying information in a graphical form.

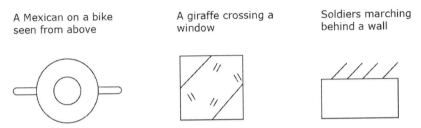

Figure 1.2. *Examples of proto-iconical images (visual jokes)*

The visual variables that Bertin distinguishes are seven: the 2D plane, scale, value (degrees of saturation and brightness), grain (simulated textures), color, orientation and form (circle, rectangle, triangle, glyphs, etc.). He then demonstrates how to use these variables according to four retinal variables [BER 05, p. 48]: 1) selective (signs are perceived as different); 2) associative (signs are perceived as similar); 3) ordered (signs are ranked); and 4) quantitative (signs are perceived as proportional to numeric factors).

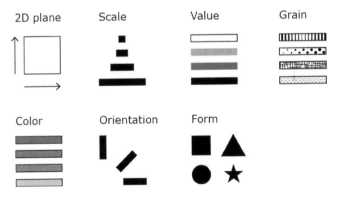

Figure 1.3. *Visual variables according to Jacques Bertin*

Furthermore, Bertin distinguishes what he calls "imposition groups", which are none other than visualization categories: networks, cartographies, diagrams and signs/symbols. Imposition groups are derived from several imposition types or spatial organization patterns: linear, circular, orthogonal and polar. Special cases occur when more than two components need to be represented: then he adds volume projections in perspective view (Chapter 4 deals with these "imposition types" from a different categorical perspective: charts, plots, network graphs, geometric sets, and variations/combinations).

Although Bertin's work was done before the use of computers, his lessons are still valid in many contemporary uses of graphics. In historical and recent accounts of graphical information, [TUF 97, LIM 11, MEI 13 DRU 14], we observe how designers use visual variables in creative manners. More recently, with the explosion of computing information visualization, it is exciting to notice models and tools that allow general users to practice with their own sets of data. In the following chapters, we will explore in detail libraries and web apps that support certain kinds of models, but it will be necessary for us to revise how such models are technically and formally implemented in order to challenge them.

1.4.4. *Visual computation*

Historically, the relationship between computer sciences and images has yielded specialized groups interested in the development of computational and mathematical methods in image processing (IP), computer vision (CV), computer graphics (CGI), and multimedia/hypermedia systems. It has also introduced new methods in established disciplines and fostered the emergence of new fields such as visual analytics, algorithmic architecture, digital art/design, digital humanities, and cultural analytics.

Simply put, the overall functions of computers can be understood from four main operations: to receive, to process, to store, and to emit information (philosopher Michel Serres observes that these operations also apply to living systems, inanimate objects and human associations. Therefore, the computer, as a universal machine, helps erase the gap between social and natural sciences because it simulates the behavior of all the objects in the world [SER 07]). From this classification, we can identify methods and techniques that have been developed for each operation. To receive information relates to digitization, image capture or image acquisition. To process information includes image representation, analysis, enhancement, generation and compression. To store information relies on bits and bytes organized in data types and formats. Finally, emitting information is concerned with image projection and image transmission through different networks and protocols.

Methods in visual computing are elaborated and used to solve practical problems. Although many foundations, concepts and techniques are shared between the specialized groups (IP, CV, and CGI), there are also specific goals. It is commonly recognized that one of the first uses of IP was in images obtained from particle accelerators and space probes in the early 1960s; the original intention was to improve quality in order to be perceived by humans. More recently, IP is concerned with all the processes that are carried out once the image has been digitized and stored in the digital format. It comprises techniques like image representation and description, image formation (quantization, sampling), image analysis (segmentation, feature extraction), image restoration, color processing, image transformations (pixel processing, geometric transformations) and image compression.

Regarding CV, it concentrates on gathering, describing and analyzing information. As we can see, it also uses image analysis, but strives to go from a syntactical description of objects and scenes to a semantic level where the system would be capable of taking decisions (such as clustering, learning and recognizing shapes). During the 1980s, the approach developed by David Marr introduced the first formalizations of vision for computing purposes. Marr was interested in deriving shape information from images, entering a sequence of representations from what he called the primal sketch (constituted by edge segments, blobs, groups, boundaries) to 2½ D sketch (local surface orientation, distance from viewer, discontinuities in depth and surface) and to 3D model representation (volumetric and surface primitives) [MAR 10, pp. 36–37]. Later, other research has extended Marr's investigations to include the particularities of the observer (human or computerized), changes in the context and evolution of internal structure of the system, such as machine learning and more recently artificial neural networks or "deep learning".

Finally, CGI deals with producing and synthetizing information. It adopts a somehow inverse direction from CV: it constructs and produces images based on a given computational model, most commonly: polygons, surfaces and volumes. In the late 1960s, the first uses of CGI appeared in the form of computer modeling, computer animation, virtual worlds, and digital art. Let's remember, for example, the "Sensorama Simulator" by Morton Heiling (1960), the artworks "Aku" (1977) and "Transjovian Pipeline" (1979) by David Em, and "Legible City" (1989) by Jeffrey Shaw.

IP, CGI and CV integrate their methods in applied areas such as scientific visualization, multimedia/hypermedia systems, video games, and digital art. The way in which this integration takes place is in the form of software. While each of the applied areas have dedicated tools, libraries, APIs and SDKs, it is interesting to note that software packages might implement the same techniques and algorithms, but by adapting its functionality according to the domain conventions and vocabulary. Consider how programs like ImageJ, Processing, Unity, Photoshop or QGIS use interface metaphors and organize workflow through their command menus.

In the past 10 years, we have seen emergent areas that have started to use extensively visual methods in their research agendas. In 2005, the well-known report *Illuminating the Path*, edited by Thomas and Cook, introduced the notion of visual analytics and defined it as: "the science of analytical reasoning facilitated by interactive visual interfaces" [THO 05, p. 4]. In the same year, the media editor Tim O'Reilly called for the era of "Web 2.0" [ORE 05], broadening the scope of data mining to the social Internet and into what is called today big data. The massive creation of texts, images and videos by any user with access to a connected computing device accelerated the development of procedures to analyze and visualize information using high-level languages like R, Python and JavaScript. We have seen that fields like "information design" are now labeled "data and information visualization", with dedicated compendiums of creative projects by designers and developers [MEI 13, LIM 11].

In 2008, Lev Manovich oriented his work on software studies towards "cultural analytics" with the aim of studying cultural data (i.e. data that is produced by everybody on an everyday basis, as opposed to scientific data for example) through IP techniques, opening the path to techniques such as media visualizations, image plots, image histograms, and motion structures. Also in 2008, the former field known as "humanities computing" started to redefine itself into "digital humanities" [SCH 08]. While the primary emphasis of scholars and practitioners seemed to be in text analysis and processing, visual methods can be found in metadata descriptors, cartography, and diagrammatic visualizations of texts (word clouds, word trees, network topologies). Other researchers use image reconstruction techniques with heritage and historical data to produce 3D models and simulations of ancient buildings and cities.

Finally, arts and design have also embraced visual computing. From the early development of CAD systems dedicated to architecture and industrial design, we observe new trends such as "algorithmic architecture" where programming code and scripts are used to create variations and generative design [TER 06, PET 13]. Researchers like Anthony Dunne, Fiona Raby, Johanna Drucker and Bettany Nowviskie have approached speculative and critical visions of design applied to graphical interfaces and devices. In art, visual computing has been considered as a means of expression, of subjectivity, of political contestation, and to represent the complex and contradictory nature of human condition. Finally, the school of pioneering artists such as John Whitney, Saul Bass, John Maeda, Jean-Pierre Balpe, Jean-Louis Boissier and Roy Ascott, among many others, has a strong influence on new generations of scholars that create, code, prototype and teach with their own productions – from artistic visualizations to computer games – as intellectual objects (to mention only a couple of recent examples, the reader can consult the recent volumes of the collection Digital Tools & Uses published by ISTE-Wiley [SZO 17, REY 17, BOU 17]).

2

Describing Graphical Information

Before we represent images and interfaces in a graphical form on a computer screen, the underlying digital information is subject to different processes. Although the surface level is always based on screen pixels, the description of images follows different forms and formats: from bitmap images to 2D and 3D vector graphics, etc. Accordingly, the kind of processes that can be performed varies for each type of image.

When we use a software application to process graphical information, we have at our disposition a series of predefined options, parameters and operations for working with information. This is a practical entry point to start discovering the functionalities harnessed by the software environment. However, we are often also confronted with the necessity of understanding what is happening "under the hood" and sometimes we even want to go further than the given possibilities at hand.

This chapter is devoted to the foundations of graphical information. In this part, we consider images as data and digital information. We look at the technical aspects that define a digital image: from data types and data structures required to render an image on the computer screen to seminal algorithms and image processing techniques. Our aim is to offer a technical overview of how images are handled by the computer and to identify how they are implemented at higher levels of description, that is, in graphical visualizations of data, user interfaces, and image interfaces for exploring information.

2.1. Organizing levels of description

Digital images can be seized from different angles: as a series of pixels on screen, as a computer code, as mathematical descriptions of vertices and edges, or as sequences of bits and bytes. Different forms depend on the *level of description* at which we study them. Generally speaking, a *level of description* uses its own language, notation system, and model rules in order to understand and explain the components of a lower level.

Scientist Douglas Hofstadter observes that any aspect of human thinking can be considered a "high level description of a system [the brain] which, at a lower level, is managed by simple and formal rules" [HOF 85, p. 626]. Lower levels can be so complex that for practical reasons, we take for granted their internal mechanisms and we produce a semantic abstraction of them. Thus, "the meaning of an object is not located in its interior" [HOF 85, p. 653]; it rather comes from multidimensional cognitive structures: previous experiences, intuitions, mental representations, etc. Following this argument, we will understand software from its material components and material relationships: programming languages and graphical interfaces that allow using algorithms that have been designed according to determinate data structures and electronic circuitry, that rely on more basic data types that give shape to bytes and bits.

So how and where should we start analyzing digital images and interfaces? If we choose the software level as entry point, then we would have to take for granted lower layers that might be useful in our account. Moreover, which aspect of software should we consider: the compiled application, the source code or the graphical user interface? And what about the relationship between software and hardware, including display, storing and processing components?

With these questions in mind, the model called "generative trajectory of expression", proposed by semiotician Jacques Fontanille [FON 08] (briefly introduced in section 1.4.2), will help us distinguish among different layers of meaning and description. The term "generative" is borrowed from semiotician Algirdas Greimas, who uses it to accentuate the act and mode of production– creation. The term "trajectory" makes reference to the fact that there are several components that intervene and cooperate in the production mode. This trajectory goes, similar to Hofstadter, from simple to complex, from abstract to concrete levels. Although Fontanille has continued to develop his model in the analysis of practices and forms of life, we have discussed it and adapted it to more fundamental levels regarding digital images.

Table 2.1 summarizes the different levels through which digital images are used and produced. Each level claims a double face (or interface as Fontanille calls them [FON 08, p. 34]), where there is always a formal part that points to a lower level structure, and a material–substantial part directed towards the manifestation in a higher level. In other words, what is formal at one level derives from what is substantial in a lower level; and what is substantial is delimited by its formal support. To study the intricacies at any given level, it is necessary to revise how it is produced from its different components.

In the following parts of this chapter, we will follow this generative trajectory to offer a technical overview of how images are handled by the computer and to identify how they are implemented at higher levels of description. We will develop formally the first three levels: signs, texts and objects. The remaining levels can be implied in the following chapters.

In Table 2.1, the emphasis is made on the "expression plane" rather than on the "content plane". In semiotic studies, the expression is part of the meaning process that is perceptible, while the content is the abstract, internal and interpretative part that is evoked or suggested in front of an expression.

For a different look at how semiotics has been approached to study computing processes, or if the reader desires more insights from the "content" perspective, we might point to seminal works by Peter Andersen [AND 97], Clarisse de Souza [DES 05] and Kumiko Tanaka-Ishii [TAN 10]. Historically, Heinz Zemanek [ZEM 66] was among the first to study relationships between language and compilers, asking for instance, what do different translating principles and what do different compilers do to the language? The articulation of Zemanek's semiotic thinking is grounded on the Vienna Circle, which was influenced by Bertrand Russell and Charles Morris, the latter being a follower of Charles Peirce and who distinguished formalization in terms of syntactic, semantic and pragmatic dimensions. More recently, the linguistic turn is also considered by Frederica Frabbeti [FRA 15], who connects saussurean signifiers to voltages and micro-circuitry and to their signified meaning according to the rules of programming languages in which the code is written. She is interested in how the formalization of language makes them an instrument [FRA 15, p. 134]; reading Hayles, Kittler, Derrida and Stiegler, among others, to investigate the larger question of code and metaphysics.

Level of pertinence	Interface	Expression in digital image (Formal/Material)	Experience
1. Signs	Source of formants	Electron diffusion, binary code	Figuration
	Recursive formants	Data types, data structures, algorithms (logical and mathematical rules)	
2. Texts	Figurative isotopies of expression	Syntax and semantics of programming languages, programming styles, elements of the graphical user interface (GUI)	Interpretation
	Enunciation/ inscription device	Programming code, graphical user interfaces, file formats, application software	
3. Objects	Formal support of inscription	Raster grid	Corporeity
	Morphological praxis	Display technologies (screens CRT, LCD, LED, DLP); capturing devices (CCD, CMOS); printing devices (2D and 3D)	
4. Scenes of practice	Predicative scenes	Manipulating, retouching, drawing, designing, experimenting, discovering, etc.	Practice
	Negotiation processes	Different practices, e.g. artistic, aesthetic, commercial, educational, professional	
5. Strategies	Strategic management of practices	Fields and domains such as image processing, computer vision, computer graphics, digital humanities, UX/UI	Conjuncture
	Iconisation of strategic behaviors	Working with images as a scientist, or as an artist, or as a designer, or as a social researcher	
6. Life forms	Strategic styles	Digital culture, digital society	Ethos and behavior

Table 2.1. *Levels of description. Semiotic trajectory of expression with an adaptation to digital images*

2.2. Fundamental signs of visual information

At the beginning of the trajectory, meaning starts to take form in basic units of expression. In the case of digital information, such units are essentially abstract. Digital computers are considered multipurpose precisely because they can be programmed to perform a wide variety of operations. That means the same hardware components can be configured to support many diverse uses and applications. This is possible because the fundamental type of information that digital systems handle is in abstract binary form.

In this section, we explain how fundamental units of expression are configured from abstract to more concrete idealizations that help achieve envisioned operations with digital computers. In other words, our goal is to take a glance at the basic pieces underlying software environments. To do that, we go from data types to data structures in order to identify how they allow the implementation of solutions to recurrent problems. Conversely, it also occurs that the nature of problems dictates how information should be organized to obtain more efficient results.

2.2.1. *From binary code to data types*

The binary form is represented with binary digits, also called *bits*. Each bit has only two possible values: 0 or 1. A series of bits is called *binary code*, and it can express notations in different systems. For example, human users use different notation systems to refer to numbers: instead of using a 4-digit binary code such as 0101, we will likely say 5 in our more familiar decimal system, or we could have written it using another notation: "V" in Roman.

Hence, all sign systems that can be simulated by computers are ultimately transformed into binary code. As we can imagine, sequences of binary code become complex very rapidly because they increase in length while using the same elementary units. On top of binary code, other number systems exist with the intention to overcome this difficulty. While octal and hexadecimal number systems have been used, the latter remains more popular; it compacts four binary digits into one hex digit. Table 2.2 summarizes the equivalencies for numerical values, from 0 to 15, in hexadecimal code and in 4-digit binary code.

Decimal number	Hexadecimal	4-digit binary code
0	0	0000
1	1	0001
2	2	0010
3	3	0011
4	4	0100
5	5	0101
6	6	0110
7	7	0111
8	8	1000
9	9	1001
10	A	1010
11	B	1011
12	C	1100
13	D	1101
14	E	1110
15	F	1111

Table 2.2. *Numerical notations: decimal, hexadecimal and binary*

In terms of memory storage of bits, the industry standard since early 1960s are 8-bit series also called bytes or octets. Generally speaking, a byte can accommodate a keyboard character, an ASCII character, or a pixel in 8-bit gray or color scale. Bytes also constitute the measure of messages we send by email (often in kilobytes), the size of files and software (often in megabytes), or the capacity of computing devices (often in giga or terabytes). As we will see, the formal description in terms of 8-bit series is manifested at higher levels of graphical interface: from the specification to the parameterization of media quality and visual properties.

In practice, binary code is also called machine language. Bits represent the presence or absence of voltage and current electrical signals communicating among the physical components of digital computers such as the microprocessor, the memory unit, and input/output devices. Currently, machine language is of course hardly used. What we use to write instructions to computers are higher-level languages. One step above machine language we find assembly language and, at this level, it is interesting to note that the literature in electrical, electronic and computer engineering distinguishes between "system software" and "applications software" [DAN 02, p. 9].

In general terms, assembly language is used for developing system software such as operating systems (OS), and it is specific to the type of hardware in the machine (for example, a certain kind of processor). On the other hand, applications software run on the OS and can be written in languages on top of assembler, such as C. The passage from one level to another requires what we would call "meta-programs". An assembler converts assembly into machine language, while a compiler does the same but from higher-level language.

Before moving from the formal level of binary signs into a more material level of programming languages, we should clarify that this level (as it may occur in any other level of the generative trajectory) could be further elaborated if we operate a change of "scale". We could be more interested to know how, for instance, signals behave among digital components, or how they are processed by more basic units such as the algorithmic and logic unit (ALU), or how circuits are designed logically, or how they are interconnected. In order to do that, we should turn to the area of study called "digital and computer design".

2.2.2. *Data types*

As we have seen, bits are assembled to represent different systems of signs. Our question now is: which are those different systems and how do computers describe them? We already saw that binary code is used to describe numbers and letters, and from there we can create words and perform mathematical operations with numbers.

Data types represent the different kinds of values that a computer can handle. Any word and any number are examples of values: "5", "V", or "Paris". From the first specifications of programming languages, we recognize a handful of basic data types, or as computer scientist Niklaus Wirth called them: "standard primitive types" [WIR 04, pp. 13–17]:

– INTEGER: for whole numbers

– REAL: numbers with decimal fraction

– BOOLEAN: logical values, either TRUE or FALSE

– CHAR: a set of printable characters

– SET: small sets of integers, commonly no greater than 31 elements

These particular data types were first used in languages in which Wirth was involved, from Algol 68 and Pascal in 1969 to Oberon in 1985. Currently, many programming languages use the same data types although with different names and abbreviations. As a matter of fact, the situation of identifying which data types are supported by any language is experienced most of the time when we learn a new language. Considerable time is spent in distinguishing those syntax differences.

Data types allow performing, programming and iterating actions with them. For example, basic operations with numbers include addition, subtraction, division and multiplication, while operations with words are conjunction and disjunction of characters. However, data types can be combined and organized in order to support more complicated operations, as we will see in the following section.

In the case of graphical information, there are two fundamental approaches to data types. From the standpoint of image processing and computer vision, the accent is placed on *bitmap* and *raster graphics* because many significant processes deal with capturing and analyzing images. A different view of data types is that of computer graphics whose focus is on *vector graphics* as a model to describe and synthetize 2D figures and 3D meshes that can be later rasterized or rendered as a bitmap image. We will now take a brief look at both perspectives.

2.2.2.1. *Data types and bitmap graphics*

The bitmap model describes an image as a series of finite numerical values, called picture elements or *pixels*, organized into a 2D matrix. In its most basic type, each value allocates one bit, thus it only has one possible brightness value, either white or black. The described image in this model is also known as monochrome image or 1-bit image.

In order to produce gray scale images, the amount of different values per pixel needs to be increased. We refer to 8-bit images when each pixel has up to 255 different integer values. If we wonder why there are only 255 values, the explanation can be made by recalling Table 2.2: the 4-bit column shows all the different values between 0000 and 1111 and their corresponding decimal notations. An 8-bit notation adds 4 bits to the left and counts from 00000000 to 11111111, where the highest value in decimal notation is 255.

Nowadays, the most common data type used for describing color images is 24-bit color. Taking as primary colors the red, green and blue, every pixel contains one 8-bit layer for each of these colors, thus resulting in a 24-bit or "true color" image. As such, the color for a given pixel can be written in a list of three values. In programming languages such as Processing, the data type COLOR[1] exists together with other types, like BOOLEAN, CHAR, DOUBLE, FLOAT, INT and LONG.

The red, green and blue color combination has been adopted as the standard model for describing colors in electronic display devices. From the generic RGB color model, there are more specific color spaces in use, for example:

– *RGBA*: adds an extra layer for the alpha channel that permits modification of transparency. In this case, images are 32-bit.

– *sRGB*: a standardized version by the International Electrotechnical Commission (IEC) and widely used in displaying and capturing devices.

– *HSB (Hue, Saturation, Brightness) or HSL (Hue, Saturation, Lightness)*: a color representation that rearranges the RGB theoretical cube representation into a conical and cylindrical form (we will revise those models in section 2.4).

In the form of data types, colors are handled as binary codes of 24 or 32 bits. Table 2.3 shows some RGB combinations, their equivalent in HSB values, in hexadecimal notation, in binary code, and their given name by the World Wide Web Consortium (W3C).

---

1 https://processing.org/reference/color_datatype.html

Name	RGB	HSL	Hex	24-digit binary code
Black	0, 0, 0	0, 0%, 0%	#000000	00000000 00000000 00000000
Red	255, 0, 0	0, 100%, 50%	#FF0000	11111111 00000000 00000000
Lime (Green)	0, 255, 0	120, 100%, 50%	#00FF00	00000000 11111111 00000000
Blue	0, 0, 255	240, 100%, 50%	#0000FF	00000000 00000000 11111111
Cyan or Aqua	0, 255, 255	180, 100%, 50%	#00FFFF	00000000 11111111 11111111
Magenta or Fuchsia	255, 0, 255	300, 100%, 50%	#FF00FF	11111111 00000000 11111111
Yellow	255, 255, 0	60, 100%, 50%	#FFFF00	11111111 11111111 00000000
Gray	128, 128, 128	0, 0%, 50%	#808080	10000000 10000000 10000000
White	255, 255, 255	0, 0%, 100%	#FFFFFF	11111111 11111111 11111111
Tomato	255, 99, 71	9, 100%, 64%	#FF6347	11111111 01100011 01000111

Table 2.3. *Color notations: W3C name, RGB, HSB, hexadecimal, binary code*

In domains like astronomy, medical imagery, and high dynamic range imagery (HDRI), 48- and 64-bit images are used. For these types, each image component has 16 bits. The reason for adding extra layers is to allocate space for different light intensities in the same image, or to describe pixel values in trillions of colors (what is also called "deep color"). However, although software applications that allow us to manipulate such amounts of data have existed for some time, the hardware for capturing and displaying those images is still limited to specialized domains.

2.2.2.2. Data types and 2D vector graphics

Vector graphics describe images in terms of the geometric properties of the objects to be displayed. As we will see, the description of elements varies depending on the type of images that we are creating – currently 2D or 3D. In any case, such description of images occurs before its restitution on screen; this means that graphics exist as formulae yet to be mapped to a position on the raster grid (such positions are called *screen pixels*; see section 2.4.1.).

The equivalent to data types in vector graphics are the *graphics primitives*. In 2D graphics, the elementary units are commonly:

– *Points*: represent a position along the X and Y axes. The value and unit of measure for points in space are commonly real (or float) numbers expressed in pixels, for example, 50.3 pixels. Furthermore, the size and color of points can be modified. Size is expressed in pixels, while color can be specified with values according to RGB, HSL or HEX models (see Table 2.3).

– *Lines*: represent segments by two points in the coordinate system. Besides the position of points and the color of points, the line or both, line width and line style can also be modified. The latter with character strings (solid, dot or dash pattern), and the former with pixel values.

– *Polylines*: connected sequences of lines.

– *Polygons*: closed sequences of polylines.

– *Fill areas*: polygons filled with color or texture.

– *Curves*: lines with one or more control points. The idea of control points is to parameterize the aspect of the curve according to the polygonal boundary created by the set of control points, called the *convex hull*. Thus, we can position points in space but also the position of control points, both expressed in real number values. There are several kinds of curves, each of them representing different geometrical properties, conditions and specifications:

– *Quadratic curves*: curves with one control point.

– *Cubic curves*: curves with two control points.

– *Spline curves (or splines):* curves with several cubic sections.

– *Bézier curves:* curves based on Bernstein polynomials (mathematical expressions of several variables).

– *B-splines (contraction of basis splines)*: curves composed of several Bézier curves that introduce *knots*, a kind of summarization including different control points from single Bézier curves.

– *Circles, ellipses* and *arcs*: a variety of curves with fill areas properties. That means that while a circle can be easily imagined to have a color or texture fill, it is also the case for only a fragment of its circumference. In that instance, the segment is an arc that closes the shape at its two points. The ellipse is a scaled circle in a non-proportional manner.

Today, many programming languages provide combinations of already made prototypical shapes. The most common examples are ellipses and rectangles, which means that triangles and other polygons (pentagons, hexagons, irregular shapes with curved edges, etc.) have to be specified through vertices points. Another case is text, which typically needs to load an external font file (file extensions OTF (OpenType Font) or TTF (TrueType Font)) containing the description of characters in geometrical terms.

2.2.2.3. *Data types and 3D vector graphics*

In 3D graphics, the notion of graphics primitives depends on the modeling technique used to construct a digital object. In general, we can identify two major approaches: *surface methods* and *volumetric methods*. The first method implies the description and representation of the exterior surface of solid objects while the second method considers its interior aspects. Allow us to explore briefly both the approaches.

– *Surface methods*: polygons can be extended to model 3D objects, in an analogous fashion to 2D graphics. Today, many software applications include what are called *standard graphics objects*, which are predefined functions that describe basic solid geometry such as cubes, spheres, cones, cylinders and regular polyhedra (tetrahedron, hexahedron, octahedron, dodecahedron and icosahedron, containing 4, 6, 8, 12 and 20 faces, respectively).

For different kinds of geometries, another technique of modeling objects consists of considering basic graphics units in terms of *vertices*, *edges* and *surfaces*. In this respect, it is necessary to construct the geometry of an object by placing points in space. The points can then be connected to form edges, and the edges form planar faces that constitute the external surface of the object.

Besides polygons, it is also possible to model surfaces from parametric curves. We talk about spline surfaces, Bézier surfaces, B-spline surfaces, beta-splines, rational splines, and NURBS (*non-uniform rational B-splines*). The main advantage of using curves over polygons is the ability to model smooth curved objects (through *interpolation* processes). Overall, a spline surface can be described from a set of at least two orthogonal splines. The several types of curves that we mentioned stand for specific properties of control points and boundary behaviors of the curve[2].

– *Volumetric approaches*: we can mention volume elements (or *voxels*) as basic units for a type of modeling that is often used for representing data obtained from measuring instruments such as 3D scanners. A voxel delimits a cubic region of the virtual world, in a similar manner to pixels, but of course a voxel comprises the volume of the box. If an object exists in a particular region, then it could be further described by subdividing the interior of the region into octants, forming smaller voxels. The amount of detail depends on the necessary resolution to be shown adequately on the screen.

A couple of other different techniques for space-partitioning representation can be derived from combining basic elements. For instance, *constructive solid geometry* methods unveil superposed regions of two geometrical objects. Basically, there are three main operations on such sets: union (both objects are joined), intersection (only the intersected area is obtained) and difference (a subtraction of one object from the other). The second case is called extrusion or *sweep representations*. It consists of modeling the volume of an object from a curve that serves as a trajectory and a base model that serves as the shape to be extruded.

The other example of the volumetric approach considers scalar, vectors, tensors and multivariate data fields as the elementary type for producing visual representations (in the next section, we will cover vectors such as data structures in more detail). These cases are more used in scientific visualization, and they consist of information describing physical properties such as energy, temperature, pressure, velocity, acceleration, stress and strain in materials, etc. The kind of visual representations that are produced from these kinds of data types usually take the form of surface plots, isolines, isosurfaces, and volume renderings [HEA 04, pp. 514–520].

---

2 Detailed explanations of spline surfaces can be found in computer graphics literature such as [HEA 04, pp. 408–472].

As can be inferred from the last example, an object should be further described in order to parameterize its color, texture, opacity, as well as how it reacts to light (reflecting and refracting it, for instance). Without this information, it could be impossible to explore or see inside a volumetric object. Together with its geometrical description, a digital object also includes data called *surface normal vectors*, which is information that defines the simulated angle of light in relation to the surface.

Finally, for all cases in 3D graphics, we can also think about triangles as primitive elements. Any surface of an object is tessellated into triangles or quadrilaterals (the latter being a generalization of the former because any rectangle can be divided into two triangles) in order to be rendered as an image on screen. Even in the case of freeform surfaces, they often consist of Bézier curves of degree 3 as they can be bounded into triangles more easily.

2.2.3. *Data structures*

Generally speaking, we can approach data structures or information structures as a special form of organizing data types. We create data structures for practical reasons; for example, a data structure can hold information that describes a particular geometrical form or, more simply, it can store a bunch of data as a list. In fact, the way in which data is structured depends on what we intend to do with that data. Therefore, data structures are intimately related to algorithms – which are the specific topic of section 2.2.4.

Computer scientist Niklaus Wirth considered data structures as "conglomerates" of already existing data types. One of the main issues of grouping and nesting different types of information has always been arranging them efficiently, both for retrieval and access, but also for storing. Data representation deals with "mapping the abstract structure onto a computer store... storage cells called bytes" [WIR 04, p. 23]. Wirth distinguished between static and dynamic structures that he implemented in the programming languages where he was involved as a developer. *Static structures* had a predefined size, and thus the allocated memory cells were found in a linear order. Examples of this type are arrays, records, sets and sequences (or files). On the contrary, *dynamic structures* derivate from the latter but vary in size, values, and can be generated during the execution of the program. In this case, the information is distributed along different nonsequential cells and accessed by using links. Examples of this type are pointers, linked lists, trees and graphs.

With similar goals but different perspective, computer scientist Donald Knuth categorized information structures into linear and nonlinear. Porting his theoretical concepts to his programming language MIX, Knuth counts as linear structures: arrays, stacks, queues and simple lists (circular and doubly linked) [KNU 68, p. 232]. Nonlinear structures are mainly linked lists and trees and graphs of different sorts: binary trees, free trees, oriented trees, forests (lists of trees) [KNU 68, p. 315].

Data structures are used extensively at different levels of the computing environment: from the design and management of OS to the middleware to the web applications layer. Moreover, data structures can be nested or interconnected, becoming larger and complex. In some cases, it is necessary to transform them, from one structure to another. Although it is out of our scope to study data structures in detail, we review those that seem to be fundamental for visual information.

2.2.3.1. *Data structures for image processing and analysis*

In the last section, we mentioned that common techniques for image processing are performed on bitmap images, which are composed of picture values named pixels. Such values are orderly arranged into a bi-dimensional array of data called a matrix. A bitmap is thus a kind of array data structure.

– *Arrays*: the array is one of the most popular data structure of all time. It defines a collection of elements of the same type, organized in a linear manner and that can be accessed by an index value that is, in its turn, an integer data type.

– *Matrices*: elements of the array can also be themselves structured. This kind of array is called a matrix. A matrix whose components describe two element values is a 2D matrix. In the case of bitmap images, those values constitute the rows and columns of the pixel values that describe an image (X and Y coordinates). Of course, different kinds of matrices exist: multi-dimensional matrices (as in 3D images) or jagged arrays (when the amount of elements in arrays is not regular), to mention a couple.

– *Quadtrees*: these are known as nonlinear data structures. They are based on the concept of trees or graphs. A quadtree structure is created on top of a traditional rectangular bitmap in order to subdivide it in four regions (called quadrants). Then the structure decomposes a subregion into smaller quadrants to go into further detail. The recursive procedure extends until the image detail arrives at the size of a pixel. In the following section, we will illustrate some of the uses and applications of quadtrees.

– *Relational tables*: Niklaus Wirth thought of them as matrices of heterogeneous elements or records. Tables associate rows and columns by means of keys. By combining a tree structure to detect boundaries and contours, the table can be used to associate semantic descriptions with the detected regions.

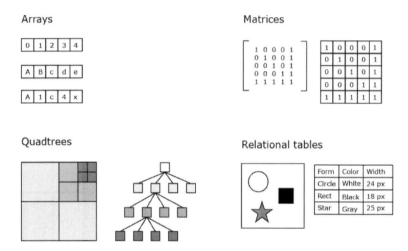

Figure 2.1. *Data structures for image processing*

2.2.3.2. *Data structures for image synthesis*

Image synthesis is a broad field interested in image generation. In visual computing, it is the area of computer graphics that deals more specifically with image synthesis. From this perspective, we observe three main models for image representation: 1) meshes; 2) NURBS and subdivisions (curves and surfaces); and 3) voxels. The first model has been widely adopted for image rendering techniques (for rasterizing vector graphics), the second in object modeling (shaping surfaces and objects), and the third in scientific visualization (creating volumetric models out of data).

Each one of these models takes advantage of the fundamental data structures (arrays, lists, trees) in order to build more complex structures adapted to special algorithmic operations. These structures are known as *graphical data structures*, including geometrical, spatial and topological categories. By abstraction and generalization of their properties, they have been used to describe and represent 1D, 2D and 3D graphics.

At the most basic level, graphics consist of vertices and edges. One way to describe them is according to two separate lists: one for the coordinates of vertices and the other for the edges, describing pairs of vertices. The data structure for this polyline is called *1D mesh* [HUG 14, p. 189].

Of course, points coordinates are not the only way to describe a line. *Vector structures* are a different approach that exploits two properties: magnitude and direction. In this sense, the line is no longer fixed in the space, but becomes a difference of points. It maintains its properties even if the positions of points are transformed. The magnitude property defines the distance between two points while the direction defines the angle with respect to an axis. As we mentioned earlier, vectors are used in scientific domains because it is straightforward to simulate velocity and force with them as both the phenomena show magnitude and direction properties. The latter quantity is the amount of push/pull and the former quantity refers to the speed of moving an object.

Here we should evoke briefly *tensors*, which are a generalization of vectors. Tensors are defined by coefficient quantities called ranks, for example, the number of multiple directions at one time. They are useful, for instance, to simulate transformation properties like stress, strain and conductivity. For terminology ends, tensors with rank 0 are called scalars (magnitude but no direction); with rank 1 are called vectors (magnitude and direction); with rank 2 are called matrices; with rank 3 are often called triad; and with rank 4 tetrads, and so on. As we will explore in further chapters, vectors and tensors have gained popularity as they are used for modeling particle systems, cellular automata, and machine learning programs.

In 2D and 3D, vertices and edges are grouped in triangles. A series of triangles connected by their edges produce a surface called *triangle mesh*. In this case, the data structure consists mainly of three tables: one for vertices, one for triangles and one for the neighbor list. The latter table helps identify the direction of the face and the normal vectors (this is important when surfaces are illuminated, and it is necessary to describe how light bounces off or passes through them).

Besides triangle meshes, it is also possible to model objects with quadrangles (also named *quads*) and other polygons of more sides. A simple case of using quads would be to insert a simple bitmap image (a photograph, an icon, etc.) inside a container plane (sometimes called a *pixmap*). There is today some debate around the reasons to choose quads over triangles (most notably in the digital modeling and sculpting communities); however, current software applications often process in the background the necessary calculations to convert quads into triangles. Triangles anyhow are preferred because of their geometric simplicity: they are planar, do not self-intersect, they are irreducible and therefore are easier to join and to rasterize.

With the intention to keep track, find intersections, and store values and properties of complex objects and scenes, the field of computer graphics has developed *spatial data structures*. Such structures are built on the concept of polymorphism, which states that structures of some primitive type be allowed to implement their operations on a different type. We can cite two main kinds of spatial data structures: lists and trees.

– *Lists*: they can be considered as a sequence of values whose order is irrelevant for the operations that they support. Lists are among the most basic and earliest forms of data structure. Donald Knuth, for example, identified and implemented two types of lists still popular today: stacks and queues. *Stacks* allow deleting or inserting elements from one side of the list (the top, for instance, representing the latest element added and the first element deleted). *Queues* allow deleting data from one side (for example, the first element) while adding new data to the other end. In the case of visual information, lists can be generalized to higher dimensions: each element of the list can be a different structure, for instance, an array containing two or three position values.

– *Trees*: as we mentioned earlier, trees are nonlinear structures that store data hierarchically. The elements of trees are called nodes, and the references to other nodes are edges or links. There are several variations of trees (some lists have tree-like attributes): linked lists (where nodes point to another in a sequential fashion); circular linked lists (where the last node points back to the first); doubly linked lists (where each node points to two locations, the next and the precedent node); binary trees and binary search trees (BST) (where each node points simultaneously to two nodes located at a lower level).

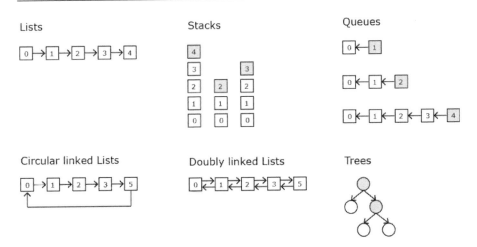

Figure 2.2. *Data structures: types of lists and trees*

Applied to visual information, there are three important variations of trees:

– *Binary space partition (BSP) tree:* while a 2D spatial tree will divide the space by means of 2D splitting lines, a BSP will partition the inner space of volumes into subspaces. Depending on the algorithmic operations, subspaces can be 2D polygons, 3D polyhedra or higher-dimensional polytopes [HUG 14, p. 1084].

– *Octrees*: octrees extend the idea of quadtrees from two dimensions to three dimensions. The tree structure consists of nodes pointing to eight children that describe the volume space. The principle is to start from the cube volume that surrounds a model and to recursively subdivide it into smaller cubes. As in the case of quadtrees, each division is performed at the center of its parent.

– *Bounding volume hierarchy (BVH) tree*: this structure separates space in nesting volumes by means of axis-aligned boxes (bounding tight clusters of primitives). Its implementation requires first a BSP tree and then boxes form bottom-top (from the leaves to the root). Even though boxes at the same level often overlap in this passage, it has demonstrated better efficiency over octrees and has gained recent popularity for ray tracing and collision detection operations.

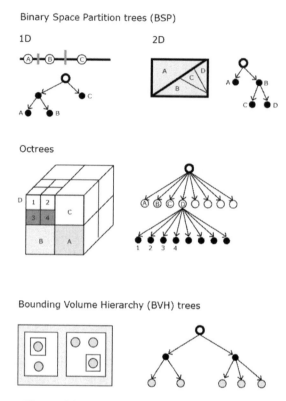

Figure 2.3. *Data structures for image synthesis*

To close this section, we should point to the fact that image synthesis considers the generated or modeled graphical object together with the virtual world, or environment, where it exists. For example, in 3D graphics, the data structure *scene graph* arranges the whole universe of the image, from the scene to the object to its parts.

2.2.4. *Algorithms*

If we imagine data structures as objects, algorithms then would be the actions allowed on those objects. The close relationship between both can be seized from what we expect to do with our data. Just as in dialectic situations, a data structure is conceived to support certain operations, but algorithms are also designed based on the possibilities and limits of data structures.

Computer scientist Donald E. Knuth defined algorithms simply as a "finite set of rules that gives a sequence of operations for solving a specific type of problem" [KNU 68, p. 4]. In this approach, the notion can be related to others like recipe, process, method, technique, procedure or routine. However, he explains, an algorithm should meet five features [KNU 68, pp. 4–6]:

– Finiteness: an algorithm terminates after a finite number of steps. A counter example of an algorithm that lacks finiteness is better called a computational method or procedure, for example, a system that constantly communicates with its environment.

– Definiteness: each step must be precisely, rigorously and unambiguously defined. A counter example would be a kitchen recipe: the measures of ingredients are often described culturally: a dash of salt, a small saucepan, etc.

– Input: an algorithm has zero or more inputs that can be declared initially or that can be added dynamically during the process.

– Output: it has one or more quantities that have a relation with the inputs.

– Effectiveness: the operations must be basically enough so that they could be tested or simulated using pencil and paper. Effectiveness can be evaluated in terms of the number of times each step is executed.

Algorithms have proliferated in computer science and make evident its relationship to mathematics. Because data types are handled as discrete numerical values, an algorithm takes advantage of calculations based on mathematical concepts: powers, logarithms, sums, products, sets, permutations, factorials, Fibonacci numbers, asymptotic representations. Besides those, in visual computing, we also found: algebra, trigonometry, Cartesian coordinates, vectors, matrix transformations, interpolations, curves and patches, analytic geometry, discrete geometry, geometric algebra. The way in which an algorithm implements such operations varies enormously, in the same sense that various people might solve the same problem very differently. Thus, there are algorithms that are used more often than others, not only because they can be used in several distinct data structures, but also because they solve a problem in the most efficient yet simple fashion.

To describe an algorithm, its steps can be listed and written in a natural language, but it can also be represented as mathematical formulae, as flow charts, or as diagrams depicting states and sequences[3] (Figure 2.4). The passage from these forms to its actual execution goes through its enunciation as a programming code (the topic of section 2.3.1).

Algorithm E (*Euclid's algorithm*). Given two positive integers m and n, find their *greatest common divisor*, that is, the largest positive integer that evenly divides both m and n.

E1. [Find remainder.] Divide m by n and let r be the remainder. (We will have $0 \leq r < n$.)

E2. [Is it zero?] If $r = 0$, the algorithm terminates; n is the answer.

E3. [Reduce.] Set $m \leftarrow n$, $n \leftarrow r$, and go back to step E1. ∎

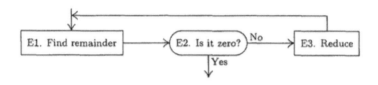

Figure 2.4. *Euclid's algorithm and flowchart representation [KNU 68, pp. 2–3]*

Before diving into algorithms for visual information, we briefly review the two broadest types of algorithms used in data in general: sorting and searching.

2.2.4.1. Sorting

Sorting, in the words of Niklaus Wirth, "is generally understood to be the process of rearranging a given set of objects in a specific order. The purpose of sorting is to facilitate the later search for members of the sorted set" [WIR 04, p. 50]. D. E. Knuth exemplifies the use of sorting algorithms on items and collections by means of keys. Each key represents the record and establishes a sort relationship, either a < b, or b < a, or a = b. By the same

---

3 Algorithms can also be simulated in an interactive or animated manner. Examples of websites dedicated to *algorithm visualization* are: https://visualgo.net/, http://algovisualizer. jasonpark.me/, http://sorting.at/

token, if a < b and b < c, then a < c [KNU 73, p. 5]. There exist many different sorting algorithms and methods; among the most used, we have:

– *Sorting by insertion*: items are evaluated one by one. Each item is positioned in its right place after each iteration process of the steps.

– *Sorting by exchange*: pairs of items are permutated to their right locations.

– *Sorting by selection*: items are separated, or floated, starting with the smallest and going up to the largest.

The first and the most basic algorithms evolved as the amounts and type of data to be sorted increased and differed. Examples of advanced algorithms invented around the 1960s but still in use today are: Donald Shell's diminishing increment, polyphase merge, tree insertion, oscillating sort; Tony Hoare's quicksort; J. W. J. William's heapsort.

2.2.4.2. Searching

Searching is related to processes of finding and recovering information stored in the computer's memory. In the same form of sorting, data keys are also used in searching. D. E. Knuth puts the problem as: "algorithms for searching are presented with a so-called argument, K, and the problem is to find which record has K as its key" [KNU 73, p. 389]. Generally speaking, there have been two main kinds of searching methods: sequential and binary.

– *Sequential searching* starts at the beginning of the set or table of records and potentially visits all of them until finding the key.

– *Binary searching* relies in sorted data that could be stored in tree structures. There are different binary searching methods. Knuth already identifies binary tree searching (BTS), balanced trees, multiway trees, and we observe more recent derivations such as red-black trees or left-leaning red-black trees (LLRB) (which were evoked at the end of the last section as an example of esoteric data structure). Anyhow, the overall principle of these searching methods is to crawl the tree in a symmetric order, "traversing the left subtree of each node just before that node, then traversing the right subtree" [KNU 73, p. 422].

We will now discuss some algorithms introduced specifically within the context of visual data. For practical reasons, we continue distinguishing techniques from different fields in visual computing[4], and we also relate how these techniques apply on specific data structures.

2.2.4.3. Geometric Transformations

Geometric transformations imply modification of the coordinates of pixels in a given image. They are based consistently on arrays and matrices data structures. They define operations for translating (i.e. moving linearly along the axes), rotating (along two or three axes) and scaling (i.e. dimensioning an image). These techniques can be applied globally – that is, to the entire bitmap image – or only onto smaller layered images contained in the space, such as *sprites* in 2D graphics or *meshes* in 3D graphics.

Common variations of these methods include: stretching or contracting, shearing or skewing, reflecting, projecting (rotating and scaling to simulate perspective). More complex methods exist such as *nonlinear distortions*. In this case, the points are mapped onto quadratic curves resulting in affine, projective, bilinear, twirl, ripple and spherical transformations, for example.

2.2.4.4. Image transformation (image filtering)

The second important family of transformations that are also based on arrays and matrices of pixels are *filters*. The general idea of filtering is to define a region of pixels inside the image (also called a neighborhood or spatial mask, kernel, template, window), then to perform an operation on that region before applying it to the entire image space [GON 08, p. 167]. There are two main types of filtering in visual computing literature. First, those performed on the image space:

– *Intensity transformations*: such as negative transformations, contrast manipulation, and histogram processing.

– *Smoothing filters*: used for blurring and noise reduction, either by averaging or ranking (ordering) the pixels in the mask.

– *Sharpening filters*: enhance edges by spatial differentiation [GON 08, p. 179].

---

4 Our main reason is to orient the reader towards more detailed literature in case they are interested in going deeper into details. We note that in a real-world project, it is common to cross boundaries from one field to another. As a matter of fact, one aim of this book is to foster disciplinary border crossing and to invite techniques and practices from other fields into our own.

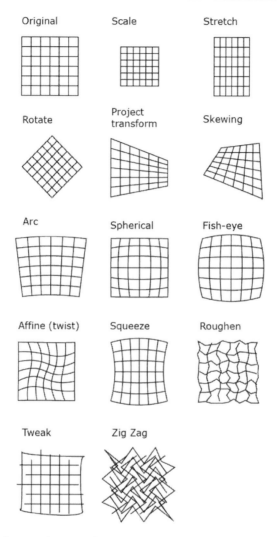

Figure 2.5. *Geometrical transformations (created with Adobe Illustrator filters)*

Second, there are filters that perform better when the image is viewed as a signal. As with sound frequency and amplitude, images also show variations of visual information that can be associated with frequencies. The standard mechanism to transform image coordinates into frequencies is the Fourier transform.

– *Fourier transform*: this helps to determine the amount of different frequencies in a signal. To do this, the surface of the image is first converted to sine and cosine curves. "The values of the pixels in the frequency domain image are two component vectors" [PAR 11, p. 254]. Variations of this transform are discrete Fourier transform or DFT (applied to sampled signals) and the fast Fourier transform or FFT (an optimization of the latter).

– *High-pass filters*: these are based on small frequencies; they apply transformations to edges and small regions.

– *Low-pass filter*: refer to slow variation in visual information such as big objects and backgrounds.

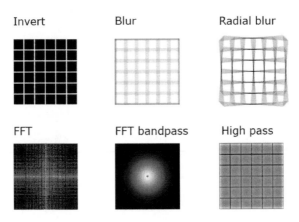

Figure 2.6. *Image filtering. FFT images were produced with ImageJ, all other with Adobe Photoshop*

As it might be guessed, some filter operations can be achieved faster in the frequency space than in the image space, and vice versa: particular methods like correlation and convolution[5] address those issues. Nowadays, there are new techniques and ongoing research that extend the use of image filtering into specialized fields within the domains of image processing and computer vision dedicated to image enhancement, image correction, image restoration, image reconstruction, image segmentation, image measurement,

---

5 These are mathematical operations on a pair of functions that give a third function as result. Applied to visual information, the original image is considered a function; a mask filter would be the second function. The resulting third function would then be applied and transformed back to the spatial field.

image and object detection, and image and object recognition. Among many other standalone or combined filters introduced for special uses, we may cite: noise, noise reduction, thresholding, and motion blur.

2.2.4.5. Color quantization (color segmentation)

Color quantization refers to those procedures by which the amount of colors available in a bitmap image is reduced or mapped or indexed to a different scale. Today, this is mainly used for image acquisition (for example, when an image is captured through the camera lens, the colors of the natural world have to be sampled for digital representation) and for image content-based search [PAR 11, p. 399].

Two main categories of methods for color quantization can be identified: 1) the scalar method, which converts the pixels from one scale to another in a linear manner; and 2) the vector method, which considers a pixel as a vector. The latter technique is used more for image quality and counts more efficient algorithms, including: the popularity algorithm (takes the most frequent colors in the image space to replace those which are less frequent); the octree algorithm, which as we saw in the last section is a hierarchical data structure. It partitions the RGB cube consecutively by eight nodes, where each node represents a sub-range of the color space); and the median cut algorithm (similar to the partitions in the octree, but it starts with a color histogram and the representative color pixel corresponds to the median vector of the colors analyzed) [BUR 09, p. 89].

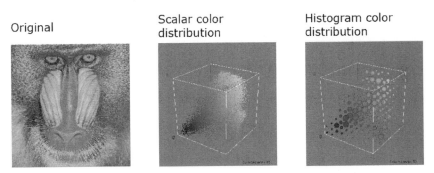

Original   Scalar color distribution   Histogram color distribution

Figure 2.7. *Color segmentation. Images were produced with Color Inspector 3D for ImageJ. For a color version of the figure, see www.iste.co.uk/reyes/image.zip*

As with the frequency space view, vector-based color segmentations work better with the 3D view of the RGB color space in order to facilitate the evaluation of color distributions and proximities.

2.2.4.6. *Image compression*

Another family of algorithms that builds on pixel values is dedicated to image storing and transmission purposes. Broadly speaking, the goal of image compression algorithms is to reduce the amount of data necessary to restitute an image. Such algorithms can be classified as lossless or lossy: the former is used to preserve in its entirety the visual information that describes an image, while the latter reduces the file size mainly through three methods [GON 08, p. 547]: by eliminating coding redundancy, by eliminating spatial redundancy, and by eliminating information invisible for human visual perception.

Lossy algorithms have been successfully implemented in image file formats like JPEG and PNG (section 2.3.3 deals with image formats in more detail). The way in which pixel values are handled implies transforming them into code symbols that will be interpreted at the moment of image restitution (the process is called encode/decode; *codecs* are the programs in charge of performing these operations). PNG files, for example, are based thoroughly on spatial redundancies. The format uses the LZW algorithm (developed by Lempel, Ziv and Welch in 1984) for assigning predefined code symbols to visual information.

On the other hand, formats like JPEG use the Huffman coding algorithm (introduced in 1952 and also used for text compression) in order to determine "the smallest possible number of code symbols" [GON 08, p. 564] based on ordering probabilities. Moreover, just like the Fourier transform, JPEG formats also use a frequency field representation called discrete cosine transform. The difference image describes visual variations "only with cosine functions of various wave numbers" [BUR 09, p. 183] which are ordered by their importance to represent those visual variations (spatial regions, chromatic values, etc.)

2.2.4.7. *Image analysis and features*

Image analysis also constructs on pixel values. It extends image-processing techniques by taking a different direction towards feature detection and object recognition techniques. The algorithms designed for such tasks analyze a digital space according to two categories: image features and shape features.

– *Image features* are those properties that can be measured in an image such as points, lines, surfaces and volumes. Points delimit specific locations in the image (the surrounding area is called keypoint features or interest points, for example, mountain peaks or building corners [SZI 10, p. 207]), while lines are used to describe broader regions based on object edges and boundaries. Formal descriptors for these features are SIFT (scale invariant feature transform) and SURF (speeded up robust features).

– *Shape features* constitute the metrics or numerical properties of descriptors that characterize regions inside an image. There are several types, classifications and terminologies of shape descriptors:

– *Geometrical features*: they are algorithms to determine the perimeter, area and derivations based on shape size (eccentricity, elongatedness, compactness, aspect ratio, rectangularity, circularity, solidity, convexity [RUS 11, p. 599]).

– *Fractal analysis*: mostly used to summarize the roughness of edges into one value. A simple calculation implies starting at any point on the boundary and follow the perimeter around; "the number of steps multiplied by the stride length produces a perimeter measurement" [RUS 11, p. 605].

– *Spectral analysis (Fourier descriptors or shape unrolling)*: this describes shapes mathematically. It starts by plotting the X and Y coordinates of the region boundary and then converting the resulting values into the frequency field.

– *Topological analysis*: these descriptors quantify shape in a structural manner, which means they describe, for example, how many regions or holes between borders are in an image. Algorithms for optical character recognition (OCR) are an example where topological analysis is applied: they describe the topology of characters as a skeleton.

Later in this book, we will show some applications using shape descriptors and we will note that they can be combined. They can also be generalized to 3D shapes and, more recently, they are available as programmatic categories in order to implement machine learning algorithms.

2.2.4.8. *Image generation (computational geometry)*

These types of algorithm make reference to methods and techniques that generate or synthesize geometric shapes. From a mathematical perspective, a distinction is made between a geometrical and topological description of shapes. Geometry simply defines positions and vertices coordinates, while topology sees the internal properties and relationships between vertices, edges and faces. When pure geometrical description is needed, a set of vertices or an array of positions is enough, but it is common to use a vertex list data structure that organizes the relations between vertices and faces and the polygon. We will now explore prominent techniques for image generation.

– *Voronoi diagrams and Delaunay triangulation*: these geometric structures are closely interrelated although they can be studied and implemented separately. Voronoi diagrams are commonly attributed to the systematic study of G. L. Drichlet in 1850 and later adapted by G. M. Voronoi in 1907 [DEB 08, p. 148]. Basically, they divide planar spaces into regions according to a "mark" or "seed" (which can be a given value, or a cluster or values, or a given shape inside an image); the following step consists of tracing the boundaries of regions by calculating equal distances from those "marks". On its own, the resulting geometry of the diagram can help identify emptier and larger spaces, and also to calculate distances from regions and points (through the nearest neighbor algorithm, for example).

Voronoi diagrams can be extended into Delaunay triangulations by relaying the marker points and tracing perpendicular edges to the boundaries. While there are several triangulation methods, the popularity of Delaunay's algorithm (named after its inventor, mathematician Boris Delone) resides in its efficiency for reducing triangles with small angles (a situation that is desired for their subsequent uses such as creating polygonal and polyhedral surfaces)[6].

– *Particle systems*: these are typically collections of points where each dot is independent from the others, but follows the same behavior. More clearly, single points have physics simulation attributes such as forces of attraction, repulsion, gravity, friction and constraints such as collisions and flocking clusters. It is documented that the term "particle system" was coined in 1983 by William Reeves after the production of visual effects for

---

6 The reader can consult the complete Delaunay algorithm in [DEB 08, p. 200] and the Voronoi algorithm in [DEB 08, p. 157].

the film *Star Trek II: the wrath of Khan* at Lucasfilm [SHI 12, ch. 4]. As in that case, particle systems are used to generate and simulate complex objects such as fire, fireworks, rain, snow, smog, fog, grass, planets, galaxies or any other object composed of thousands of particles. Because particle systems are often used in computer animation, algorithms for velocity and acceleration are also used. Common methods involve considering particles as vectors and adapting array list data structures to keep track and ensure collision detection procedures.

– *Fractals*: these are geometric shapes that, following the definition by mathematician Benoît Mandelbrot who coined the term in 1975, can be divided into smaller parts, but each part will always represent a copy of the whole. In terms of image generation, fractals use iteration and recursion. That means a set of rules is applied over an initial shape and, as soon as it finishes, it starts again on the resulting image. Famous examples of fractal algorithms are the Mandelbrot set, the Hilbert curve, the Koch curve and snowflake.

Fractals have been adapted into design programs by using grammars. The idea of grammar-based systems comes from botanist Aristid Lindenmayer, who in 1968 was interested in modeling the growth pattern of plants. His L-system included three components: an alphabet, an axiom, and rules. The alphabet is composed of characters (e.g. A, B, C), the axiom determines the initial state of the system, and the rules are instructions applied recursively to the axiom and the new generated sentences (e.g. (A→AB)) [SHI 12, ch. 8].

– *Cellular automata*: these are complex systems based on cells that exist inside a grid and behave according to different states of a neighborhood of cells. The states are evaluated and the system evolves in time. The particularity of these systems is their behavior: it is supposed to be autonomous, free, self-reproducing, adapting, and hierarchical [TER 09, p. 168]. Uses and applications of cellular automata can be seen in video games (such as the famous Game of Life by John Conway in 1970), modeling of real-life situations, urban design, and computer simulation.

– *Mesh generation*: procedures of this kind are related to 3D reconstruction techniques, tightly bounded to surface and volumetric representation as well as mesh simplification methods. Mesh generation is commonly associated with creating 3D models, useful in medical imaging, architecture, industrial design, and recent approaches to 3D printing. The design of these algorithms first considers the kind of input data because clean mesh surfaces are not always the starting points (i.e. planar, triangle-based, with explicit topology that facilitate interpolation or simplification).

– *Points*: these algorithms consider scattered points around the scene. They can be seen as generating a particle system as a surface. A simple method tends "to have triangle vertices behave as oriented points, or particles, or surface elements (*surfels*)" [RUS 11, p. 595].

– *Shape from X*: this is a generalization of producing shapes from different sources, for example, shades, textures, focuses, silhouettes, edges, etc. The following section will give an overview of shading and texturing, but the principle in here is to reconstruct shapes by implying the illumination model and extracting patterns of texture elements (called *textels*).

– *Image sequences*: let's suppose we have a series of images positioned one after another along the Z-axis, like a depth stack. Algorithms have been designed to register and align the iterated closest matches between the surfaces (the ICP algorithm). Then, another algorithm such as the marching cubes can help generate the intersection points between the surface and the edges of cubes through vertices values. In the end, a triangulation method can generate the mesh tessellation. Of course the differences between a clean mesh surface and one generated as an isosurface reside in the complexity and quantity of vertices and edges. It is precisely for these cases that mesh decimation or mesh triangulation are used to reduce and simplify the size of models.

2.2.4.9. *Image rendering*

Once an object has been generated, either within a 2D or a 3D world, there is a necessary passage from the geometrical information to the visual projection on the screen. In other words, we go from image pixel values to "screen pixel values", a process generally called image rendering. There are actually two main rendering methods, rasterization and ray casting. Both take into account more visual information than geometry.

– *Viewing and clipping*: image viewing is related to the virtual camera properties. This is the same as choosing the right angle, position, tilt and type of lens before we take a photograph. In the case of visual information, image viewing consists of four main transformations: position, orientation, projection (lens, near and far plans, or view frustrum), and viewport (shape of the screen). In parallel, image clipping relates to eliminating geometrical information outside the viewing volume of the scene. Algorithms such as Sutherland and Hodgman are adapted to clip polygons [HUG 14, p. 1045].

– *Visible surface determination*: this family of algorithms is also called hidden surface removal depending on the literature and specificities ([HEA 04] argues that the case of wire-frame visibility algorithms might invigorate the term visible surface determination as it is more encompassing). Anyhow, their main goal is to determine which parts of the geometrical information will be indeed shown on the screen. Although there are abundant algorithms depending on the hardware, software or type of geometry, we can exemplify two broad approaches. On the one hand, the family of image space methods, such as the depth-buffer or z-buffer algorithms, builds on hardware graphics power to trace, screen pixel by screen pixel, all polygons existing in the virtual world, and showing only those closest to the view point. On the other hand, the family of object space methods, such as the depth sorting or the painter's algorithm, first sort objects according to the view point. Then, they render from the farthest object to the closest, like layers on a canvas or celluloid sheets. It is interesting to note that the latter method is currently implemented in graphical user interfaces (see section 2.3.2).

– *Lighting and shading*: objects and meshes do not have only solid colors to be visible. Mainly for photorealistic objectives, the visual aspect of surfaces can be considered a combination of colors, textures and light that bounces around the scene. This is essentially what we call shading. The model of light underlying shading algorithms consists of the light source itself (its location, intensity, and color spectrum) as well as its simulated behavior on surfaces:

- *Diffuse reflection* (Lambertian or matte reflection): distributes light uniformly in all directions.

- *Specular reflection* (shine, gloss or highlight): mostly depends on the direction of the bouncing light.

- *Phong shading*: a model that combines diffuse and specular with ambient illumination. It follows the idea that "objects are generally illuminated not only by point light sources but also by a general diffuse illumination corresponding to inter-reflection" [SZI 10, p. 65].

The BDRF (bidirectional reflectance distribution function) is a model that also takes into account diffuse and specular components; nevertheless, more recent programming environments embrace vertex and fragment shaders functions that allow for integrating more complex models in real-time rendering.

– *Texturing*: another visual feature of objects is their simulated texture. That means that instead of geometrically modeling the tiniest corrugation, we use 2D images as textures that simulate such depth. Lastly, the 2D image is handled as an array whose elements are called *textels*. In terms of [ANG 12, p. 366]: "The mapping algorithms can be thought of as either modifying the shading algorithm based on a 2D array (the map), or as modifying the shading by using the map to alter surface parameters, such as material properties and normal." There are three main techniques:

– *Texture mapping*: this is the texture in its common sense meaning. One way to do this is to associate a texture image with each triangle of the mesh. Other methods unwrap the surface onto one or more maps (called UV mapping).

– *Bump mapping*: the goal of this technique is to alter the normal vectors of models in order to simulate shape imperfections (recall that normal vectors designate the direction of faces according to the convex hull).

– *Environment mapping*: this refers to techniques where an image is used to recreate how objects in the scene reflect light, but without tracing the actual rays of light. Most of the time, these maps are built on polar coordinates or parametric coordinates [HUG 14, p. 549].

– *Ray tracing*: in contrast to the last paragraph, these algorithms actually trace the path of light rays in a scene. The method consists of starting from a screen pixel and then searching for intersections with objects. Of course although in the physical world there are endless light bounces, in here it is necessary to delimit the depth of level of intersections (often three levels). In the end, it is possible to "combine the color of all the rays which strike our image plane to arrive at the final color for each pixel" [GOV 04, p. 179]. An alternative contemporary method to ray tracing is called radiosity, which is inspired by thermal heat transfer to describe light as energy emitters and receivers.

2.3. Visual information as texts

The next level in our generative trajectory refers to texts, which we understand in a broader sense. Texts have to do with configurations that are made out of the entities encountered at the fundamental level (data types, data structures, and algorithms). Texts are enunciations: manifest interpretations of how and which information is present (to the emitter and the receiver). Thus, for text to be comprehensible and transferable, it should follow some syntactic and semantic rules shared by the sender and the receiver. Moreover, as occurs with texts in general (for example, a narrative prose and a poem are structurally different from scientific texts), programming codes have writing styles that reflect on computation models underlying the representation they make of data.

In this section, we describe how the units of the fundamental level are manifested in the form of text. We have chosen three main entry points. The first is in terms of programming code, and we will discuss programming languages and their categorizations. The second concerns graphical user interfaces. At the end of the section, we take a look at file formats as they can also be seen as texts.

2.3.1. *Programming languages*

In section 2.2.1, we evoked different levels of programming languages. At the closest part to the binary code (the lowest level), there are machine languages. Then, on top of them, we identify assembly languages, which facilitate programming by conventionalizing instructions, that is, using mnemonic conventions instead of writing binary code. A third layer consists of high-level programming languages, which assist in focusing on the problem to be tackled rather than on the lower-level computing details (such as memory allocation). These languages are essentially machine-independent (we can write and execute them in different OS) and generally can be regarded as *compiled* or *interpreted*. Compiled languages are commonly used for developing standalone applications because the code is converted into its machine language equivalent. On the other hand, interpreted languages use a translator program to communicate with a hosting software application (that means the code executes directly on the application). Examples of the first category include languages like Java and C++, while the second is associated with languages such as JavaScript and Python, among many others.

Programming languages provide the means to manipulate data types and data structures as well as to implement algorithms. Computer scientist Niklaus Wirth has observed analogies between methods for structuring data and those for structuring algorithms [WIR 04, p. 129]. For instance, a very basic and recurrent operation in programming is to "assign an expression's value to a variable". This is done simply on scalar and unstructured types. Another pattern is "repetition over several instructions", written with loop sentences on an array structure. Similarly, the pattern "choosing between options" would build on conditional sentences using records. As we will see, in programming terms, sentences are called statements (also known as commands or instructions): they contain expressions (the equivalent of text phrases), and they can be combined to form program blocks (the equivalent of text paragraphs).

In this section, we will observe the overall characteristics of programming languages, from the syntactic, semantic and pragmatic point of view. Then we will present some programming styles (also called paradigms or models) and conclude by revisiting major programming languages for visual information.

2.3.1.1. *Syntactics, semantics and pragmatics*

In contrast to natural languages such as English, French, Spanish, etc., programming languages are formal languages. That means they are created artificially to describe symbolic relationships, like in mathematics, logics, and music notation. One way of studying programming languages has been to distinguish between the syntactic, semantic and pragmatic dimensions, just as they were originally envisioned by semiotician Charles Morris (see section 2.1) and early adopted in computer science literature [ZEM 66].

Syntactics refers broadly to the form of languages. We can say it encompasses two main parts: the symbols to be used in a language, and their correct grammatical combinations.

The first part of syntactics is known as *concrete syntax* (or context-free grammars); it includes the character set (alphanumerical, visual or other alphabet), the reserved special words (or tokens, which are predefined words by the language), the operators (specific symbols used to perform calculations and operations), and grouping rules (such as statement delimiters – lines or semicolons – or delimiter pairs – parentheses, brackets, or curly brackets).

The second part is named syntactic structure or abstract grammar. It defines the logical structure or how the elements are "wired together"

[TUR 08, p. 20]. This part gives place to language constructs where we can list, ranging from simple to complex: primitive components, expressions, statements, sequences and programs. Expressions like "assigning value to a variable" demand using the dedicated token for the data type, the identifier of the variable, an assignment operator and the assigned value (for example, *int num* = *5*). Regarding statements, there are several types (conditional, iteration and case), each identified with their own tokens (*if-else*, *for* or *while*, *switch*) and delimited by grouping rules. A statement is considered by many languages as the basic unit of execution.

Semantics refers to the meaning of programs at the moment of their execution. In other words, it is about describing the behavior of what language constructs do when they are run. Because programs are compiled or interpreted on machine and layers of software, it is said that semantics depends on the context of execution or the computational environment. Although most of the time we express the semantics in natural language prose as informal description (as it occurs in language references, documentation, user's guides, the classroom, workshops, etc.), there are a several methods to formalize the semantics of programming language, which are mainly used for analysis and design.

Even though it is not our intention to deal with semantic issues, we only evoke two common methods for specifying programming languages. First, *denotational semantics,* which explains meaning in terms of subparts of language constructs. And, complementary, *operational semantics*, which observes language constructs as a step-by-step process. Examples of programming language subparts are: 1) the essential core elements (the kernel); 2) the convenient constructs (syntactic sugar); and 3) the methods provided by the language (the standard library) [TUR 08, p. 207]. Examples of operations at execution are naming, states, linking, binding, data conversions, etc. Together, these methods are useful for identifying and demonstrating language properties (for instance, termination[7] or determinism[8]).

---

7 Programs are not expected to handle infinite loops, for example, but rather to terminate at some point, otherwise they could "crash".

8 The execution of a program as it was precisely specified. Nondeterministic behavior is associated with "glitch" effects.

Before tackling pragmatics, we illustrate two practical cases of syntactics and semantics at the heart of most programming languages. Table 2.4 summarizes different operators: the symbol and its meaning at execution. Table 2.5 extends operators by showing their implementation, from a mathematical notation into programming language syntax. We have chosen JavaScript language syntax for both the tables.

Operator symbol	Description
+	Addition
-	Subtraction
*	Multiplication
/	Division
%	Modulus (division remainder)
++	Increment
--	Decrement
==	Equal to
===	Equal value and equal type
!=	Not equal
!==	Not equal value or not equal type
>	Greater than
<	Less than
>=	Greater than or equal to
<=	Less than or equal to
&&	And
||	Or
!	Not

Table 2.4. *Common operator symbols and their description in the JavaScript language*

Pragmatics refers to the use and implementation of programming languages. It has to do with the different forms of solving a problem, like managing the resources available in the most efficient way (memory, access to peripherals). In computer science literature, pragmatics is associated with programming models (also referred to as programming styles and programming paradigms).

Mathematical notation	Description	Programming code
$\sqrt{(x)}^2 = x$	Square root.	```Math.sqrt(x);```
$i = \sqrt{-1}$	Complex numbers. JavaScript requires an external library such as MathJS.	```var math = require('mathjs'); var a = math.complex(3, -1); var b = math.sqrt(-1); math.multiply(a,b);```
3k o j	Vector multiplication. Other variations are: Dot or scalar product of a vector (K o j) and cross product k × j.	```var s = 3; var k = [1, 2]; var j = [2, 3]; var tmp = multiply(k, j); var result = multiplyScalar(tmp, s); function multiply(a, b) { return [a[0] * b[0], a[1] * b[1]] } function multiplyScalar(a, scalar) { return [a[0] * scalar, a[1] * scalar] }```
$\sum_{i=1}^{100} i$	Sigma or summation. Some derivations are: $\sum_{i=1}^{2}\sum_{j=4}^{6}(3ij)$ $\sum_{i=1}^{2}\sum_{j=4}^{6}(3ij)$	```var sum = 0; for (var i = 1; i <= 100; i++) { sum += i }```
$\prod_{i=1}^{6} i$	Capital Pi or big Pi.	```var value = 1; for (var i = 1; i <= 6; i++) { value *= i; }```
$|x|$	Absolute value.	```Math.abs(x);```
$\|\mathbf{v}\|$	Euclidean norm. "Magnitude" or "length" of a vector.	```var v = [0, 4, -3]; length(v); function length (vec) { var x = vec[0]; var y = vec[1]; var z = vec[2]; return Math.sqrt(x * x + y * y + z * z); }```
$|\mathbf{A}|$	Determinant of matrix A.	```var determinant = require('gl-mat2/determinant'); var matrix = [1, 0, 0, 1]; var det = determinant(matrix);```

$\hat{a}$	Unit vector.	```js\nvar a = [0, 4, -3];\nnormalize(a);\nfunction normalize(vec) {\n var x = vec[0];\n var y = vec[1];\n var z = vec[2];\n var squaredLength = x * x + y * y +\n z * z;\n\n if (squaredLength > 0) {\n var length =\nMath.sqrt(squaredLength);\n vec[0] = vec[0] / length;\n vec[1] = vec[1] / length;\n vec[2] = vec[2] / length;\n }\n\n return vec;\n}\n```
$A = \{3, 9, 14\},$ $3 \in A$	An element of a set.	```js\nvar A = [3, 9, 14];\nA.indexOf(3) >= 0;\n```
$k \in \mathbb{R}$	Set of real numbers.	```js\nfunction isReal (k) {\n return typeof k === 'number' &&\nisFinite(k);\n}\n```
$f(x,y) = \sqrt{x^2 + y^2}$	Functions can also have multiple parameters.	```js\nfunction length (x, y) {\n return Math.sqrt(x * x + y * y);\n}\n```
$f(x) = \begin{cases} \frac{x^2 - x}{x}, & \text{if } x \geq 1 \\ 0, & \text{otherwise} \end{cases}$	Functions that choose between two "sub-functions" depending on the input value.	```js\nfunction f (x) {\n if (x >= 1) {\n return (Math.pow(x, 2) - x) / x;\n } else {\n return 0;\n }\n}\n```
$sgn(x) := \begin{cases} -1, & \text{if } x < 0 \\ 0, & \text{if } x = 0 \\ 1, & \text{if } x > 0 \end{cases}$	The signum or sign function.	```js\nfunction sgn (x) {\n if (x < 0) return -1;\n if (x > 0) return 1;\n return 0;\n}\n```
$\cos \theta$ $\sin \theta$	Cosine and sine functions.	```js\nMath.cos(x);\nMath.sin(x);\n```
$f'(x) = 2x$	A value similar to another, while keeping the same name. It can describe the "next value" after some transformation.	```js\nfunction f (x) {\n return Math.pow(x, 2);\n}\n\nfunction fPrime (x) {\n return 2 * x;\n}\n```

$floor(x) = \lfloor x \rfloor$ $ceil(x) = \lceil x \rceil$	Floor and ceil functions to round float numbers.	Math.floor(x); Math.ceil(x);

$A \Rightarrow B$	Used in logic for material implication. That is, if A is true, then B is also true.	if (A === true) {
		    assert(B === true);
		}

$k \gg j$	Significant inequality. That is, k is an order of magnitude larger than j.	orderOfMagnitude(k) >
		orderOfMagnitude(j);
		
		function log10(n) {
		    return Math.log(n) / Math.LN10;
		}
		
		function orderOfMagnitude (n) {
		    return Math.trunc(log10(n));
		}

$k > 2 \wedge k < 4 \Leftrightarrow k = 3$	Logical conjunction ∧. Analogous to operator AND.	if (k > 2 && k < 4) {
		    assert(k === 3);
		}

$A \vee B$	Logical disjunction ∨. Analogous to operator OR.	A || B

$x \neq y \Leftrightarrow \neg (x = y)$	Symbols ¬, ~ and ! are used to represent logical NOT.	if (x !== y) {
		    assert(!(x === y));
		}

$x \in [0,1]^3$	Intervals. Numbers restricted to some range of values, e.g. a point x is in the unit cube in 3D. Also related are set operations: union ∪, intersection ∩ and difference −.	var nextafter = require('nextafter') var a = [nextafter(0, Infinity), nextafter(1, -Infinity)]; var b = [nextafter(0, Infinity), 1] ; var c = [0, nextafter(1, -Infinity)] ; var d = [0, 1] ;

Table 2.5. *From mathematical notation to programming syntax, adapted from Math as code by Matt DesLauriers[9]. A reference of mathematical symbols for UTF-8 formatting is also available online[10]*

From this standpoint, programming languages have been divided into styles by the way in which they adapt a computational model. For example, two prominent paradigms used today are the imperative model and the object-oriented model. The former is implemented by procedural languages and is based on the use of sequences or blocks to compute step-by-step procedural hierarchies. The latter defines objects that have properties and

---

9 https://github.com/Jam3/math-as-code
10 https://www.w3schools.com/charsets/ref_utf_math.asp

behaviors previously declared as a data class. Classes thus have class variables and class methods, which can also be nested and combined with other classes (something called inheritance). Other paradigms that we might cite are: functional, logic, declarative, concurrent[11] and, more recently, multi-paradigms and emerging ones such as reactive programming. Of particular importance for our study will be the visual programming approach, which adds functionalities of graphical user interfaces to languages (see next section 2.3.2).

Let's now present some of the main programming languages that are used to handle visual information, namely Java, C++, Python, JavaScript and OpenGL. These languages are of course very popular and too vast; they are used for a large number of different applications. The following account has no intention to introduce programming techniques, but only to have a glance at the main characteristics and general behaviors, for "a programmer is greatly influenced by the language in which programs are written" [KNU 68, p. ix]. In the next chapter, we will explore concrete implementations for specific image-interface scenarios.

2.3.1.2. *Java*

Java 1.0 was introduced in 1996 by Sun Microsystems. At the moment of writing these lines, its current version is Java 8, maintained by Oracle Corporation (which acquired Sun). In little more than 20 years, the Java programming language has grown from roughly 200 classes organized in 8 packages to more than 4000 and 200 packages (we will see later what classes and packages are).

Java can be seized as a programming ecosystem that includes the language specification, a compiler, the run-time environment, and its various APIs (application programming interfaces) that extend its basic functionalities. Moreover, because Java is general-purpose, there are actually several versions: Java Mobile Edition (Java ME), Java Standard Edition (Java SE), Java Enterprise Edition (Java EE) and Open Java Development Kit (JDK). However, vendors and companies (Apple, IBM, Red Hat, among others) have worked together on interoperability standards to maximize compatibility.

---

11 Peter Van Roy produced in 2009 a poster identifying 27 programming paradigms and their relationships. Available at: https://www.info.ucl.ac.be/~pvr/paradigms.html

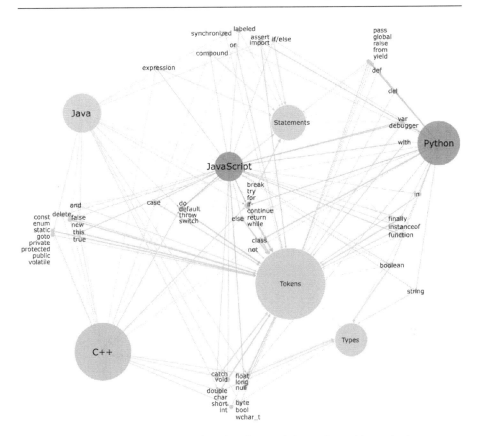

Figure 2.8. *Network graph of main tokens, statements and types in Java, Python, C++ and JavaScript programming languages. For a color version of the figure, see www.iste.co.uk/reyes/image.zip*

As with the other programming languages, the Java syntax can be seen in a hierarchical categorization. From simple to complex, we may list: tokens, data types, statements, methods, classes, packages and programs. In Figure 2.8, we summarize the differences and similarities between tokens, primitive types, and statements supported in the languages reviewed here[12].

---

12 The figure shows nodes with more than three links for all four languages. The main reason is legibility, as the whole network we created consists of 200 nodes and 500 links. The algorithm used is Yifan Hu in Gephi. The idea is to visualize how different languages use the same words and terms, but also how they differ and how they can also function as token, type and statement.

For Java in particular, the syntax levels are based on 53 tokens and 8 primitive types.

One of the strengths of Java is the manner in which it supports object-oriented programming, where methods and classes play a major role. A method has been defined as "a named sequence of Java statements that can be invoked by other Java code. When a method is invoked, it is passed zero or more values known as arguments." [EVA 15, p. 66], and classes are "a named collection of fields that hold data values and methods that operate on those values" [EVA 15, p. 72].

The idea of classes is built on the concept of data structures. Classes define new types by combining several primitive types within a constructor, which is a block of code that specifies the properties and behaviors of the class. However, a class exists only virtually, as a formal and abstract rule that needs to be materialized. The instance of a class is called an *object* which holds the same properties and behaviors of its class, and which can be instantiated indefinitely. Another interesting part of objects is that they can be nested and can inherit properties from other classes.

In the following upper level of syntax complexity, classes are grouped into packages. In Java, all predefined packages start with the token "java", such as java.util, java.lang, and it is also possible to create our own packages. The highest level of syntax is a program: it consists of one or several files of source code. If a Java file contains a class, it is expected to be named according to that class (e.g. Filename.java would contain the class Filename). Then, when they are compiled, the file is transformed into Java byte code, creating a file with extension ".class" (i.e. Filename.class) that can be executed by the run-time environment for a given type of computer processor.

Among the many APIs available to extend the basic functionalities of Java, there are mainly two devoted to synthesizing images: Java 2D[13] and Java 3D[14]. Furthermore, there is also a binding for the OpenGL library called

---

13 Documentation available at: http://www.oracle.com/technetwork/java/index-jsp-138693. html

14 Java 3D's current version is 1.5.2., well documented Javadoc (a Java API documentation generator) at: https://java3d.java.net/

JOGL[15] (later in this section, we present OpenGL). Finally, Java is also the foundation for the development of seminal programming environments dedicated to working with visual information, among others: RStudio, ImageJ and Processing.

2.3.1.3. C++

C++ was initiated in 1985 at Bell/AT&T and was standardized in 1988 by ISO/IEC. Although it was initially inspired by the C language with the intention to facilitate some tasks, it has grown separately and can be considered a different language. Currently, the latest published version is C++14 (from 2014), maintained by the Standard C++ Foundation (a non-profit organization with members from Google, Microsoft, Intel, among others).

C++ is a compiled language that might feel of lower level than Java because of its abstractions (e.g. access to memory management, pointers and preprocessing). It supports a generic programming paradigm that constructs mainly on procedural and object-oriented (recall Pragmatics in section 2.3.1.1). To work with C++ programming code, it is necessary to have an editor and a compiler, or an IDE (integrated development environment, offering an editor, a compiler, and a file management system in a bundle such as Eclipse[16] or NetBeans[17], both multi-language, multiplatform, and freely available tools). Anyhow, there also exist commercial implementations of C++ that extend the primary functions of the language.

C++ comprises 74 tokens and 15 primitive types. As we mentioned before, Figure 2.8 shows a map of relationships of types, tokens and statements used in languages of this section. Besides that, the hierarchical syntax of C++ is similar to Java, from expressions to statements, classes, templates, the standard library, projects and programs.

The particular notion of template is similar to the classes and objects behavior in Java; it makes reference to a model for creating classes or functions as instances of the template. However, in C++ template-based programming, a class or a function can be defined "independently of its parameters (which can be values, types, or even other templates)" [LIS 03,

---

15 Available at: https://jogamp.org/jogl/www/

16 Maintained by the Eclipse Foundation: https://www.eclipse.org/

17 Originally developed by Sun Microsystems: https://netbeans.org/

p. 174]. The C++ standard library concerns types, macros, functions and objects that can be used in programs: these all are called headers. In C++14, there are 51 headers and it is mandatory to add the directive #include, for example: #include <header> (third-party libraries are also called projects, like Boost[18] and many others[19]).

At compilation time, the header is entirely replaced by the content of the file to which it makes reference. A C++ program may consist of several files, each containing zero, one or more headers. Conventionally, files comprising headers only bare the file extension .h or .hpp, while their implementation is in files with extension .c or .cpp.

The main form in which C++ handles visual information is through libraries (also called C++ projects). One of the most famous is the OpenGL library for computer graphics, but there are others specially designed for computer vision (OpenCV), image processing (Magick++), and artistic images (Cinder and OpenFrameworks). Given its lower level nature, ultimately many software applications can be developed or extended with C++, including Pure Data, RStudio and MATLAB.

2.3.1.4. Python

Python was initiated by Guido van Rossum in 1990, and it is currently maintained by the non-profit Python Software Foundation. It supports procedural and object-oriented programming styles and is considered of higher level than C++ and Java mainly because it is run on an interpreter and does not require any further compilation (thus it is known as an interpreted language).

Python can also be seen as a software ecosystem containing the language, an interpreter, and a series of extension modules. There are two main modes of using Python: Classic Python (CPython), which is the most widely used, and Jython, which is an implementation of the language for Java. In the first case and for basic operations, it is recommended to install the Python IDE (called IDLE) that offers an editor, an interpreter and a debugger available for multiple platforms. For complex operations using different libraries and

18 http://www.boost.org/
19 http://en.cppreference.com/w/cpp/links/libs

packages, [MON 16] recommends to install a Python distribution like Anaconda[20].

The syntax of Python programs follows the previously explored principles, constructing from expressions to statements, modules, packages and programs. The 33 keywords reserved in Python 3 are summarized in Figure 2.8. In Python terminology, sets and dictionaries would be the equivalents to lists and arrays in other languages. Actually, dictionaries support mapping; therefore, they can be thought of as associative arrays (the equivalent of "map," "hash table," or "hash" in other languages). Another difference that should be mentioned is that lines of code written in Python are equal to physical lines. That means there is no semicolon to indicate the end of a statement, but it is rather the end of the line itself. The same situation occurs with indentation, which is used to "express the block structure of a program" [MAR 06, p. 34].

One of the central notions in Python is the module. Modules are chunks of programming code, stored in different files with the idea of making them reusable and portable. Modules can be called between them using the import statement (creating a namespace to access the properties of such modules) and, because in Python all types are objects, "a function can return a module as the result of a call. A module, just like any other object, can be bound to a variable, an item in a container, or an attribute of an object" [MAR 06, p. 140]. The standard library has predefined objects known as built-ins (hence, they do not require the import statement, contrary to extensions), covering 68 functions dedicated to types and algorithms.

A complete Python program may have different files. The file extension used for modules is .py (.pyc is also used for compiled files in bytecode). Given the popularity of the language, a large number of libraries exist as extension modules that can be bundled in packages. Of special interest to this book is PIL (Python Imaging Library) and its derivative Pillow adaptation. Furthermore, it is often the case to use a visual information library together with other packages: Tkinter for graphical user interfaces, SciPy for mathematics and graphics, Panda3D for games, to mention some.

---

20 https://www.continuum.io/anaconda-overview

2.3.1.5. *JavaScript*

JavaScript was designed by Brendan Eich at Netscape. Strictly speaking, the name JavaScript is protected by Sun Microsystems (acquired by Oracle in 2010), but the standard version received the name ECMAScript in 1997 (after the European Computer Manufacturer's Association). Currently, JavaScript 1.5 is of the same ECMAScript 5 standard, though the most recent version is 7, released in 2016.

JavaScript is largely known to be the scripting language of the Web, as it is an interpreted, high-level language that can be run on web browsers (although there are derivations of the language used to script software applications such as ExtendScript for Adobe Photoshop, Illustrator, and After Effects). JavaScript has evolved to support several programming styles (functional and object-oriented) thanks to its API for understanding and manipulating a document model (most notably HTML).

The overall lexical structure of JavaScript is inspired from Java. It delimits 29 keywords to formulate expressions and statements. Besides the five primitive types (numbers, strings, Boolean, and null or undefined), everything else can be an object. For example, basic arithmetic expressions combine values with operators (+, −, /, *), but when it is necessary to perform more complex operations, we have to use the Math object and its predefined methods: Math.sin(), Math.cos(), Math.floor(), Math.random(), etc.

There are three important kinds of objects in JavaScript: arrays, functions and objects. Arrays represent an ordered collection of elements with dedicated methods to access them. It is interesting to note that elements of an array can be of different types, making it possible to create complex data structures such as arrays of arrays, arrays of objects, multidimensional arrays, etc. Functions are objects with "executable code associated with it" [FLA 11, p. 30]. They can be launched asynchronously from other objects and return a computed value, that could be yet another function. Finally, functions are widely used to create new objects via constructors, in the fashion of object-oriented programming. For practical matters, there are several predefined classes of objects such as Date, RegExp and Error, which help create methods and objects that represent dates, regular expressions and syntax bugs at runtime, respectively.

As can be guessed, objects in JavaScript constitute the main component of the language. We have already said that objects can have properties and methods of different types and that can also be inherited and nested. When JavaScript is run on web browsers, for example, it starts by creating a model of the document (the DOM, or Document Object Model). But the document is already included in a larger object, which is the browser window. The Window object allows access to properties such as name, innerWidth, innerHieght, screenLeft, screenTop, etc., and methods such as alert(), scrollTo(), prompt(), confirm(), etc.[21] Then, at the Document level, the object describes the HTML elements displayed as the content of the page through methods like getElementById()[22]. Further down the Document object, there is the Element object, which distinguishes HTML elements individually. This functionality is important for manipulating visual attributes associated with styles defined in the Cascade StyleSheets (CSS) standard but also to event handler properties triggered by input devices (e.g. typing a key of the keyboard, click or double-clicking the mouse). Besides Document and Element objects and the Window object, there are also properties and methods for Location[23], Screen[24], Navigator[25] and History[26] objects.

A complete JavaScript program might consist of one or more files recognized with the file extension js. Within a web browser context, .js files can be added to an HTML document via the script tag or invoked with the javascript: protocol as an attribute of an HTML element (for instance, <button onclick="javascript:hello();">). More recently, JavaScript programs have gained popularity as distributed in the form of "bookmarklets". These are .js files stored in a server and added as a bookmark to a browser. Then, the browser executes the code "as if it were a script on the page and can query and set document content, presentation, and behavior" [FLA 11, p. 316]. Finally, it is also possible to place the JavaScript code within an HTML document itself, without any reference to external files.

---

21 Window object reference of properties and methods is available at: https://www.w3schools.com/jsref/obj_window.asp

22 Reference available at: https://www.w3schools.com/jsref/dom_obj_document.asp

23 https://www.w3schools.com/jsref/obj_location.asp

24 https://www.w3schools.com/jsref/obj_screen.asp

25 https://www.w3schools.com/jsref/obj_navigator.asp

26 https://www.w3schools.com/jsref/obj_history.asp

Regarding visual information, JavaScript on the web takes advantage of two main technologies: on the one hand, the HTML5 <canvas> element and, on the other, the SVG (Scalable Vector Graphics) language. HTML5 canvas introduced a drawing API (developed by Apple for Safari 1.3 in 2006) that defines methods for graphics such as lines, curves, polygons, text, shadows, gradients, images and pixel manipulation (these shapes also include 15 visual properties such as lineWidth, fill, shadowColor, etc.). From this perspective, graphics can be considered similar to pixel-based images or bitmaps because they exist within the 2D context of the canvas tag (specifying the width and height of the visible space). Conversely, SVG is a vector image format based on XML, that is, images are structured like a tree, similar to the HTML DOM. Of course, the SVG model varies from that in HTML, but it is worth noting that basic shape elements such as <circle>, <rect>, <line>, or <polygon> can also be grouped and nested into <path> or <g> tags, thus creating the tree-like structure. SVG files have the file extension .svg, natively supported by browsers and software applications like Adobe Illustrator or Photoshop (as smart object). Table 2.6 compares the visual properties that can be accessed with Canvas and SVG, and OpenGL.

The graphics possibilities of the web do not rely exclusively on <canvas> and SVG. As browsers evolve, CSS3 becomes tightly integrated, supporting animation and 3D graphics. Furthermore, HTML5 defines native support for <audio> and <video>, opening access to multimedia file formats to communicate with the HTML DOM (for example, via media events like playing, ended, or volumechange among a total of 22 events and recent recommendations such as WebRTC).

One final word regarding web graphics is the recent support of the OpenGL library. OpenGL ES (Embedded Systems) was adapted from the OpenGL specification in order to operate in consoles, phones, devices, vehicles and web browsers. WebGL is the name given by the Khronos Group to the 3D graphics API. While the first version of WebGL was released in 2011, based on OpenGL ES 2.0 (published in 2008), the second version appeared in 2017 and adopts OpenGL ES 3.0 (published in 2015). JavaScript can use the WebGL API via the <canvas> element. Because OpenGL ES 2.0 specifies shader-based graphics, WebGL also implements vertex and fragment shaders. This is generally a difficult task since the language gets closer to the level of Graphical Processing Units (GPU); thus, several JavaScript libraries have emerged (such as three.js[27] or PhiloGL[28]).

Canvas[29]	SVG[30]	OpenGL[31]
addColorStop(), arc(), arcTo(),beginPath(), bezierCurveTo(), clearRect(), clip(), closePath(), createImageData(), createLinearGradient(), createPattern(), createRadialGradient(), data, drawImage(), fill(), fillRect(), fillStyle, fillText(), font, getImageData(), globalAlpha, globalCompositeOperation, height, isPointInPath(), lineCap, lineJoin, lineTo(), lineWidth, measureText(), miterLimit, moveTo(), putImageData(), quadraticCurveTo(), rect(), rotate(), scale(), setTransform(), shadowBlur, shadowColor, shadowOffsetX, shadowOffsetY, stroke(), strokeRect(), strokeStyle, strokeText(), textAlign, textBaseline, transform(), translate(), width	alignment-baseline, attributeName, attributeType, azimuth, baseFrequency, baseline-shift, baseProfile, begin, bias, calcMode, class, clip, clip-path, clip-rule, color, color-interpolation, color-interpolation-filters, color-profile, color-rendering, contentScriptType, contentStyleType, cursor, cx, cy, diffuseConstant, direction, display, dominant-baseline, dur, dx, dy, edgeMode, elevation, end, fill, fill-opacity, fill-rule, filter, filterRes, flood-color, flood-opacity, font-family, font-size, font-size-adjust, font-stretch, font-style, font-variant, font-weight, from, fr, fx, fy, gradientTransform, height, href, k1, kernelMatrix, kernelUnitLength, kerning, keySplines, keyTimes, lengthAdjust, letter-spacing, lighting-color, limitingConeAngle, local, marker-end, marker-mid, marker-start, markerHeight, markerUnits, markerWidth, mask, maskContentUnits, maskUnits, max, min, opacity, operator, order, overflow, overline-position, overline-thickness, paint-order, pathLength, patternTransform, pointer-events, points, pointsAtX, pointsAtY, pointsAtZ, preserveAlpha, preserveAspectRatio, r, radius,	glutInitDisplayMode glColor glIndex glutSetColor(); glEnable(); glBlendFunc (); glEnableClientState(); glColorPointer(); glIndexPointer(); glPointSize(); glLineWidth(); glEnable(); glEnable(); glLineStipple(); glPolygonStipple(); glPolygonMode glEdgeFlag glFrontFace glEnable glGet glPushAttrib glPopAttrib();

---

27 https://threejs.org/

28 http://www.senchalabs.org/philogl/

29 https://www.w3schools.com/tags/ref_canvas.asp

30 https://developer.mozilla.org/en-US/docs/Web/SVG/Attribute

31 [HEA 04, p. 255]

	refX, repeatCount, repeatDur, restart, result, rx, ry, scale, seed, shape-rendering, specularConstant, specularExponent, stdDeviation, stitchTiles, stop-color, stop-opacity, strikethrough-position, strikethrough-thickness, stroke, stroke-dasharray, stroke-dashoffset, stroke-linecap, stroke-linejoin, stroke-miterlimit, stroke-opacity, stroke-width, style, surfaceScale, tabindex, targetX, targetY, text-anchor, text-decoration, text-rendering, textLength, to, transform, type, underline-position, underline-thickness, values, version, viewBox, visibility, width, word-spacing, writing-mode, x, x1, x2, xlink:href, xlink:show, xlink:title, y, y1, y2	

Table 2.6. *List of visual attributes in CSS, SVG and OpenGL*

2.3.1.6. *OpenGL*

The first version of OpenGL was introduced in 1994 by Silicon Graphics. It was a major achievement in separating software from hardware regarding graphics packages (or Graphics Libraries, GL), in the same line as DirectX and VRML (Virtual Reality Modeling Language). Today, OpenGL is maintained by the non-profit Khronos Group (current release is 4.5) and is widespread across multiple platforms and devices (through, as we sought, OpenGL ES and WebGL).

Technically speaking, OpenGL is not a programming language, but rather a library designed to support 3D and 2D graphics programs. As a matter of fact, it is intended to be independent of any language, yet offers bindings for at least the most common programming languages that we have seen before (Java, C++, Python, JavaScript). Thus, the programmatic capabilities of graphics will depend on the hosting system and language in which OpenGL is implemented.

The syntax of OpenGL describes more than 500 commands. The function names pertaining to the core library can be recognized by the prefix gl. In an analogous manner, the built-in data types contain the prefix GL: GLbyte, GLshort, GLint, GLfloat, GLdouble, GLboolean. Being a multi-purpose library, there are no descriptions of models and surfaces; therefore, it is necessary to construct them programmatically from basic geometry: GL_POINTS, GL_LINES, GL_LINE_STRIP, GL_LINE_LOOP, GL_TRIANGLES, GL_TRIANGLE_STRIP, GL_TRIANGLE_FAN, and GL_PATCHES [HEA 04, p. 30]. Of course, there are many OpenGL libraries specially conceived to facilitate some tasks: the famous GLUT (OpenGL Utility Toolkit), for instance, provides a screen-windowing system. If programming in C++, for example, templates can be added using the C++ syntax: #include <GL/glut.h>.

Since OpenGL 2.0, graphics are heavily based on shaders. For that matter, the GLSL (OpenGL Shading Language) was introduced. The main idea is to provide means to extend the basic data types into more complex structures such as vectors and matrices of two, three and four components (e.g. a float type can be declared as a vector with the variables vec2, vec3, vec4, and as matrices with mat2, mat3, mat4, and derivations like mat2x3; the same logic applies to integers: ivec2, ivec3, etc.). There are operations to truncate, lengthen and combine components, as long as they share the same components: (x, y, z, w) associated with positions, (r, g, b, a) with colors, (s, t, p, q) with texture coordinates [SHR 13, p. 43].

The two main kinds of shaders in the OpenGL pipeline are vertex shaders and fragment shaders. When the geometric data is stated (points, lines, and geometric primitives), the vertex shading stage is in charge of processing the data in the buffer. Then, when it is passed to the rasterizer, the fragment shading phase generates samples, colors, depth values, for the geometry inside the clipping boundaries [SHR 13, p. 35]. Finally, there are libraries and extensions for GLSL as well as additional and optional shadings that can be taken into account: precisely, tessellation shading and geometry shading that allow modifying geometry before it is rasterized.

2.3.2. Graphical interfaces

When visual information is rendered on a screen, it is hardly done in a static manner. First of all, the image on the screen is always dynamic as the computer monitor is refreshed at a rate of 60 Mhz (section 2.4.1 will address this issue). However, images are also dynamic in the sense that they might have animation properties, interaction (scrolling or orbiting around the virtual environment), and parameters for modifying specific parts in real time. In practice, a combination of these three often occurs.

As we know, the diversification of software applications to analyze or synthesize visual information is not limited to command line interfaces. Graphical interfaces constitute that special kind of visual configuration explicitly created to interact with digital information. In later chapters of this book, we will analyze productions in which images and data representations convey themselves methods to act on visual attributes, using in creative manners three aspects: the graphics or the image itself, the ambience in which it is rendered (the window and the screen), and second-order graphics that add to the scene (the graphical interface elements).

Graphical interfaces can be regarded as texts in several ways. First, the available interface components are defined at the programming language level. That means that interface elements exist in programming code, as package, extension or library. Second, interface menus and dialogs are written in natural language, using terms and notions from different domains. Third, graphical interfaces follow a model or structure (either explicit or implicit, systematic or intuitional). Several aspects, such as the hierarchical organization, the kind of values that we can manipulate, and the way in which the system makes us aware that values can be manipulated (i.e. the selected interface element) can be seized as enunciation acts, as windows that reflect the design choices behind the system, and ultimately as pieces of culture that will endure or not as the system is used.

While the first graphical interfaces were tightly bound to specific hardware and software configurations, they were eventually abstracted and generalized. Anyhow, we should notice that many of the pioneering models and ideas remain valid nowadays. In 1963, computer scientist Ivan Sutherland presented Sketchpad [SUT 63], a revolutionary system dedicated to digital drawing, by means of using a light pen directly on the screen. This scheme is recognized and implemented today as the Model-View-Constraint paradigm. In Sketchpad, many buttons existed as hardware, not as graphical representation in software. Among its many innovations, digital graphics were thought to be modular (created from other shapes) and constrained (their properties could be controlled according to geometric relationships). Images could be grasped and manipulated, just like other interactive object.

The generalized idea of graphical interfaces that largely subsists in present days is the so-called WIMP (acronym for Windows, Icons, Menus, and Pointers). A complete evolutionary account of how the model was forged requires looking at inventors, managers, users, among other actors. In here, we only want to evoke some major salient points. In 1970, Xerox PARC was established with the intention of working on the future of personal computing. In 1972, the Xerox Alto computer was introduced, developed by teams led by Alan Kay and Robert Taylor, and taking into account lessons from Sutherland and Douglas Engelbart (mainly his On-Line System). The Alto also came with an early object-oriented programming language, Smalltalk; an early word-processor, Bravo; and early drawing applications, Draw and Markup [WIN 96, p. 32].

By 1978, one of the first object-oriented software applications was developed: ThingLab, written with Smalltalk by Alan Borning. In 1981, the Xerox Star consolidated the work begun with the Alto and adapted direct-manipulation, desktop metaphor, and a WYSIWYG model (What You See Is What You Get) [WIN 96, p. 33]. In 1984, Apple introduced the Macintosh inspired by the Star and added a consistent style to all the applications: menu commands, use of dialog boxes, and windows. In 1987, the software HyperCard was delivered for free in every Mac. Bill Atkinson's hypermedia system was based on the metaphor of stacks as programs and catapulted creative uses: writing, reading and prototyping applications. In 1988 came Macromedia Director (later acquired by Adobe) and MasterArchitect (a program used for building information modeling, or BIM).

By 1990s, the era of cultural software, as media theorist Lev Manovich calls it, was already established [MAN 13b, p. 247]. Programs for image editing and design flourished such as Aldus PageMaker (1985), Director (1988), Adobe Photoshop (1989), After Effects (1993), Maya (1998), among many others. In the next chapter, we will talk in more detail about software applications; for now, we want to note by that time the emergence of visual programming environments (or associative programming) and parametric design, where the graph constructed between objects to control visual attributes is the graphical interface itself.

In this part, we focus on the state of current graphical interfaces. We start by reviewing their relevance to devices and data; then we show an inventory of major elements and models.

2.3.2.1. Graphical input data

Graphical input data is used to map numeric values from input devices. Indeed, devices can be classified from the kind of data they provide. Typically, there are six main categories [HEA 04, p. 670]:

– *Coordinate locator devices*: specify one coordinate position such as the location of the screen cursor. The mouse, the arrow keys and joysticks provide this kind of data.

– *Stroke devices*: specify a set of coordinate positions as happens upon continuous movement of a mouse while dragging.

– *String devices*: specify character and strings input, most often with a keyboard.

– *Valuator devices*: specify a scalar value like velocity, tension, volume, etc. It is common to use control dials, sliders, rotating scales, or detect the pressure of click.

– *Choice devices*: allow the selection of processing options, parameter values. We can point with the mouse and click on buttons or enter text with the keyboard, and use voice commands.

– *Pick devices*: allow the selection of a subpart or region of a picture. For example, the combination between mouse and screen cursor is used to select or to draw surfaces, faces, edges and vertices.

Graphics packages provide functions for selecting devices and data classes. In OpenGL, for example, this is carried out with GLUT because input data operates on a windowing system. GLUT specifies around 20 functions for mouse, keyboard, tablet, spaceball, dials, etc.[32] Functions look like glutMouseFunc (mouseFcn), where mouseFcn has four parameters: button (left, middle, right), event (up/down), location X and location Y. Besides GLUT, there are other libraries specially dedicated to create and handle complex graphical interfaces (see next paragraph).

---

32 Reference is available at: https://www.opengl.org/resources/libraries/glut/glut-3.spec.pdf

Inheriting from the Sketchpad tradition, several techniques have been identified for drawing pictures with input devices and data. We have already mentioned *dragging*, but there are also *constraints* (when shapes adjust to a specific delimitation), grids, *rubber-band methods* (stretching or contracting parts of shapes), and *gravity-magnetic fields* (aligning shapes to arbitrary objects rather than to grids).

2.3.2.2. *Graphical interface elements*

The state of graphical interface development has diversified with the variety of devices and hardware available today. Graphical interfaces are seldom hard-coded; it is preferable to use a toolkit that will help interface between the final result and the deeper details of computing operations. Toolkits and frameworks exist for different platforms and programming languages. For instance, Java applications might be extended with AWT (Abstract Window Toolkit) and Swing; Python with Tkinter or wxPython; JavaScript with jQuery UI or dat.GUI; C++ and OpenGL with GLUT or GTK+.

GUI libraries organize their elements into different categories. For example, GTK+, a toolkit originally designed for the GIMP software (see further section 3.6), has 13 display elements, 16 buttons, 2 entries, 16 containers, and 11 windows[33]. Another example is the Tkinter module delivered with Python. It offers simple widgets, containers, menus, text, canvas, layout management, and events[34]. For Tkinter, a simple widget could be: button, checkbutton, entry, label, listbox, radiobutton, scale and scrollbar. All widgets share common properties such as length/width dimension, color and number of characters allowed inside of it. Finally, all widgets have associated methods to graphical input data: get, config, set, quit, update, wait, info width, info height.

Although a library can be very exhaustive, its final implementation will depend on the OS or the software application that hosts the GUI. In technical terms, GUIs are programmed as objects of graphics and drawing classes. Within this context, the controls that users see on-screen are called *widgets* (buttons, sliders, etc.). In a robust environment such as Qt, controls are only a small part of a larger ecosystem.

---

33 https://developer.gnome.org/gtk3/stable/gtkobjects.html
34 https://docs.python.org/2/library/tkinter.html

Qt was initiated in 1994 in Norway by computer scientists Nord and Chambe-Eng. Today, it has grown in popularity and it is distributed in two licenses, GNU LGPL or commercial. It consists of a series of tools dedicated to the development of GUIs: Qt Designer (a GUI builder software), Qt Linguist (supporting translation services), Qt Assistant (a help browser) and Qt Creator (an Integrated Development Environment). Qt is based on C++ and can be used standalone or as a library (for example, in sophisticated software like Autodesk Maya, Adobe Photoshop, or Adobe Illustrator).

The language specification behind Qt is Qt QML, a declarative, JavaScript-like syntax programming language. It includes 13 principal modules (Qt Core, Qt GUI, Qt Multimedia, Qt Multimedia Widgets, Qt Network, Qt QML, Qt Quick, Qt Quick Controls, Qt Quick Dialogs, Qt Quick Layouts, Qt SQL, Qt Test, and Qt Widgets) and add-ons like Qt Canvas 3D, Qt SVG, Qt Data Visualization, or Qt Sensors, among 30 others.

Qt supplies two main forms of GUI: traditional widgets and QML GUIs. The first type is claimed to be more adapted for common desktop applications, with no need for multi-device scaling. Qt supports more than 100 classes in 9 categories (basic, advanced, abstract, organization, graphics, view, window, style, and layout[35]). The second type supports scaling, but also better communication with other Qt modules: render engines, coordinate systems, animation and transition effects, particles and shader effects, web engine. Figure 2.9 shows a representation of the 25 different control widgets available in the Qt Quick Controls module[36].

In web environments, controls are associated with forms and input elements. While HTML5 specifies 13 standardized form elements, and 22 different types of input tag, extensibility of GUI elements can be achieved with JavaScript libraries such as jQuery UI or dat.GUI. Table 2.7 illustrates the variety of HTML forms, input types, jQuery UI widgets and jQuery UI interaction methods.

Finally, a different manner to explore the diversity of graphical interface elements is to use a GUI builder, which are software applications that support the design and creation of GUI templates, usually by dragging, dropping and

---

35 Full reference available at: http://doc.qt.io/qt-5/widget-classes.html#basic-widget-classes
36 http://doc.qt.io/qt-5/qtquickcontrols-index.html

parameterizing the elements on-screen. Examples of GUI builders are Qt Designer or Glade[37] for GTK+, both cross-platform free software.

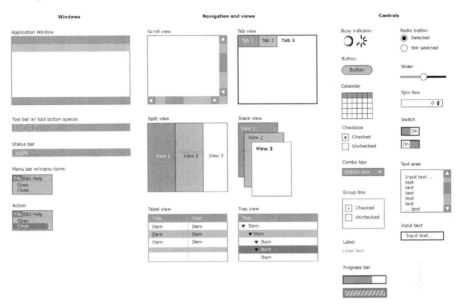

Figure 2.9. *Different types of control widgets as they are rendered on the computer screen, inspired from Qt Quick Controls module. The graphic style has been simplified. It may actually change in different platforms*

HTML form tags	HTML input tag types	jQuery UI widgets	jQuery UI interaction
<form>, <input>, <textarea>, <button>, <select>, <optgroup>, <option>, <label>, <fieldset>, <legend>, <datalist>, <keygen>, <output>	button, checkbox, color, date, datetime-local, email, file, hidden, image, month, number, password, radio, range, reset, search, submit, tel, text, time, url, week	Accordion, Autocomplete, Button, Checkboxradio, Controlgroup, Datepicker, Dialog, Menu, Progressbar, Selectmenu, Slider, Spinner, Tabs, Tooltip	Draggable, Droppable, Resizable, Selectable, Sortable,

Table 2.7. *HTML forms, input types, jQuery UI widgets and interaction methods*

37 https://glade.gnome.org/

2.3.2.3. *Graphical interface models, structures, patterns*

While the semantics of GUI elements is discovered through direct manipulation (pressing, releasing, dragging, stretching, launching actions, etc.), it is also recommended to satisfy a user's model and to fulfill the expected user's experiences. A user's model approach implies designing in terms of needs and usefulness. From this strand, developing a GUI requires to have a clear idea of the following questions: what is its purpose (what can we do, how can it help to do something)? What is the profile of a typical user (background, domain, language, age)?

Throughout the evolution of user interfaces, various approaches have placed special interest on how GUI elements will be organized. One of the most famous initiatives has been the Apple Human Interface Guidelines, initiated in 1987 and still in use today for designing desktop applications using the Mac environment and tools[38]. In a similar manner, Google introduced in 2015 its own view called Material Design including guidelines and a vast gallery of resources[39].

In a broader sense, computer scientist Siegfried Treu proposed the term *interface structures* to signify organizational and relational patterns among GUI elements. Inspired by the same logic behind object-oriented programming and taking into account research from cognitive sciences, Treu considered three types of representations: propositional (objects, ideas, symbols, words), analogical (dimensions, shapes, sizes) and procedural (instructions, actions, lists, sets) [TRE 94, p. 60]. He identified seven patterns or structures:

– *Object-oriented structures*: objects are explicitly linked as networks of nodes;

– *Set structures*: elements are grouped together according to some criteria;

– *Horizontal* and *vertical structures*: elements follow hierarchical or sequential organizations;

– *Spatial structures*: elements float around the visible space at any position (this pattern can be extended to volumes in 3D);

---

38   https://developer.apple.com/library/content/documentation/UserExperience/Conceptual/ OSXHIGuidelines/

39 https://material.io/

– *Context-providing structures*: central elements are enveloped or surrounded by other elements at determinate distance;

– *Language structures*: elements react to each other in a conversational or action–reaction sequence.

More recently, the notion of user interface has broadened with the variety of platforms, devices and software applications. In fact, interface models are no longer limited to considering widgets as the basic interface elements, but also the spatial configurations of visual components. Following interface designer Jenifer Tidwell, what we observe today are *interface idioms* (prototypical styles of a kind of interface: it is in these terms that we speak about word processor interfaces, paint interfaces, or spreadsheet interfaces) and "a loosening of the rules for putting together interfaces from these idioms" [TID 11, p. xvi]. In this respect, Tidwell also identifies patterns from a wide variety of domains. More precisely, she identifies 101 patterns or best practices organized in nine categories (see Table 2.8): navigation, layout, lists, actions and commands, trees and charts, forms and controls, social media, mobile devices, and visual style.

Navigation	Clear entry points; menu page; pyramid (tree); modal panel; deep-linked state; escape hatch; fat menus; sitemap footer; sign-in tools; sequence map; breadcrumbs; annotated scrollbar; animated transition
Layout	Visual framework; center stage; grid of equals; titled sections; module tabs; accordion; collapsible panels; movable panels; right/left alignment; diagonal balance; responsive disclosure; responsive enabling; liquid layout
Lists	Two-panel selector; one-window drilldown; list inlay; thumbnail grid; carousel; row striping; pagination; jump to item; alphabet scroller; cascading lists; tree table; new-item row
Actions and commands	Button groups; hover tools; action panel; prominent "done" button; smart menu items; preview; progress indicator; cancelability; multi-level undo; command history; macros
Trees and charts	Overview plus detail; datatips; data spotlight; dynamic queries; data brushing; local zooming; sortable table; radial table; multi-y graph; small multiples; treemap
Forms and controls	Forgiving format; structured format; fill-in-the-blanks; input hints; input prompt; password strength meter; autocompletion; dropdown chooser; list builder; good defaults; same-page error messages

Social media	Editorial mix; personal voices; repost and comment; conversation starters; inverted nano-pyramid; timing strategy; specialized streams; social links; sharing widget; news box; content leaderboard; recent chatter
Mobile devices	Vertical stack; filmstrip; touch tools; bottom navigation; thumbnail-and-text list; infinite list; generous borders; text clear button; loading indicators; richly connected apps; streamlined branding
Visual style	Deep background; few hues, many values; corner treatments; borders that echo fonts; hairlines; contrasting font weights; skins and themes

Table 2.8. *Interface patterns, from [TID 11]*

To conclude this part, we will discuss how graphical interfaces also consist of linkage structures, that is, the web of links between the visual components. Within the domain of hypertext and hypermedia, this approach is broadly studied as rhetoric of hypertext: how information is written and read through user interfaces. Computer scientist Mark Bernstein, in his seminal article [BER 98] identifies different patterns of hypertext:

– *Cycles*: the structure of a text is recognized by returning over an entry point and departing towards a new path. This can be experienced when returning to the same home page in websites. When several web pages or entire hypertexts are linked together, the cycle can be known as a web ring.

– *Mirrorworlds*: two or more different sets of nodes are put together in order to favor comparison. The structure is recognized implicitly by the reader, who identifies different parallel statements.

– *Tangle*: links do not explicitly help the reader to distinguish the destination or action that will occur upon making a choice. This structure makes the reader aware of the existence of new and unknown information.

– *Sieves*: these are tree-like structures representing layers of choice and organization.

– *Montage*: various spaces appear together, maybe overlapping or freely floating around a larger space. Spaces can be distinguished from each other, and also each space has its own information and identity.

– *Neighborhood*: similar to the context-providing structures in [TRE 94]; nodes emphasize the associative structure of texts by visual properties and proximity.

– *Missing links or nodes*: the structure is suggested by explicit missing elements (like a blank space among list items) or suggested links, using rhetorical figures like allusion or narrative techniques like ellipsis.

– *Feint*: shows the diverse entry points or the overall parts of a text. It might provide access to individual parts and, more importantly, it creates the structure of possibilities that can be navigated further after.

Although these patterns have been observed for creative writing purposes in spatial hypertext systems, they are also found in the design of multipurpose systems. Systems such as Tinderbox exploit visual attributes of nodes and links, and also provide an environment to express structure through several spatial models [BER 12a]. This is also the case in visual or associative programming software like Pure Data or Max/MSP devoted to audio signal processing (the next chapter discusses examples in more detail).

2.3.3. *Image file formats*

Image file formats refer to the stored representation of visual information. Commonly, we identify two types of formats, vector and bitmap formats, and both handle information in a sequential alphanumeric manner.

2.3.3.1. *Vector formats*

Although the name vector format derives historically from images specifically created for vector displays (also known as random-scan systems such as oscilloscopes monitors), they have been eventually replaced by raster-scan systems. Nevertheless, vector formats are recurrent in literature and denote an image representation in terms of geometric information.

We have already mentioned the SVG graphics language in section 2.3.1. The syntax and structure of SVG is defined in an XML namespace. Accordingly, an SVG image is composed of a sequence of tags and attributes in a text form. Another format based on XML is COLLADA, introduced in 1982 and currently maintained by the Khronos Group. COLLADA is a format dedicated to 3D graphics. One of its goals is to facilitate the exchange of assets (or models) between software applications. The current version is

1.5 (specified in 2008) and supports graphics defined with OpenGL ES 2.0[40].

Some vector formats support different representations, either as ASCII or as binary code. In the first case, the visual information is described with only ASCII characters, meanwhile the binary form relies on series of bits and algorithms to make the reading and writing of large files more efficient. A binary file would often be preferred if the file size is a constraint. Examples of formats that support both configurations are: DXF (acronym of Drawing Exchange Format) developed for Autodesk AutoCAD in 1982, and STL (acronym of Stereolithography), introduced in 1987 by 3D systems (a pioneer company in 3D printing systems).

Vertex data	Elements	Free-form curve/surface attributes
v: geometric vertices v vt: texture vertices vn: vertex normals vp: parameter space vertices	p: point l: line f: face curv: curve curv2: 2D curve surf: surface	cstype: rational or non-rational forms of curve or surface type: basis matrix, Bezier, B-spline, Cardinal, Taylor deg: degree bmat: basis matrix step: step size
Free-form curve/surface body statements	**Grouping and Connectivity between free-form surfaces**	**Display/render attributes**
parm: Parameter values trim: outer trimming loop hole: inner trimming loop scrv: special curve sp: special point end: end statement	g: group name s: smoothing group mg: merging group o: object name con: connect	bevel: bevel interpolation c_interp: color interpolation d_interp: dissolve interpolation lod: level of detail usemtl: material name mtllib: material library shadow_obj: shadow casting trace_obj: ray tracing ctech: curve approximation stech: surface approximation

Table 2.9. *Data keywords in the OBJ file format[41]*

---

40 https://www.khronos.org/files/collada_spec_1_5.pdf
41 https://www.cs.utah.edu/~boulos/cs3505/obj_spec.pdf

One of the most used formats is OBJ, developed in 1992 by Wavefront Technologies (later merged with Alias and later acquired by Autodesk) and available as an open format. OBJ offers a clear specification to exemplify the structure of data inside a file. It determines seven classes; each one identified with a specific keyword. Once a model or surface has been generated and exported to OBJ, the file contains a series of lines referring to the data keywords and their values.

2.3.3.2. *Raster file formats*

Raster file formats are the most common image file formats today. They can be seen as a direct interface between the visual information and the screen monitor. Indeed, for graphics systems, the color screen is represented as a series of RGB values. These values are stored in the frame buffer, which is refreshed continuously (typically at the rate of 60 Mhz). The RGB values are stored as non-negative integers and the range of values depends on the number of bits per pixel position. As we said earlier, in true color images, each pixel has three color components (red, blue and green), each of 8 bits. If we recall the binary conversions in Table 2.3, the maximum values that one component allocates is 256 (or 255 if we start to count from 0). Anecdotally, the term *bitmap image* was referred originally to monochrome images, while *pixmap* was used for multiple bits per pixel. However, the name bitmap is used indistinctly to signify raster images [HEA 04, p. 779].

In raster images, the visual information is structured in a binary form, and it might include additional information such as metadata, look-up tables, or compression types. Moreover, some formats may act as containers or metafiles (i.e. a format like PDF can contain JPEG images). Examples of raster formats are BMP, GIF, PNG and JPEG, among hundreds of others. Here, we briefly describe them.

BMP (or simply bitmap) was one of the earliest image formats, introduced by Microsoft for applications like Paint and Paintbrush in 1985. The structure of a .bmp consists of a header part (which uses 14 bytes of memory for specifying types, size and layout); the bitmap information part (which uses 40 bytes and specifies dimensions, compression type, and color format); and the bitmap data, consisting of values representing rows of the image in left-to-right order.

GIF (Graphics Interchange Format) was developed in 1987 by UNYSIS and CompuServe. It initiated as an adapted format for electronic transmission. In 1989, the format was modified to support animation (animated GIFs), which has propelled its popularity among online social networks in recent years. The file structure has five parts: the signature, the screen descriptor, the color map, the image descriptor, and the GIF terminator.

PNG (Portable Network Graphics) started as an open alternative to GIF license fees. Its first specification was published in 1996 (four years after JPEG). Among other features of PNG, we highlight the support to 48-bit images, which allow the addition of transparency layers into 24-bit color images, as well as color correction information. The structure of PNG files is given in the form of block chunks (using the PNG jargon). There are different kinds of chunks: critical, public, private, and safe-to-copy. We note that PNG files can be extended with additional metadata, such as the XMP recommendation: physically, this information goes inside the text block iTXt, with the identifier XML:com.adobe.xmp.

JPEG (Joint Photographic Experts Group) was first published in 1992 and standardized by ISO/IEC 10918-1. JPEG actually covers a variety of specifications regarding digital images: first, the coding technology; second, the compliance testing; and third, the extensions and format. As a matter of fact, it is this third part, the JFIF (JPEG File Interchange Format) which is generally referred as the JPEG file format. These specifications are not freely available.

JPEG has become the most popular format because of its great compression rate. There are actually four compression methods: lossless, sequential, progressive and hierarchical. The first two modes are almost the only ones used; they are known as Huffman-encoded with 8-bit samples. The lossless has been superseded by other standards and the hierarchical bares the barrier of its complexity. When we refer to sampling, this is the first step in the JPEG encoding scheme. Sampling implies converting RGB colors into YCbCr color space. Y stands for luminance (it is a black and white representation of the image), Cb for the blueness of the image, and Cr for its redness. After sampling, the image is compressed into data units (8 x 8 pixel blocks). The technique uses operations in the frequency domain, a DCT (discrete cosine transform) to store data as cosine functions. The third step is quantization, where non-essential cosine functions are eliminated in order to recreate the original. The last step is the Hoffman coding, where only quantized DCT coefficients are encoded.

The structure of a JPEG file is decomposed by means of markers. There are 2 bytes per marker: the first part is always FF values and the second part denotes the code of the market type. A typical structure is:

Before closing this part, it is important to recall one last format technique heavily used in web environments via the HTML5 canvas element. Base 64 is a base encoding of data used in situations where only ASCII characters are allowed (e.g. a URL name address). It is constructed from a subset of 64 characters[42]: letters from A to Z (uppercase), a to z (lowercase), numbers from 0 to 9, underscore and minus sign. The 65th character (equal sign) is dedicated to represent processing functions. Among its implementations, the HTML5 canvas method toDataURL() can be used to generate compressed images and to distribute them directly in the URL bar of web browsers. The identifier starts with the protocol and instruction: data:image/png;base64.

Values	Symbol used by JPEG	Description
FFD8	SOI	Start of image
FFE0-FFEF	APP	Application-specific data or associated information. It is in this part that metadata like EXIF and XMP is added
FFC4	DHT	Define Huffman Table
FFDB	DQT	Define Quantization Table
FFCD	SOF	Start of frame. In JPEG terminology, a frame is the equivalent of a picture
	Second tables: DHT or DQT	
FFDA	SOS	Start of scan. A scan is a pass through the pixel color values; a segment is a group of blocks, and a block is a series of 8 x 8 pixels
	Scan Data 1	This is the only part of a JPEG file that does not happen within a marker; however, it always follows an SOS marker
	N tables: DHT or DQT N SOS: start of scan n times Scan Data n times	
FFD9	EOI	End of image

Table 2.10. *Generic structure of JPEG files*

42 64 is obtained from the 6 bits allowed (contrary to 8 bits, which allow 256 characters). There is also Base 32 (5 bits) and Base 16 (4 bits, or hexadecimal). More information at the Internet Society RFC 3548: https://tools.ietf.org/html/rfc3548.html

2.4. Objectual materiality of visual information

The third level of our trajectory depicted in Table 2.1 focuses on the materialization and effects of computing, as it is perceptible in the physical world through our senses. The inscription devices that we explored in the last section (GUIs, programming languages, file formats) participate now as formal supports of image interfaces. That means the technical, material and corporal characteristics of the screen and other devices are determined and configured to respond to them. However, this is also a dialectic process. While hardware is built on top of other levels of computing, it can also modify those levels (following a downward direction in the trajectory, innovating new algorithms, new data structures, new data types).

From the perspective of visual information and visual interfaces, we often talk about graphics systems as complex apparatuses that combine CPU (central processing units), GPU (graphics processing unit), screens, and interaction devices (mouse, keyboard, etc.) The most important material support for our study will be the computer screen. But, more broadly, we will focus on the relationship between materials and visual information: how they handle it, how are they conceived to communicate with each other. Hence, we will also take a look at capturing devices (sensors, lenses) and printing devices (both 2D and 3D).

2.4.1. Screen

Images appear on screen following the canonical raster display model. This is also true for video projectors, touch screens, and as we will see later, for capturing and printing devices. The overall idea is that the surface display is represented as a rectangular grid of *screen pixels*, each one of these directly associated with the image samples (the fundamental pixel values that constitute the digital image). In the raster scan model, an electron beam sweeps across the screen, left-to-right and top-to-bottom[43], varying its intensity at each screen pixel position. Rows are named *scan lines* and the total screen area is called a *frame*. The representation of one state of the screen is saved in the frame buffer.

---

43 This is the common non-interlaced or progressive mode of displaying screen pixels. The other mode is the interlaced, which alternates odd and even rows in order to take advantage of the refresh rate.

A digital image described as pixel values (0 for black and 255 for white) has its corresponding visual representation in a raster grid. Rectangular grids are by far the most common types of sampling grids[44]. To simplify, we show in Figure 2.10 a 5 × 5 grid and, in Figure 2.11, logical operations, AND, NOT, XOR, performed on rectangular grids. These operations are applied from the new incoming values (source) to those already stored in the frame buffer (destination).

Square   Hexagonal   Triangular

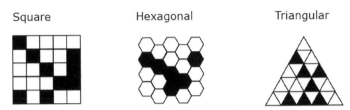

Figure 2.10. *Common types of grids*

Source   Destination   Or

And   Replace   Xor (exclusive or)

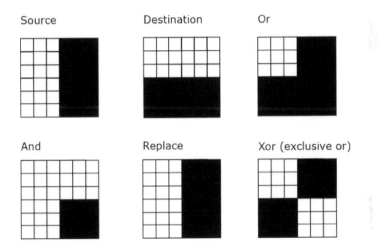

Figure 2.11. *Logical operations (transfer modes)*

---

44 An alternative model is the hexagonal grid, which supposes more organic properties and more efficient mathematical set operations. Some developments in computer vision such as fingertip sensing architectures have been based on hexagonal sampling lattices.

In current display systems, there are several properties that can be identified:

– Resolution: the amount of screen pixels to be illuminated. Different resolutions depend on the aspect ratio, but screens have evolved from 640 × 480 (4:3 ratio) in the 1990s to the more recent 1920 × 1080 (16:9 ratio) in the 2010s.

– Aspect ratio: the relation given between the number of screen pixel columns divided by the number of scan lines that can be displayed. Historically, screens have moved from square ratios (4:3) to more rectangular widescreen ratios (16:9).

– Refresh rate: the amount of time at which the frame is rescanned. From film studies, we know that below 24 frames per second (fps), the human eye might detect gaps between images. Later, with the arrival of television and video, the rate used was 30 fps according to the time in which phosphor decays. In recent systems, frame cycles are measured in Hertz. Typically, we use 60 Hz because interlaced images require twice the time to sweep a frame (30 fps per pass), but higher cycles include 80 or 120 Hz.

– Color: the common standard is the true color system, containing 24 bits per pixel in the frame buffer, "allowing 256 voltage settings for each electron gun, nearly 17 million color choices for each pixel" [HEA 04, p. 44].

Although the raster model initiated with cathode ray tube (CRT) display technologies, it remains valid in recent screen devices based on light-emitting diodes (LEDs) or liquid crystal displays (LCDs). While in CRT monitors, the screen pixels produce a glowing ("circular area containing an RGB triad of phosphors on the screen" [HUG 14, p. 20]), in LCD monitors, each screen pixel is a set of three rectangles corresponding to the red, green and blue spectra. Then, there is backlight behind the screen that is filtered by these rectangles. Even though there is a small space between color dots or stripes, they are not visible when the space is less than 200 micrometers, thus producing a continuous image [RUS 11, p. 55].

2.4.2. Cameras, sensors, lenses

Digital cameras are imaging systems composed of photosensitive sensors, a lens and electronic circuitry that digitizes the image. They are of course not the only system used for image acquisition. Given the variety of wavelengths in the electromagnetic spectrum (see section 1.1.1), there are multiple devices and components designed for different purposes (from microscopes to space probes). The example of digital cameras is worth noting because of their popularity, available in a wide range of devices.

The overall process for image acquisition through digital cameras is as follows. When visible light hits the lens, it projects the viewed scene to the sensors, which converts the light energy to voltages. Then, electronic circuitry transforms the output into analog and digital signals, resulting in a 2D digital image. Let's now analyze in more detail each component in relation to visual information.

The physical quantity measured by lenses is irradiance, also referred to as brightness or intensity. In order to match the projected scene, the ultimate goal is to make a straight ray correspond directly from the scene to the sensor (this is also called the pinhole model). In practice, this is not the case because lenses introduce optics aberrations that need to be handled in software. The five main types of aberrations are: spherical distortion, coma, astigmatism, curvature of field, and color aberration [SON 08, pp. 86–87]. Curvature of field includes geometric distortions such as barrel (dispersion away from the observed scene) and pincushion effects (dispersion towards the image center). Another example of distortion is *vignetting*, caused by the loss of visual information at the edges of the image boundaries. Figure 2.12 shows barrel and pincushion effects as they are simulated and available through Nik Colleciton[45], precisely the Analog Efex Pro 2→Lens distortion.

As we mentioned, photosensitive image sensors convert photons to electrical signals. Technically, sensors can be grouped according to two principles. On the one hand, those based on photo emission, as used in vacuum tube television cameras, and on the other hand, those based on photovoltaic principles, as used in the development of semiconductors. In this line, there have been two types applied to cameras: CCD (charged-coupled devices) and CMOS (complementary metal oxide semiconductor). The latter has become the de facto standard in devices requiring low power

45 Nik Collection is a series of plugins for Photoshop acquired by Google and made available for free in March 2016 at: https://www.google.com/nikcollection/

consumption (such as mobile devices). Sensors are commonly arranged in the form of a 2D array with an additional color filter to create a color camera. The most common filter pattern is the Bayer mosaic which assigns "twice as many detectors for green as for red or blue, which mimics to some extent the human eye's greater sensitivity to green" [RUS 11, p. 17].

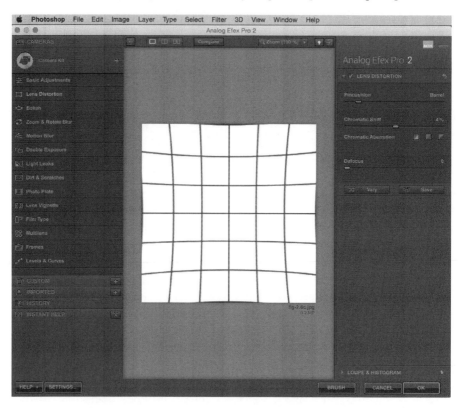

Figure 2.12. *Barrel and pincushion effects in Nik Collection*

At this level, it is interesting to note two things. First, the small capacity of CMOS chips results in lowering the brightness resolution of captured images. However, images are stored in 8-bit per channel anyway, to cope with the standard model. Second, it is the combination of color filter and the interpolation algorithms used in the camera that is used as a signature to identify the model or to check if any alteration has been made.

2.4.3. 2D and 3D printing devices

Printing implies moving an image beyond the screen into a rigid physical support. The technique to achieve this goal is also based on the raster grid model. In 2D, there are several kinds of printers, inks and papers that are used to obtain the desired result. Printing is based on two fundamental concepts: the density of dots and the pattern in which such dots are arranged.

Density of dots is also known as dpi (dots per inch). A general rule is that the lower the dpi, the lower the quality of images (characterized by a jagged or "pixelated" effect). To solve this issue, it is possible to increment the number of dpi in an image. A value of approximately 300 dpi is satisfactory for house and reports, but professional imaging material relies on 1200 dpi at least. The basic problem is that the computer screen is based on 72 dpi. Moreover, the type of ink and paper will also be important, as ink might spread and dry differently.

Dots produced by the printer are arranged through the halftone technique. This is necessary because the size and the intensity of dots cannot be modulated. Ideally, an image pixel can be represented as a halftone cell. For instance, a 4 × 4 array can group 16 dots with 17 possible gray levels (white being the absence of dots, given by the surface of the paper). In theory then, "if each pixel corresponds to a halftone cell, then an image can be printed with about the same dimension as it appears on the screen" [RUS 11, p. 143]. But if screen resolutions range from 72 to 100 dpi, it is necessary to preview with software the lack of physical space.

In the case of printing colors, there is a fundamental passage from the screen to paper. Printers are based on the subtractive color scheme (also known as CMYK), which starts from the white of the paper. Cyan, magenta and yellow are added in order to remove the complementary colors red, green and blue. The full color model includes a layer of black in order to conserve as much as possible the use of other inks and to obtain a more contrasting black tone. The way in which CMYK halftones dictates avoiding moiré patterns by rotating the CMYK rectangular layers by 45, 70, 90 and 105 degrees, respectively: "This aligns the colored screens to form small rosettes that together make up the color" [RUS 11, p. 154].

Regarding 3D printing, the process has been named more accurately as *additive manufacturing*. It is additive because the techniques involve adding layers of raw material to form a solid object. And it is more related to *manufacturing* because of the complexity and delicateness of materials: sometimes the expected result fails; sometimes the material needs special handling (masks, gloves).

The first era of 3D printers occurred during the 1980s, but it was not until the year 2005 that 3D printing received serious attention, thanks in large extent to the "maker" and DIY (do it yourself) movements. We can identify two main types of 3D printers:

– *Selection deposition printers*: this is one of the pioneering and also safest printers, available in early models for home, office and schools. The main characteristic is they "squirt, spray, or squeeze liquid, paste, or powdered raw material through some kind of syringe or nozzle". The principal raw material is plastic, which hardens once printed.

– *Selective binding printers*: these printers use light or lasers to solidify two main kinds of materials. On the one hand, a light sensitive photopolymer is used in stereolitography (SL), in which: "The printer sweeps a laser beam over the surface of a special type of plastic, a UV-sensitive photopolymer that hardens when exposed to UV light. Each sweep of the laser traces the outline and cross-section of the printed shape in consecutive layers" [LIP 13, p. 73]. On the other hand, laser sintering (SL) uses a similar process, but uses powder instead of liquid photopolymers.

In any case, just as 2D image files have a direct relationship with the printed version, the same holds true for 3D. A file format like STL organizes the geometric information (in triangles and polygons) that will be interpreted as "slices" or virtual layers by the printer firmware.

## 3

Practicing Image-Interfaces

This chapter adopts a pragmatic perspective towards image-interfaces: it studies how image-interfaces are practiced. While the last chapter helped to identify the foundations of visual and graphical information, the current chapter has the purpose of observing the different manners in which those elements are put together, notably through software applications. This chapter is organized into different categories according to practices of imaging, for example, image editing, parametric design, and also writing and web environments. As long as we talk about image-interfaces, our concern is not only the result of some software manipulation, but also the graphical elements that accompany the user to achieve such transformations. That is one of the reasons why writing and data science environments are considered (they introduce imaginative forms that treat text as image together with the corresponding graphical interface elements).

In a similar manner in which film makers and directors spend great amounts of time watching films, image-interface designers use, test, install and hack different varieties of software applications. This chapter tries to provide a practical basis before venturing into prototyping our own image-interfaces.

3.1. Mise-en-interface

This chapter can be seen as a continuation of the generative trajectory introduced in section 2.1. In this respect, our last discussion on the materiality of visual information observes the screen and other devices as the substantial or material support of the next upper level: scenes of practice.

As proposed by semiotician Jacques Fontanille, the passage from one level to another is accompanied by the addition of an *extra dimension* to the expression plane (recall section 1.4.2) [FON 08, p. 56]. Here, the notion of dimension can be associated with the proper characteristics of each level. For instance, the textual level adds a tabular and plastic dimension to signs; the level of objects adds a corporal dimension to texts; and, the level of practices adds a topo-temporal dimension to objects. We believe this theoretical approach will prove fruitful in our study of image-interfaces.

In the following sections we discuss interface assemblies, or configurations of interface elements, as they have been integrated into software applications. These assemblies can be seen not only as interface features, but also as arguments, statements and visions that reflect upon practices influenced by upper levels in the trajectory (from artistic, educational and professional strategies, and ultimately from a fragment of digital culture). We think of these configurations as unit operations. A *unit* is, in terms of media theorist Ian Bogost, a way to refer to objects or things being three things at once: (1) isolated and unique; (2) enclosing a system and (3) part of another system – often many other systems [BOG 12, p. 28]. To say that units *operate* means that they behave and interact in a procedural, logical or algorithmic form.

In a related perspective, media theorist Noah Wardrip-Fruin employs the term "operational logics" to refer to "patterns in the interplay of data, process, surface, interaction, author, and audience" [WAR 09, p. 13]. In his devoted research to games and electronic literature, he identifies a small set of *spatial logics* that underlie modern computer gaming: collision detection, navigation, simulated physics and firing projectiles. The idea of spatial logics is that, as it occurs with any other pattern, one model can be adapted in numerous situations. Other logics he recognizes are textual-based, such as *textual-transformation logic* to simulate conversational responses and *transliteral morphing logic* to replace original texts or graphics by others with the same spatial organization and behavior.

If we follow the operational logics model, the case for image-interfaces would be first a *topo-interactional logic*. The topos part indicates the context (the time and place) of the objects, where interfaces manifest. As we have said, the main material support is the screen; it is thanks to its material properties (refreshing rate, aspect ratio, resolution, color) that we can interact with the graphical elements. However, we should note that there are several kinds of display devices, ways of materializing images (such as printers and projectors) and hardware devices to interact with screen images that can be taken into account. These configurations have an influence on the physical space where we interact with images.

Our account should be understood within a two-directional scheme. On the one hand, levels of the expression trajectory (signs, texts, objects) can be described in terms of its constitutive parts: how is it made? How does it follow or challenge the expected experience? How does it establish a communicative and semiotic relationship between actors? This is important because objects, seen as interfaces between texts and practices, host, locate and define modalities of interaction: to believe, to do and to know. It is a process of enunciation where actors choose among a series of possibilities that, at another level (that of practices), will complete their meaning. On the other hand, levels are bounded and it is from an upper level that we can verify the functioning. In this case, practices need to be put in perspective. Our premise is to study how interfaces work in order to produce, create and speculate about new models; not only as concepts but also as objects (or units), in the form of technical prototypes or sketches. If this chapter focuses on the interface as image, the following chapter will adjust the lens to focus on the image as interface.

3.2. Studying graphical interface features

For this part of our study, we opted to concentrate on interfaces designed for desktop software. This choice comes with obvious drawbacks. First, the large amount of applications that have been developed in different fields by professional and independent developers bring omissions that make any study incomplete. We have tried to favor image-oriented interfaces that have been considered seminal by the community of users, those of which we have had personal experience, those that are available as free/open cross-platform software or a combination of the above.

In general terms, our discussion will follow a chronological order. That means we have simplified the multiplicity of dates associated with software versions[1]. In this respect, valuable sources are always the official documentation, release notes, user manuals and scientific papers written by the designer, as well as the user communities, tutorials, emulators and press reviews. The screenshots presented should also be taken generally. They have been adapted from the earliest version we found for all software applications because at that moment they introduced a new vision among the galaxy of existing applications. Of course, the screenshots do not do justice to all the spaces, menus, panels and actions that we discover and experience only through software manipulation. Despite all this, we hope this tour will prove valid to observe overall traits in interface logics.

3.3. 1970s: Xerox PARC years

As we have mentioned, Xerox PARC pioneered many fundamentals of modern graphical interfaces during the 1970s. Among other exemplary applications where innovations can be appreciated, we highlight Bravo, Draw and ThingLab (Figure 3.1). These applications were written in Smalltalk and ran on the Xerox Alto computer, whose original monitor size was the same as a standard US letter sheet of paper in portrait mode. Bravo, designed in 1974 by Butler Lampson and Charles Simonyi, was conceived as a program for creating, editing and printing text documents. Draw, designed by Patrick Baudelaire in 1975, was an illustrator program for creating pictures made of lines, curves and text. ThingLab, conceived by Alan Borning in 1977, was an environment for constructing geometric models within a constraint-based approach.

Sized together, all the three interfaces dedicate a blank region to creating and editing content; this region also takes the largest part of the screen. In Bravo, the top region is called the *system window* and it offers three lines of text with contextual information (previous action; next possible action; and delete, insert and search keys). Below, in the bold bar separating both windows appears the name of the file. In Draw, the upper region is called the *message area* and also shows contextual information such as file name and font parameters. The menu area contains graphical symbols that refer to brushes, commands and fonts. The lower part is reserved for typing text that

---

1 Some applications are invented for exclusive in-house use within a company, others are sometimes released to the public years later; others are acquired or merged with other companies.

might be added to the document. In ThingLab, the upper region is divided into four panes. First there is the class pane, which lists graphical objects (point, line, rectangle, etc.). When a selection is made, the format pane displays options for the selected object (values, subclasses, etc.). The messages pane includes commands such as insert, delete, move and constrain. In addition, the arguments pane contains classes that can be used with the previous commands.

Bravo   Draw   ThingLab

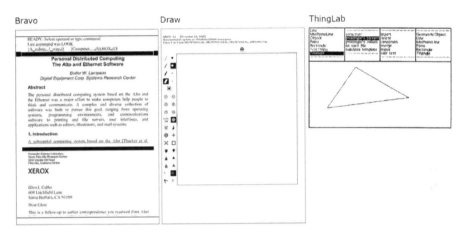

Figure 3.1. *Xerox Alto interfaces*

In 1975, Richard Shoup, with contributions by Alvy Ray Smith, introduced an enhanced version of the interface for his SuperPaint system (started in 1972). This is considered one of the first programs to use the frame-buffer approach for creating and editing static and animated images. SuperPaint was written in BCPL and assembly language, developed in a Data General Nova 800 computer connected to a commercial RGB display and several other components. Figure 3.2 shows the interface main menu, which was available on demand by the user; that is, when a selection was made the menu disappeared for a full screen view of the painting area. There were four main parts: a color selector (three sliders for each component of the HSB color mode); menu items (sixteen pictograms that refer to commands); a color palette; and a series of predefined shapes for drawing (line, round, rectangle, etc.)

1977, SuperPaint   1986, Trillium

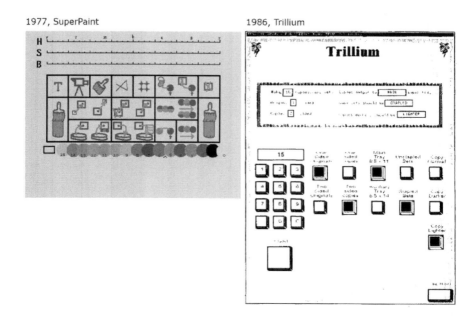

Figure 3.2. *SuperPaint and Trillium interfaces. For a color version
of the figure, see www.iste.co.uk/reyes/image.zip*

By 1981, with the increasing number of applications, it became
paramount to create interfaces not only for software but also for hardware. In
those years, D. Austin Henderson started working on Trillium, an early
interface designer program. Trillium was successfully used across Xerox
sites as an environment for simulating and experimenting mechanical–
machine interfaces (copiers and printers commercialized by Xerox). Trillium
included predefined types of widgets (buttons, labels, and decorations) along
with window editors to modify their values. The program was written in
Interlisp-D, running on Xerox 1100 series processors.

The fact that these applications were not designed according to a unitary
style recalls their developing and innovative momentum. For instance,
images of icons vary in all systems even though they would refer to a same
action or command. In other words, these systems were monolithic in the
sense that they were tightly coupled to the hardware machine in which they
ran and not easily portable to other systems (although the exchange of files
was supported via Ethernet). Nevertheless, these applications opened up new
graphical possibilities and spread a new way of spatial reading (moving the

gaze and displacing the mouse from one position to another in a constant manner).

3.4. 1984–1996: Classic Mac OS years

While the Xerox Star computer introduced the WIMP GUI paradigm in 1981, it is acknowledged that it was widely popularized by the Apple Macintosh in 1984. The envisioned strategy by Apple was to confer a unified look and experience to all applications running on its operative system. This was achieved through, among other things, a series of guidelines known as the Macintosh User Interface Guidelines, based on a formalization of the interface elements.

The first version of the Guidelines was published for the first Macintosh system, which was based on a monochrome CRT display with a resolution of 512 × 342 pixels and a refresh rate of 15.6 Mhz. The estimated size of a rectangular screen pixel was 1/74 in. [APP 85b, p. 18]. The interface toolbox contained routines to manage memory, fonts, menus, events, windows, controls and other utilities that appear on screen. Graphics were handled by QuickDraw, an API that allowed bitmap graphic operations across applications. As QuickDraw was integrated with the environment, it furnished a way to exchange information between different windows, to manage clipping inside areas and to prepare graphics for printing. Moreover, it could also communicate with controls and events of the standard Mac interface. The Guidelines were specified for Pascal and assembly language; developers could use one or combine both languages.

The overall Apple strategy was to deploy applications that were easy to use and learn for an audience considered as non-programmers and even "people who have previously feared and distrusted computers" [APP 85a, p. 27]. For this, the qualities of a program interface should ensure consistency with the look and feel of the operative system. For example, developers were encouraged to include the standard Apple, File and Edit menus; to address the user with verbs in menu commands; to use as much graphics as possible: "use controls and other graphics instead of just menu commands" [APP 85a, p. 70].

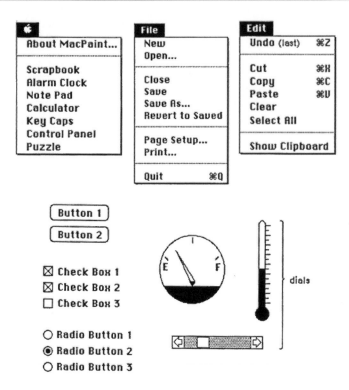

Figure 3.3. *Menus and controls from Macintosh User Interface Guidelines*

In terms of the Guidelines, a collection of icons enclosed within a rectangular region was called a palette. Palettes existed in Draw and SuperPaint, and were also used by MacDraw and MacPaint, both programs released together with the first Macintosh. The former, developed by Mark Cutter, was dedicated to vector graphics and the later, developed by Bill Atkinson (who also wrote QuickDraw), to bitmap images.

With the intention of extending the capabilities of MacDraw, Adobe Systems introduced Illustrator in 1987. Designed by Mike Schuster, Bill Paxton and John Warnock (also co-founder of Adobe and formerly at Xerox PARC), the first version of Illustrator added support to more sophisticated manipulations of vector graphics such as editing Bézier curves. This was done in a similar manner as we still do today (through direct manipulation of control points) and led to the development of the technique *image tracing* (importing a photograph and tracing the contours with curves). The use of vector images was exemplified in logos, technical drawings, illustrations and typography.

Two years later, in 1989, Adobe acquired Photoshop from its designers, Tom and John Knoll, who had started its development in 1987. It soon became the most popular software for photo-retouching, image-editing and color painting for raster images and has been since that moment. Photoshop organized its tools in a floating palette called the toolbox, granting easy access to image processing techniques. Attributes and properties for each tool could be modified through contextual menus (containing controls, sliders, input areas for modifying visual attributes) and extra techniques such as filters could be accessed from the Image menu. Photoshop introduced original tool icons (many of them remain the same in contemporary versions) and interfaces, such as the Photoshop Color Picker (by 1990 Photoshop 1.0 was running in Macintosh II computers, which supported colors).

The use of graphics took another dimension when, also in 1987, Bill Atkinson developed the celebrated HyperCard. This application included several features from MacPaint but with hypertext functionalities. Following the metaphor of desk and stacks, every window in HyperCard was called a card and it was possible to add text, pictures and buttons. One of the features that attracted users was the possibility of linking and navigating between cards without advanced programming skills. This was possible with HyperTalk, a high-level language developed by Dan Winkler especially for HyperCard.

HyperCard was regarded as an authoring system and it attracted a large community of users from different fields. When a stack of cards was created, it could be navigated as a full-screen presentation. At that time, another authoring system was conceived as a writing and reading environment for both fiction and non-fiction authors: Storyspace. First demonstrated in 1987, it was designed by scholars and authors Jay Bolter and Michael Joyce, with computer scientist John Smith, and was inspired by hypertext theory, practice and applications. The fundamental building blocks were of course nodes and links. Nodes were writing spaces known as *places*. Within a Map view, places could be situated spatially inside the window, then linked or grouped into *areas*. The reader could follow "paths across hierarchies in one or more documents; and choose among what we call Outline, Chart, or Map views of an emerging document" [JOY 88, p. 621]. The other views, Outline and Chart, were accessible from the tool icons palette. Since 1991, Storyspace has been managed and maintained by Eastgate Systems [BER 16].

During the 1990s, perhaps the most famous authoring system was Macromedia Director (later acquired by Adobe in 2005). The predecessor of Director, called Videoworks, was designed by Marc Canter, Mark Pierce and Jaime (Jay) Fenton at Macromind in 1985. The distinctive Director user interface was already present at that moment: the Stage, the Cast and the Score. Inspired from the film and theatrical domain, the Stage represented the main screen where objects appeared; the Cast was the multimedia database where images, video, sound and text were stored; the Score was an innovative grid of frames for animating members of the Cast. The software gained popularity not only because of its relative simplicity to create animations and multimedia productions, but also because of its programmability. By 1988, Videoworks was officially named Director and, in 1990, version 2.0 included its own high-level scripting language: Lingo, developed by John Thompson.

The multimedia boom of the 1990s was marked by animation, motion graphics and nonlinear editing, with techniques including transitioning, layering, keying, masking and tempo modification. Productions were broadcast in real time or distributed in physical supports such as VHS videocassettes, CDs, DVDs and multimedia kiosks. A common production studio would include a computer with two or more display monitors. Two applications that introduced novel interfaces for the Macintosh were the Avid/1 Media Composer (developed in 1989 by Avid Technology) and Adobe After Effects (appeared in 1993, designed at the Company of Science and Art, and soon acquired by Adobe in 1994).

The first Avid/1 Media Composer demonstration separated the main window in two areas for previewing video footage. A secondary window showed all video segments in three modes: as timeline (thumbnails of video fragments), as timecode (as lines and text showing duration and other information) and as film mode (frames of video sequences). The secondary window could be expanded in order to adjust the size of thumbnails. Both windows, the preview and the editor, were synchronized: the position of the timeline in the editor window would preview the frame in the main window. Finally, two monitor displays were connected to Macintosh II. Avid would release a family of Media Composers and became the professional reference in video editing.

The other application, After Effects, presented a similar interface to that of Avid/1 in its first versions. However, the principal focus of the program was on visual effects. It included visual mechanisms to animate elements, such as tracing Bézier curves as animation paths. Another innovation was the use of diamond-shaped key frames to indicate critical positions where visual attributes of the element could be modified. The program would then use interpolation algorithms to calculate the transition between key frames. In Figure 3.4, the interface corresponds to version 3.0 (1995), when the Timeline editor was introduced, which marked new ways to edit motion graphics. The idea was that visual effects had their own layers. Thus, a *composition* in After Effects would consist of layers of visual elements, each having different layers of effects.

Before taking a look at other software in different operative systems, we evoke some applications that developed novel manners to interact visually with information, although not particularly oriented towards the production of figurative images.

In 1986, researcher and composer Miller Puckette conceived MAX, an implementation of real-time audio processing for the 4X system at IRCAM, Paris. While MAX proved to function efficiently, its use was difficult without a graphical interface. The Patcher, designed by Miller in 1988, had the intention of controlling MAX objects in a graphical environment. The idea was to connect objects and to pass information as messages between them. The original idea envisioned by Puckette can be recognized visually nowadays and gave birth to a family of patcher programming languages including Max/MSP, Pure Data, Max/FTS, ISPW Max and jMax. Max/MSP is managed by Cycling'74 since version 4.1 (2002), resulting in many improvements such as Jitter, a module dedicated to patching 3D graphics and video. What is appealing from the standpoint of graphical interfaces is that patcher programs are determined by the objects, their values and their interactions. The complexity of a program might lead to very complex diagrams of objects, which reflect directly on how the programmer designs a musical composition.

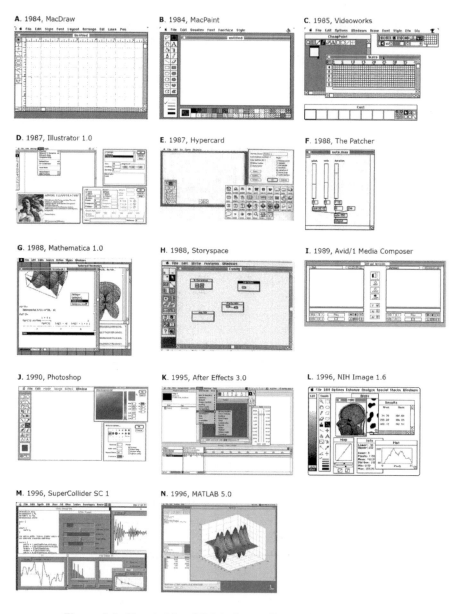

Figure 3.4. *Classic Mac OS interfaces. For a color version of the figure, see www.iste.co.uk/reyes/image.zip*

A different approach to audio synthesis came with SuperCollider, developed by computer scientist and composer James McCartney in 1996, but whose origins date back to 1990, when he worked on programs like Synth-O-Matic and a MAX object called Pyrite [MCC 96, p. 257]. SuperCollider provided a windowed environment comprising an interface builder for controlling signal processing and synthesis functions (through the common Mac controls), and a graphical interface for creating wave tables. Supercollider is a free software package under the GNU license and has become popular among algorithmic composers and musicians since 2002. It also includes its own programming language, called sclang, inspired by Smalltalk, with similar syntax to C or JavaScript[2].

Just as digital music employed signal-processing imaging, the scientific domain also started to develop applications that run on personal computers. The first version of the widely renowned Wolfram Mathematica was released in 1988, designed by scientist Stephen Wolfram. It was capable of performing numerical, symbolic and graphical operations. The resulting graphics could be enhanced with shading color and lighting effects. Mathematica introduced *notebooks*, which were like documents containing text, graphics and Mathematical notation that could be edited and with built-in contextual menus to provide assistance with the code.

In 1984, scientist Cleve Moler, and control engineers Jack Little and Steve Bangert, founded Mathworks with the intention of developing MATLAB commercially. The application was first written in Fortran in the late 1970s, with an approach focused on numerical analysis and signal processing. Versions for Macintosh, Windows and UNIX were available by 1996 with MATLAB 5. The environment was augmented into a series of tools, available as separate windows (commands, history of commands, workspace), capable of plotting mathematical functions, performing data analysis, importing files (images, spreadsheets, audio and video) and managing scripts with the MATLAB programming language.

Within the medical imaging domain, software engineer Wayne Rasband started developing in 1987, at the National Institutes of Health (NIH), a Macintosh version of his previous program called Image. Among the capabilities of NIH Image 1.6, released in 1996, was that of measuring regions of interest (or ROI) defined by the user, performing particle analysis,

---

2 http://supercollider.github.io/

and applying spatial and density calibration. Results of measures could be saved or copied as text files, but also visualized in different manners, simultaneously in different windows: along with the input images or as data plots. Since 1997, Rasband develops and maintains a public-domain cross-platform Java-based version named ImageJ.

3.5. 1995–2005: Windows 95, 98 and XP years

Before Microsoft Windows 95 was released, the popular operating system was DOS (disk operating system). Developers programed directly in assembler or BASIC, among other low-level languages, and the user interface was text-based. However, early graphics applications were designed on DOS systems, for example, the Fairlight CMI I (Computer Musical Instrument), created by artists and inventors Kim Ryrie, Peter Vogel and Tony Furse in 1979 for reproducing sounds and doing audio synthesis. The instrument consisted of different keyboards, hardware and a display monitor. It included an innovative graphical interface developed in QDOS for representing sound in the form of waves[3]. The CMI systems series became very influential in pop-rock music production during the 1980s.

Another example is AutoCAD, developed in 1982 by John Walker (also founder of Autodesk). AutoCAD was a pioneering computer-aided design software, addressed specially to industrial design: 3D, solid modeling, conceptual design in architecture, interactive mechanical engineering, facility planning, geographic information systems and integrated flexible manufacturing. The graphical interface allowed drawing lines, solids and texts and other primitives that could be manipulated independently. AutoCAD rapidly became one of the most popular CAD software applications, mainly maintained for Windows operating systems (indeed Macintosh support was not granted from 1994 to 2011).

Since its introduction in 1981, MS-DOS remained the most popular DOS system throughout the 1980s and part of the 1990s. At the same time, Microsoft unveiled the Windows operating system in 1985 and developers and designers started to create new types of applications and interfaces based

---

3 In 2013, Peter Vogel announced the release of the CMI-30AX to commemorate the 30th anniversary of the first sale of the CMI systems (see http://petervogelinstruments.com.au/specs/). The reader interested in 3D visualization software for sound can also refer to sndtools from the Sound Lab at Princeton University (see http://sndtools.cs.princeton.edu/).

on the WIMP paradigm. The now ubiquitous Microsoft Word, for example, was originally developed for MS-DOS in 1983, but it was not as popular as Word Perfect at that time. However, when it was refashioned for Windows in 1989 by Charles Simonyi (ex-Xerox PARC developer of Bravo) and Richard Brodie, it quickly became the standard application for text processing. Its graphical organization of commands for text formatting has been adapted to different applications.

A turnover in graphical interfaces for Windows occurred in 1991, with the introduction of the first version of Visual Basic, the product of the vision of software programmer Alan Cooper (who sold the precursor of Visual Basic to Microsoft in 1988). In the similar style of current interface builders, Visual Basic offered an environment and programming language to design applications based on widgets, geared toward the user interface style of Windows itself. By 1995, Windows was a robust and stable system when it became available to the public. Visual Basic was upgraded to version 4.0 and, since 1997, it is part of the Windows IDE (integrated development environment) Visual Studio.

The software applications that were dedicated to working with images and visual information became very complex as the entertainment industry consolidated visual special effects and 3D animation. Although production studios behind the cameras of blockbuster movies from the 1990s usually had their own version of software, plug-ins and in-house development departments, some of their software tools became publicly available.

Autodesk 3D Studio Max (version 1.0 published by Kinetix in 1996) and Autodesk Maya (version 1.0 released by Alias Wavefront in 1998) popularized user interfaces devoted to 3D modeling, texturing and animation. The common digital artists' workspace divided the screen in four views (usually top, left, front and perspective views, but these could of course be customized). Menus surrounded the views and were constructed with different nesting levels (i.e. a menu contained submenus with more submenus and options). The complexity of using such multi-purpose yet highly specialized applications was the amount of features and the difficulty of locating them in the interface. Thus, users could be identified according to their practices: generalists, animators, riggers, modelers, texturers, etc. Each of these roles only accessed determined portions of the same application. Among the innovations to ease the complexity, Maya embraced an implementation of *marking menus* in its interface: keeping the right-button of the mouse clicked over an object would reveal a floating menu of options. Another practice was to use and customize enhanced mice and devices (three or more buttons, side buttons, scrolling wheel, Wacom tablets, etc.). Therefore, together with keyboard shortcuts, it was easier for users to access options instead of navigating menus in windows.

Learning, mastering and obtaining a certification in a software package became a career strategy for entertainment artists. In this context, one of the main drawbacks for the general public was the elevated cost of software licenses. While 3D Studio MAX and Maya were expensive (expressed in thousands of US dollars), there were high-end software like Autodesk Flame, Smoke and Inferno that charted in the hundreds of thousands. In some cases, it was preferable to rent an equipped studio with the adapted hardware or to choose a diploma in recognized schools with modern equipment and instructors.

In 1993, computer scientist and film graduate Bill Spitzak developed NUKE at Digital Domain. As with many other software applications of that time, NUKE started as an in-house improvement to existing tools with the intention to facilitate tedious repetitive tasks of staff. In the beginning, NUKE combined command-line compositing techniques with Flame and Inferno. Later, in 2002, it was released to the public and since 2007 has been managed by The Foundry, a Digital Domain partner. Among the characteristics that attracted NUKE users was the possibility of connecting compositing objects in the form of a node graph, while also being able to script their behavior. The graphical interface was indeed simple and organized in tabs for different panels. Moreover, instead of using Visual Studio, the overall interface used the Qt GUI framework.

Just as motion graphics combined two domains (2D graphic design with animation techniques), the idea of digital sculpting was implemented into software by combining 3D models with 2D-like techniques. In 1997, technologist Ofer Alon designed ZBrush and co-founded Pixologic, the company that has been in charge of its development. In 1999, the first licenses of the software went on sale and it was rapidly recognized by both digital artists and non-technical users. The ZBrush vision of digital sculpting conceived 2.5D in the sense of using techniques common to 2D paint programs but with a sculpturing metaphor (knives, clay, etc.) to model and create 3D objects. This was constructed on the notion of *pixol*, a data structure for 2.5D situated between pixels (2D) and voxels (3D). The visual information that a pixol stores includes: positions, color, depth, material, lighting and orientation. Other innovations introduced by ZBrush are ZSpheres, which act like wire skeletons in clay modeling. The distinctive look and style of the ZBrush interface can be personalized and enhanced via the programming language ZScript.

While the entertainment industry was using software for hyper-realistic and high-definition graphics, the industrial design community identified their own tools. In practice, AutoCAD was more used by architects and planners, but industrial design included: automobiles, furniture, jewelry and all kinds of objects. Rhinoceros (also called Rhino 3D) aimed at that kind of industry. Created by Robert McNeel & Associates, version 1.0 was released in 1998 but was not publicly available until version 2.0 was released in 2000. A distinguishing feature against AutoCAD was its modeling approach based on NURBS, while AutoCAD was based on solid geometry. In 2008, it introduced the plug-in Grasshopper for Rhino, which added a node-based interface for parametric modeling.

In parallel to all these applications, another approach to graphics was taking shape in the 1990s. In 1989, physicist Tim Berners-Lee invented and settled the basis of the web with the invention of three key technologies: HTML (Hypertext Markup Language), HTTP (Hypertext Transfer Protocol) and URL (Unified Resource Locator). Based on the broader SGML language, the first HTML documents were text based and displayed on web browsers. In 1993, computer scientists Marc Andreessen and Eric Bina created Mosaic, the first browser with support for images (the <img> tag). The web started to develop and by 1995 the World Wide Web Consortium was already established; there were several browsers (Netscape and Internet Explorer became very popular) and new tags and specifications were constantly submitted: <object>, <embed>, and the graphic style language CSS.

The graphics potential of the web fostered the development of FutureSplash Animator, a project initiated in 1994 by software programmer Jonathan Gay and software entrepreneur Charlie Jackson. While Macromedia Director was widely used for multimedia production, FutureSplash appealed to designers of light motion graphics who wanted to distribute their creations across networks. Macromedia acquired the software and renamed it as Flash in 1996. The graphical interface of Flash recalled the Director key frame timeline. It also included basic drawing tools and interactive graphics functionalities controlled from the properties and actions windows (alpha channels, animation interpolation, actions and events, support for vectors, bitmap images, etc.). Flash became the favorite tool for designing interactive and animated images for the web (banners, advertising, welcome pages, artworks, experiments and entire web sites) until HTML5 and CSS3 became mainstream.

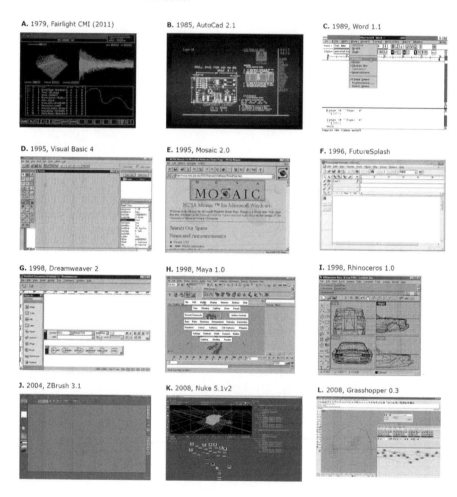

Figure 3.5. *Windows 95, 98, XP interfaces. For a color version of the figure, see www.iste.co.uk/reyes/image.zip*

Although productions made with Flash could be displayed natively in web browsers (files with the swf extension), it was also necessary to encapsulate the animations in HTML to combine them with text and static images. In 1997, Macromedia Dreamweaver was positioned as a product to create and manage web sites following the features of text-processing editors. It proposed three different views of the same document: code view (HTML tags), layout view (similar to a text-processing application) and split view (offering both code and layout views). A toolbox palette assisted the user to insert graphic elements: images, Flash animations, tables, layers (<div> tags) and controls (widgets for HTML forms).

3.6. 2005–2017: Free software years and web as platform

The free software movement started in 1983, when activist and computer programmer Richard Stallman called for the development of GNU (acronym for "GNU's Not Unix"), a 100% free operating system based on Unix. In 1985, he founded the Free Software Foundation (FSF) and, in 1990, the GNU was almost finished. Computer science graduate student Linus Torvalds released Linux as free software in 1992 and GNU/Linux appeared shortly after as a complete operating system. The GNU Project currently maintains the operating system, as well as a wide range of software applications, packages, tools, games and licenses.

In this section, we present software applications released under some kind of open and free license. Specifically, the GNU has four: General Public License (GPL), Lesser General Public License (LGPL), Affero General Public License (AGPL) and Free Documentation License (FDL). Software distributed under these licenses highlights that, in the words of the FSF, "users have the freedom to run, copy, distribute, study, change and improve the software"[4]. Alternatives to GNU licenses are listed by the Open Source Initiative, among others: BSD, MIT, Apache, Mozilla or Eclipse[5].

One characteristic of free software is that applications are often initiated by an individual (or a small group of people) and then a community of users and developers has access to the source code and can contribute to shape and polish its functionalities. This is not exactly the same as free licenses offered

---

4 https://www.gnu.org/philosophy/free-sw.html

5 https://opensource.org/licenses

by proprietary software applications, whose source code remains closed and maintained by the vendor. It has been a common practice that commercial software offers to users a trial period to install and test an application. Today, we also see free licenses for personal, educational and non-commercial use. This is the case with various Autodesk applications[6] (including Maya, AutoCAD, 3ds Max); Apple software (macOS, Xcode IDE); Unity[7] (a very popular game engine developed by Unity Technologies since 2005); Sculptris[8] (a digital sculpting software distributed by Pixologic since 2009) and web-based services like Google's universe.

However, we have to distinguish between commercial software maintained by big enterprises and proprietary software developed by small and independent groups. Eastgate Systems' chief scientist Mark Bernstein calls this *artisanal software*: "Artisan software is opinionated (...) It expresses the views of someone who thought about it and crafted it, not those an investment team has convinced itself to find in a focus group" [BER 12a, p. 18]. Examples of software that fall into this category could be Sublime Text[9], a popular text-code editor whose current license model offers an unlimited free trial period (license fee is 70 USD); Scrivener[10], an original and efficient writing environment (45 USD); Papers[11], a PDF organizer (70 euros); or, Tinderbox[12], a hypertext tool for notes (249 USD).

GNU imaging software originated in 1995, when computer science students Peter Mattis and Spencer Kimball started working on GIMP[13] (GNU Image Manipulation Program), an image-editing program for raster graphics. If GIMP can be seen as similar in functionalities to Adobe Photoshop, Inkscape[14] (initiated in 2003) would be similar to Adobe Illustrator, with additional plug-ins contributed by the community. In the 3D domain, the free software application with similar capabilities to Maya or

---

6 http://www.autodesk.com/education/free-software/all

7 https://unity3d.com/

8 http://pixologic.com/sculptris/

9 https://www.sublimetext.com/

10 https://www.literatureandlatte.com/scrivener.php

11 http://papersapp.com/mac/

12 http://www.eastgate.com/Tinderbox/

13 https://www.gimp.org/

14 https://inkscape.org/

3ds Max is Blender[15]. Publicly released in 2002 and maintained by the Blender Foundation, it includes tools for modeling meshes, video tracking, visual effects, texturing, rendering and further customization with Python.

When GIMP version 1.0 was released in 1998, Mattis had also started developing GTK, the GIMP Toolkit for creating graphical interfaces. GTK was upgraded to GTK+ and became a constitutive part of the GNOME[16] project, which is devoted to building a desktop environment for GNU/Linux. Nowadays, GTK+ can be used with Glade[17], an interface designer (or GUI builder) program, and it is the GUI framework behind Inkscape. The other popular GUI framework today is Qt (under GPL/ LGPL license; See section 2.3.2), which powers the interface of Adobe Photoshop and Autodesk Maya.

When the 2000s arrived, there was a manifest interest in experimenting with computational design, generative art and creative coding. By 1999, artist-designer and computer scientist John Maeda had been practicing (and published a book) on Design By Numbers[18] (DBN), an environment and programming language for visual artists. DBN led to the origins of Processing in 2001, conducted by Casey Reas and Ben Fry, both then graduate students at the Aesthetics and Computation Group at MIT. Processing 1.0 was released in 2008 and soon became one of the most popular languages and environments for digital art. Processing is based on Java, using a simplified version of the language and enhanced with libraries for different sorts of tasks, from OpenGL graphics to computer vision, image processing, Internet and physical computing. The minimalist graphical interface of Processing proposed a menu bar with commands to run and stop the programming code. Complex programs would distinguish classes and objects in different tabs. Processing has been used as a complete development environment for software applications (such as the RGB+D Toolkit used in the documentary CLOUDS[19]) and has aggregated a community of designers and amateurs sharing their codes (or *sketches*, in terms of Processing).

---

15 https://www.blender.org/

16 https://www.gnome.org/

17 https://glade.gnome.org

18 http://dbn.media.mit.edu/

19 http://jamesgeorge.org/CLOUDS

DBN inspired a generation of digital artists. In 2003, DesignRobots was developed as a Python application for drawing 2D graphics by Just van Rossum, Erik van Blokland and Frederik Berlaen. It soon became DrawBot[20] which, in its turn, inspired Frederik De Bleser and Tom De Smedt to develop NodeBox in 2004. NodeBox 1 added animation and interactivity to 2D graphics. In 2012, NodeBox 3 was published as a major release, including a node-based interface especially dedicated for generative design and data visualization.

In 2005, Context Free[21] appeared with a similar interface to DrawBot and NodeBox 1. Chris Coyne had created a context-free grammar for 2D graphics, and Mark Lentczner and John Horigan developed interactive versions for Mac and Windows. The program interface is divided into three main panels. The left panel is used for writing grammars, the right panel shows the graphical result (when clicking the Render button) and the third panel, in the bottom, shows code errors. While every variation seems different according to rules and changes in parameters, they can be referenced by their variation ID, located in the menu bar. Graphic designs can be saved as static or animated images; the latter depicting in time the steps the grammar follows to generate a shape.

Based on the concept of context-free design grammars, physicist and software developer Mikael H. Christensen designed Structure Synth[22] in 2007. While the graphical interface keeps the same organization as Context Free, Structure Synth generates 3D structures. The obvious modification of grammar commands concerns the support of 3D objects (boxes, spheres, meshes, cylinders, tubes, etc.), but Christensen also added ray-tracers, renderers and export to OBJ format.

A common trait of these tools is that the programming code is exposed to the designer. The minimalist GUI leaves the entire interface space to working with code. When this code is written with aesthetic intentions, we call the practice *creative coding*. The fact that Processing, for example, uses Java as its underlying technology raises problems and advantages. Depending on the final desired result, Processing might or might not be the best choice mainly because of efficiency and stability issues. Professional

---

20 http://www.drawbot.com/
21 https://www.contextfreeart.org/
22 http://structuresynth.sourceforge.net/

digital artists who exhibit in museums or who are commissioned to create artwork often choose more robust environments.

openFrameworks[23] (oF) and Cinder[24] are two projects designed with creative coding in mind that build on top of C++. oF was inspired by Processing and initiated in 2004 by digital artist Zachary Lieberman, who continues its development together with digital artists Theodore Watson and Arturo Castro and an international community of users. It offers components dedicated to work with 2D and 3D graphics, audio, video and OpenCV[25] (Open Source Computer Vision Library), a popular free software library for computer vision and machine learning.

Cinder, started as a spare time project by computer scientist Andrew Bell in 2010, also offers libraries for working with geometry, math, OpenGL, audio, video and images. The advantage of using a low-level language like C++ is the more rapid access to the operating system and devices, creating applications and communicating with input-output data. Cinder offers a couple of tools designed to facilitate the setup of projects: Tinderbox, a template assistant, and Cinderbox, a place where the different libraries are listed. However, neither Cinder nor openFrameworks offers a graphical interface to write code. They rely on an IDE, such as Xcode in macOS or Visual Studio in Windows.

As we see, creative coding relies mostly on writing interfaces (although visual programming languages are also used). What would be the difference with other interfaces for different practices of writing? Allow us now to take a brief look at systems for writing code, documentation and for creative writing.

Professional development environments like Xcode and Visual Studio remain proprietary tools. This means that they cannot be easily extended and modified by end users: it is up to Apple or Microsoft to integrate or not any new feature or improvement. Open-source alternatives exist. We have already talked about Eclipse and NetBeans as robust environments for Java and C++. The case of Eclipse is worth noting. At first, it was IBM proprietary software but, precisely because users demanded to extend the

23 http://openframeworks.cc/
24 https://libcinder.org/
25 http://opencv.org/

software, it became open source in 2001. Eclipse is now maintained by the Eclipse Foundation and distributed under a license compliant with the Open Software Initiative.

The typical graphical interface of modern code editors features syntax highlighting (different colors are assigned to texts according to their function in the program, for example, variable, function, numbers, etc.); auto-completion (as the user types, the software guesses the word, so it is less common to make syntax errors); and code-text folding (blocks of code can be stretched and expanded). Recent applications have also added different themes and styles (e.g. dark background) and support for many different languages.

In 2008, technologist Chris Wanstrath (co-founder of GitHub) envisioned Atom[26] as a code editor that could be customizable to the point that it could lead, in fact, to different and new code editors. The first version of the software was released in 2015, developed in collaboration with software programmers Corey Johnson and Nathan Sobo. The application was received with enthusiasm and lots of packages have been developed to extend its functionalities, among others the well-known zoom code view (which shows the entire code length together with the normal zoom view, popularized by Sublime Text) and content previews of different files. Its customization can be done with JavaScript and it gave birth to Nuclide[27], an editor designed at Facebook to support their specific workflow and technologies, available to download free but not as free software.

Besides writing code, another kind of writing is what is called *creative writing*, as it is associated with fiction and storytelling. As we saw earlier in this chapter, hypertext tools such as HyperCard and Storyspace were developed for creative writing practices. Today, tools such as Twine[28] draw on the same ideas. Developer, designer and writer Chris Klimas created Twine in 2009 with the intention to assist the creation of nonlinear stories such as "choose your own adventure" or game narratives. Twine is now in version 2 and it has promoted a simple graphical interface based on nodes and links. A node, called a *passage*, is similar to a book page. Inside a page there can be one or more links to other passages. From the author's

---

26 https://atom.io/
27 https://nuclide.io/
28 https://twinery.org

perspective, the story can be viewed as a structure of nodes and links. When the story is finished, it can be exported to HTML format, which can be further modified with CSS and JavaScript.

Another kind of writing concerns documentation. When discovering a new piece of software it is always useful to read the documentation and reference in order to understand the syntax and semantics of components. The kind of tools used for these tasks are called documentation generators. They often extract comments in the source code and output the documentation in HTML, GitHub or JSON format. Among the most popular generator tools and styles are Javadoc[29] and Doxygen[30].

From a different perspective, art researcher Clarisse Bardiot conceived in 2007 a tool for documenting the creative process behind live arts such as theater, performance, circus, etc. (although her approach can be easily extended to any creative project). In 2012, developers Guillaume Jacquemin and Guillaume Marais started working on the beta versions of the project and, in 2015, the version 1.0 was released. Rekall[31] software allows one to import all kinds of documents associated during the production (e-mails between persons, PDFs, photographs, videos, audio, scripts, programming code). The graphical interface follows a layering organization for timeline events. Each resource is assigned a different color and can be visualized according to an event in the timeline. Moreover, Rekall makes it possible to add notes, to extract and search metadata from imported files, and to publish a project in HTML form (an associated online project is Memo Rekall[32]).

Moreover, using methods for code extraction, the branch of computer science concerned with analyzing how the program is structured, how it executes and how it evolves is *software visualization*. In broad terms, it develops and investigates "methods and uses of computer graphical representations of various aspects of software" [DIE 07, p. 3]. Among those aspects there is of course the source code and also its requirements, documentation, changes, bug reports and files.

29 http://www.oracle.com/technetwork/java/javase/documentation/index-jsp-135444.html
30 http://www.doxygen.org
31 http://www.rekall.fr
32 http://www.memorekall.fr/

Besides the list of software visualization tools elaborated by [DIE 07, p. 163], more recently, researchers from the Università della Svizzera Italiana in Switzerland have been active in software visualization projects. For example, in 2008, graduate student Jacopo Malnati developed X-Ray[33], a plug-in for the Eclipse IDE to graphically represent Java programs. It used mainly two layout methods (a hierarchical polymetric view and a bi-dimensional circle view) whose position and color scheme were associated with *software metrics*. Moreover, in 2008, Richard Wettel made available CodeCity[34] as a software application. The first version presented a menu bar and two panes. In the left and biggest pane, the visual result is shown. The default model is 3D, associating the distribution of elements symbolically with a city, with skyscrapers, parking lots, office buildings and small houses. In order to identify which shape corresponds to which package or class, the user hovers over buildings and the information is displayed in the right panel. The menu bar offers access to view configurations. In 2009, the latest version was released with an improved interface based on user evaluations: it featured an additional panel (for displaying a tree view of the structure), a redesigned menu bar and scripting support to customize visualization beyond the graphical user interface.

We have put forward the notion of *metrics* in software visualization, that is, the quantification of programming code components. However, metrics has much larger implications. It has become a keyword with the increasing interest in data visualization. For metrics, everything is subject to being counted, formalized in the form of a database and analyzed through graphical models. For example, a classic scenario in digital humanities research involves working with a large corpus of texts (such as entire books, mail exchanges, etc.). Some *text metrics* are word frequency, n-grams, vocabulary density and topic modeling.

Data visualization modules exist in a variety of software applications, for example, the histogram panel in Photoshop, word clouds in Tinderbox, etc. However, we focus now on software specifically designed for data visualization tasks.

---

33 http://xray.inf.usi.ch/xray.php
34 https://wettel.github.io/codecity.html

Audio visualization considers sound data metrics. The common graphical representation of sound is as waveform: a series of sinusoidal functions where we can see variations in frequency (the horizontal axis) and amplitude (the vertical axis). Other relevant models for specialists can be found in the application Sonic Visualiser[35], developed since 2006 by the Centre for Digital Music at Queen Mary University of London. The graphical interface is organized to facilitate the creation of stacks of views. As in other multimedia packages, where layers are video channels or audio tracks, in Sonic Visualiser they are different representations of the same sound information. Among other views, there are: spectrogram, time-ruler, spectrum, time-instants, time-values, notes and color 3D plots. Each layer is accompanied with a right panel for parameters and additional information. During a user session, all layers are synchronized and might have different zoom detail of an audio region.

Geographic information systems (GIS) allow combining data tables of different nature. In QGIS[36], a software application initiated by geologist Gary Sherman in 2002, it is possible to add layers of spatial information that overlay on top of map views. Besides GPS data, it supports vector and raster data. The former relates to geometric figures from data values and the latter refers to photographs and satellite imagery.

In a broader perspective to data visualization, our account shall mention Gephi and RStudio as exemplary tools for general-purpose visualization. Gephi[37] was originated in 2008, with initial contributions by computer scientists Mathieu Bastian, Sebastien Heymann and Mathieu Jacomy. It is oriented towards graph analysis and visualization. Hence, its modules facilitate working with routines within a network sciences framework (the terms used for commands and actions reflect this degree of specialization; in other words, while it might be easy to explore its functionalities, the user is expected to have or to develop some knowledge about the discipline). Panels and windows that surround the main area can be redistributed or hidden. For example, exploring visual layouts (ForceAtlas, Fruchterman-Reingold, YifanHu Multilevel, OpenOrd, Circular Layout, Radial Axis Layout, Geographic map, Node overlapping) implies leaving a larger space to

---

35 http://www.sonicvisualiser.org
36 http://www.qgis.org
37 https://gephi.org

visualize the graph, but running filters and investigating modularity and clustering pops up special windows to the fore.

RStudio[38], on the contrary, is a dedicated IDE for the statistics programming language R (initially written by Robert Gentleman and Ross Ihaka in 1997). Indeed, the proper execution of RStudio depends on having R already installed in the same computer. Although R distributes a basic graphical interface, RStudio has gained acceptance because it effectively extends it with a robust code editor, code execution, and tools for plotting, debugging, command history, and workspace management (workspace in R is the place where objects, variables and functions are stored). Such features have their own default organization in the graphical interface, in the form of panels.

When we mentioned that software applications for data visualization accept formalized models of data, we were thinking about databases and data tables. Basically, the formalization is similar to spreadsheets as they are practiced with Microsoft Excel or Google Spreadsheets. To conclude this section, we make reference to Open Refine[39], a peculiar tool for cleaning and formatting data. Initially developed as Freebase Gridworks in 2010 by software engineer David Huynh at Metaweb Technologies, it was later acquired by Google and renamed Google Refine. However, since 2012 it has been released as BSD software and renamed Open Refine. The peculiarity of Refine is that it runs as a web server, that is, its graphical interface is accessible from a web browser, pointing to a local URL. Another commonality is how it handles data. Instead of a regular spreadsheet, it uses scripting code (such as GREL (General Refine Expression Language)) and filters in order to unveil patterns in data. Then, it would be possible to do manipulations: modifying, deleting, exporting, etc.

With the example of Refine, we conclude this section by evoking the current importance of web apps and the web as platform. As editor and entrepreneur Tim O'Reilly heralded in 2005, the Web 2.0 changed the Internet paradigm and attracted industries and users because of its technical possibilities (social platforms, access to media content, genres like wikis, blogs, podcasts) and new communication model (anyone can become a sender or an active receiver who selects what to read).

---

38 https://www.rstudio.com
39 http://openrefine.org

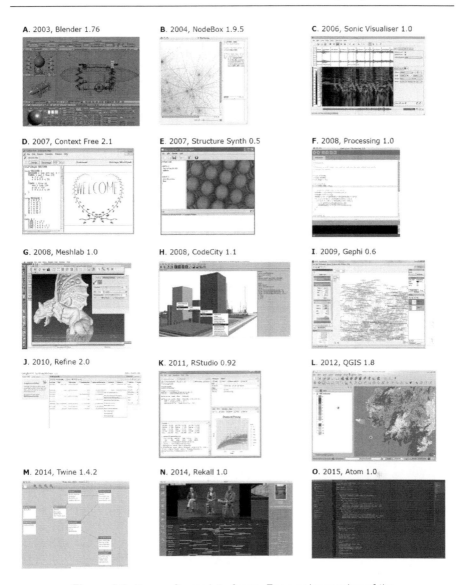

A. 2003, Blender 1.76

B. 2004, NodeBox 1.9.5

C. 2006, Sonic Visualiser 1.0

D. 2007, Context Free 2.1

E. 2007, Structure Synth 0.5

F. 2008, Processing 1.0

G. 2008, Meshlab 1.0

H. 2008, CodeCity 1.1

I. 2009, Gephi 0.6

J. 2010, Refine 2.0

K. 2011, RStudio 0.92

L. 2012, QGIS 1.8

M. 2014, Twine 1.4.2

N. 2014, Rekall 1.0

O. 2015, Atom 1.0

Figure 3.6. *Free software interfaces. For a color version of the figure, see www.iste.co.uk/reyes/image.zip*

Utilizing the web today would signify to some users creating a social media profile, or a simple web page using free online services (e.g. with Wix or Wordpress). For big industries, the web opens new possibilities to develop media and data services, from Netflix to Amazon, from watching TV series online to tracking and commercializing user data. Yet another kind of users, image-interface researchers and designers, might observe new graphical possibilities that exploit HTML5, CSS3, JavaScript and new standards such as WebRTC (Real-Time Communication), Web Audio API and WebSocket API[40].

In has been a while now that new JS libraries, CSS frameworks, HTML templates, best practices, UI patterns and UI experiments have emerged on an everyday basis. Just to mention a few examples, we summarize in Appendix 2 some libraries dedicated to images and visual information on the web. The selected libraries build on top of JavaScript, and some of them act as *meta-libraries*, that is, they are secondary libraries that build on top of another library, for example, the popular jQuery, initiated by software engineer John Resig in 2006[41].

3.7. Interface logics

The intention of our brief review of software interfaces was to identify configurations of interface elements that are put in practice for interacting with visual information. From this account, we can now distinguish some *interface logics* (following the idea of operational logics, see section 3.1), which are patterns combining spatial and visual configurations. In other words, visual patterns take place on screen, as they organize widgets, controls, regions, panes, interactions and other interface elements. However, they also act in the physical space as different screens vary in size, brightness, projection and controlling device.

The following list of interface logics should be considered non-exhaustive and not definitive. They derive from a small sample of units. As we mentioned at the beginning of this chapter, we have only reviewed seminal desktop software interfaces. The field is wide open for more inclusive studies, taking into account games, digital art, mobile apps, web sites, web apps, urban devices (kiosks, subway, buildings, stores) and objects (Internet of Things, automobiles). All in all, we believe that these logics, detected at the early stages of software interfaces, remain valid in

---

40 https://www.w3.org/TR/

41 https://jquery.com and library directories like jqueryscript.net or jqueryrain.com

contemporary designs and across domains (consult Appendix 1 for a table of current versions, licenses and scope of the software reviewed):

– *Feedback*: simple graphical means that indicate the state of the program. It could be, for example, in the form of text, such as the messages in Bravo and Draw. Otherwise, it could be in visual form such as inverting the brightness of a button when a cursor is over or when it is activated (white over black and vice versa). Feedback is extensively used nowadays and explored in different materializations: sound alerts or device vibrations.

– *Symbolization of commands*: interfaces convey the meaning of actions or procedures or algorithms by means of symbolic mediations. Pictograms and computer icons generalize expectations, for example, selecting the fill circle in the Draw menu creates the expectation that the drawing brush will take a circular shape. Symbolization is also practiced in text form, for example, when using word abbreviations that stand for the whole action or object (H for Hue, DEL for delete, etc.). Visual attributes are generally communicated through sliders, text fields and other widgets (while color pickers offer a visual preview, other attributes might be simply conveyed as text or as applied to a preview image, like the filter selector in Adobe Photoshop).

– *WIMP 2*: the original WIMP paradigm continues to play an active role. Windows and panes are designed today according to different screen sizes where the user might potentially encounter an interface. Responsive design practitioners even redesign a completely different organization for different sizes. Icons and pointers proliferate and there is a trend, in web design, of using fonts and typography to type icons instead of using them as images. Menus might keep their classical hierarchical organization and are enhanced with imbricated menus (submenus inside submenus inside submenus), with icons as items instead of texts, preview vignettes (such as in 3ds Max, ZBrush, and Substance Painter, where the user is offered a thumbnail of the material and textures).

– *Framework*: in relation to standardization strategies, graphical interfaces might use one or more development frameworks. These apply not only at the level of operating systems (such as Apple's guidelines, Visual Studio, Qt, GTK+, etc.), but also in web platforms: for example, Bootstrap and Foundation for CSS, and Angular and React for JavaScript. Although the use of a framework is not mandatory, ultimately the interface manifests its relationship to the system through the look of pointer, cursors, scroll bars and other elements whose style varies from one system to another.

– *Customization*: graphical interfaces are malleable in several ways. First, they can be rearranged and customized to suit a user's desire (in Adobe and Autodesk software, this is located in the Window menu). Second, the information on which a user is working (for instance, a photograph that is being retouched, a 3D model being texturized, etc.) can be viewed or represented in different modes. Depending on the nature of the image, it could be solid or wire-frame, opaque or transparent. In 3D interfaces, there could be multiple perspectives or views of the same object (a window subdivided into different views). Furthermore, the scale, direction and zoom detail can be modified (image dimension, text size, model orbiting), while another pane indicates the region being inspected (in code editors like Atom or Sublime, there is a right pane that shows the whole lines of code in a program).

– *Transformation sequencing*: in analogy to hypertext fiction, where a reader discovers a story by making choices and getting to know the characters, in software interfaces the user performs a series of transformations. A user gets to know commands and their functions in a cycle manner then, to achieve a particular goal, she experiments with less common commands. This occurs more often in complex environments like Autodesk Maya, and also in web browsing, documentation writing, data cleaning and environments with a large amount of information and options. Some systems trace and keep record of the history of a user, so she can come back in time or save a series of steps to be reproduced automatically.

– *Domain crossings*: interfaces combine different domains and fields. Most obviously, this can be appreciated in the language and names of menus. The canonical bureau terms File, Edit, Cut and Copy integrate with more specialized Process, Batch and Set Scale (as in ImageJ). Less evident are the use of techniques forged in a foreign domain: this is the case with some filters from signal processing adapted to images (although we have seen that they relate to the frequency domain of image processing), but the same happened when Director and After Effects adapted Bézier curves into animation techniques.

– *Programming expandability* and *code demystification*: as it was shown in interfaces for generative design, programming code appears hand in hand with images. A user can modify the code and see immediately its result. In web browsers, this can be seen with the option Console or Inspect Element.

Other environments, like CodeCity or Open Refine, keep a module to access all programmatic options with a code, since they cannot be fully depicted in the graphical interface. The programming code, then, serves to expand properties, customize parameters and analyze behaviors. Interfaces make us aware that they are made with code when errors occur (the 404 error, or "Line 10: ';' expected") but they can also contribute to better understanding its internal mechanisms.

– *Dynamic and live data*: the information that an interface depicts can be dynamic, that is, it only exists upon request of the user or it refreshes constantly (because it comes from a live stream or information flow such as financial information, RSS news, requests to a server, etc.). The use of animations is a well-known technique to convey dynamic behaviors: for example, the spinning wheel and the progress bar. Live data also refers to automatic upgrades, when users validate a new version by restarting the application. When this happens, some interfaces offer a guided tour of new features, a sort of tutorial to discover major changes.

As it can be guessed, interface logics require active engagement and manipulation to be appreciated. Our approach tries to contribute to other existing methodologies for interface analysis:

– Eye-tracking devices, heat maps[42], mouse-tracking[43] techniques.

– Recorded video of user sessions and interview and focus groups with users.

– Structural analysis where interface parts (panes, palettes, etc.) are outlined.

In fact, we could propose a different mapping on top of an interface by locating how interface units relate. For example, when we click on an icon from the toolbox, which parts of the entire interface are affected or changed? What are those changes? How is data affected or transformed? Which data structures and algorithms are executed in the background? How can we perceive that change: as text message, as visual variation, or some other way? How is the reading model of the interface designed? How does the interface place itself and contribute to already existing practices?

---

42 See, for example, heatmap.js: http://www.patrick-wied.at/static/heatmapjs/
43 See, for example, IOGraph: http://www.iographica.com

Figure 3.7 shows a quick glance of such a mapping technique, applied to a generic Photoshop interface scheme. Figure 3.7(a) shows three icon buttons linked to those places where information changes upon clicking on them. Figure 3.7(b) shows the work area (the canvas) linked to all potential buttons that can be clicked at a given time. Figure 3.7(c) is a different representation of Figure 3.7(a), isolating interface units from the whole.

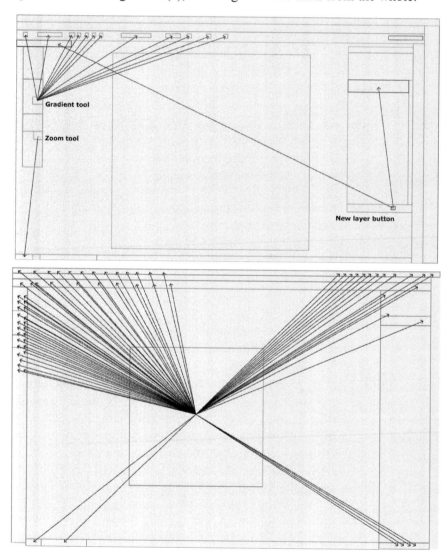

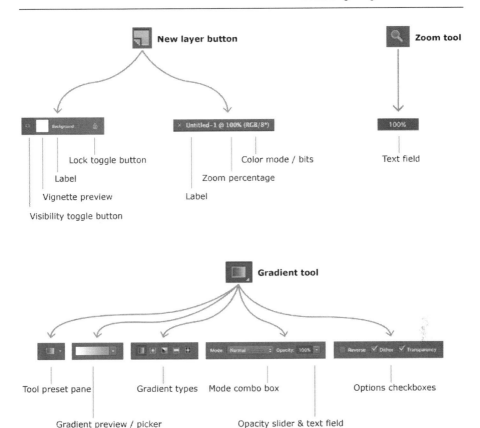

Figure 3.7. *Sketches for mapping interface logics*

The possible answers to the questions above should be thought within the context of a specific practice and in comparison to another. Interface diagrams can help as inscription supports to add annotations or trace different relations between components. Once our intuitions are discussed, we can design and speculate about our own new interfaces.

## 4

Designing Image-Interfaces

Using interfaces routinely paves the way to different *predicative scenes* that can be identified, such as editing a photo, making a digital draw, compositing channels of video and audio, writing a novel or essay and discovering a new programming language. These scenes are the underlying ground for establishing processes that will be recognized as *kinds of practices*, for example, using an interface with educational, professional or artistic intentions. When a scene of practice is identified, we may then talk about fields, domains and disciplines.

In Chapter 3, we saw numerous examples of graphical interfaces designed to support practices associated mostly with image creation (we also displayed some examples where the interface is graphical enough to convey plastic dimensions of texts and other types of information). In this chapter, we pay special attention to those cases where the image being manipulated acts as the graphical interface itself.

We are thinking about multidisciplinary fields at the crossroads of several disciplines such as graphic design, data science, computer science and humanities. The kinds of results that are produced from those perspectives include data visualization, networks graphs, infographics, cultural analytics and data art.

As we mentioned earlier, our intention with this book is to inform creative practices with the constituent and technical aspects behind the design of graphical interfaces. The kind of practice that we adopt occurs within the academic and scientific scene. That being said, our productions should be regarded more as prototypes or sketches, but also as visions, statements, hypothetical theories and pedagogical detonators, instead of fully developed systems. With respect to the design and development of complex systems, we locate ourselves at the level of interface and visualization tools. However, we believe that the use of new creations by different users and in different contexts re-launches the processes of practices, leading to potential applications in diverse domains or to the emergence of new fields (such as speculative and critical design[1]).

4.1. Precursors to data visualization

The idea of studying images as interfaces can be associated with their diagrammatic properties. In section 1.4.3, we evoked the fundamental notion of *icon* according to philosopher and logician Charles Peirce. Icons are signs that stand for something else by virtue of similarity. Peirce further subdivided icons into three categories: *images* can be appreciated as visual attributes; *diagrams* represent relations that convey a general predicate and *metaphors* map structures from one domain into another. In practice, these types of signs exist in combination with other classes of signs. Figure 4.1 situates images, diagrams and metaphors in the bigger picture of sign categories elaborated by Peirce.

Pre-computational uses of images as interfaces can be found in the literature, in the form of diagrams and illustrations from a wide range of fields. Indeed, when diagrammatic functions are explicitly added to pictures, they convert images into powerful supports for observation, abstraction and reasoning. As insisted by Stjernfelt, "manipulability and deductibility is what makes diagrams icons with the special feature that they may be used to think with" [STJ 07, p. 278]. Reading and interpreting a diagram happens in the mind of the viewer; this implies that she could manipulate mentally its properties and project more into it. Stjernfelt continues: "What is gained by realizing the diagrammatical character of picture viewing is not least the close relation between picture and thought. Seen as a diagram, the picture is a *machine à penser*, allowing for a spectrum of different manipulations" [STJ 07, p. 288].

---

1 In the words of Anthony Dunne: "Conventional roles for design include addressing problems set by industry, designing interfaces that seduce the user into cybernetic communication with the corporate cultural values embodied... But design could also develop new attitudes to electronic technology... create alternative contexts of use and need" [DUN 08, p. 75].

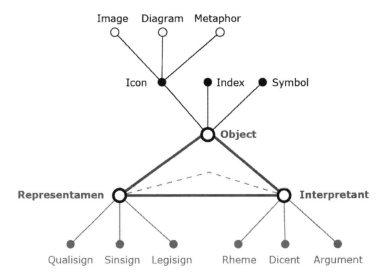

Figure 4.1. *Peirce's types of signs*

To mention some examples, we have already discussed a few names in sections 1.3.1, 1.3.3 and 1.4.3 who can be considered precursors to data and image visualization, in the sense of depicting relations, complex concepts and quantities in diagrammatic form. We can now try to draw a larger map of inspirational sources in Table 4.1. This is of course an ambitious goal and we had to make choices among many examples. The interested reader can find more resources in [DRU 14, TUF 97, BUS 07, ECO 61, GIE 13, GLE 17].

4.2. Data visualization

Data visualization is a transformation process that takes us essentially from one symbolic state to a visual representation, sometimes linearly but most of the times by taking steps back and forth. In an attempt to explain the process as simply as possible, we can recall the seven steps in data representation identified by designer and developer Ben Fry (who co-started with Casey Reas the programming language and development environment Processing): acquire, parse, mine, represent, refine and interact [FRY 08, p. 5]. Another perspective is the ASSERT model, which proposes six phases to guide the design of data visualizations: ask a question; search for information; structure that information; envision the answer; represent the visualization and tell a story [FER 13, p. 43].

Year	Author	Work title
c. 300 BC	Euclid	Elements
1305	Ramon Lull	Ars generalis ultima
c. 1370	Nicolas Oresme	Tractatus de configurationibus qualitatum et motuum
1478–1519	Leonardo da Vinci	Codex Atlanticus
1637	René Descartes	La géométrie
1802	Leonhard Euler	Letters of Euler to a German princess
1810	Johann von Goethe	Theory of colors
1854	Goerge Boole	Laws of thought
1866	Bernhard Riemann	On the hypotheses which lie at the foundation of geometry
1875	Etienne-Jules Marey	La méthode graphique dans les sciences expérimentales
1878	Eadweard Muybridge	The horse in motion
1879	Gottlob Frege	Begriffsschrift
1880	John Venn	On the Diagrammatic and Mechanical Representation of Propositions and Reasonings
1893	Etienne-Jules Marey	Le mouvement
1912	Frank Gilbreth	Primer of scientific management
1925	Paul Klee	Pedagogical sketchbook
1926	Wassily Kandinsky	Point and line to plane
1932	Lazlo Moholy-Nagy	The new vision
1934	Jacob Moreno	Who shall survive?
1935	Walter Gropius	The new architecture and the Bauhaus
1935	Kurt Koffka	Principles of gestalt psychology
1939	James Joyce	Finnegans Wake
1958	Martin Gardner	Logic machines and diagrams
1958	Yona Friedman	Mobile Architecture
1967	Jacques Bertin	Sémiologie graphique
1975	Buckminster Fuller	Synergetics
1977	Christopher Alexander	A pattern language
1990	Abraham Moles	Les sciences de l'imprécis
1993	Scott McCloud	Understanding comics

Table 4.1. *Some precursors to data visualization and diagrammatic reasoning*

A common aspect in both models is to start gathering information according to a question or a research interest. In terms of their sources and functions, data can be empirical, abstract, meta-data, spatial, visual, scientific, biological, physical or all of the above in a single project. Briefly speaking:

– *Empirical data* are collected from observations of the real world. These are often defined as qualitative data, as they are constructed from subjective interpretations made by domain specialists.

– *Abstract data* or quantitative data define measures and numerical values that can be analyzed or derived from formal models, such as "variables consisting of series, lattices, and other indexing schemes" like time, counts and mathematical functions [WIL 05, p. 48].

– *Metadata* are data about the data.

– *Spatial data* refer to geography, geo-location, Earth coordinates, etc.

– *Visual data* are associated with visual attributes, features and descriptors (also associated with *aesthetics* in statistics literature [WIL 05, p. 255]).

– *Scientific data* is an umbrella term for astronomical, nuclear, subatomic, biological and medical data among others.

In general terms, the types of the data[2] determine the graphical representation: bar charts, pie charts, scatterplots, network graphs, word clouds, media visualizations, etc. However, current practices tend to combine several types: perhaps by transforming data from one type into another (e.g. quantifying words or adding semantic annotations to images) or by designing complex and hybrid interfaces that support several views and types of data.

4.2.1. *Data models and data tables*

When data are obtained, they are either structured or unstructured. The latter case is often the most common. Consider the result of digitizing documents. A digital book can be represented not only as a sequence of texts but also as images where no text can be individually selected. If it is a picture, we have a raster format. If it is a transcription of an interview, we

---

2 Note we use "type of data" to denote different things in comparison to the "data structures" and "data types" that we explored in Chapter 2.

have plain text. There are of course data in native digital format, and the World Wide Web is an exemplary case. While a web search returns lists of links or a web site contains documents in HTML format, to think about these views as structured is misleading. Web scrapping and web data mining provide tools and methods to extract information from the web into a unified data table that is the basis of structured data.

We say that data are structured when they are stored and organized in a pertinent format that describe their content. The canonical practice of structuring data follows the form of a data table where columns define fields or dimensions, whereas rows are the individual entries. We can imagine a simple spreadsheet. One column can be assigned to names, another to dates, and so on. Then, each row is expected to be filled in with the corresponding types of data that make sense to the field (i.e. strings for names, numbers for dates).

A data model is precisely the formal description of all the columns that constitute a data table. Sometimes, users might have formulated in advance the information that is required to represent formally a subject through data. In this case, we elaborate an empty table or define a database that will be populated later. However, in other cases, the process is a cooperation between technical possibilities and access to data. In the case of web scrapping, for instance, the resulting table is organized by the document model itself: titles (<h1>), subtitles (<h2>), paragraphs (<p>), images (<img>), links (<a>), etc. Although we can give arbitrary names to our fields, the values will inherit from the technical mechanism of scrapping[3].

A proper format to store a data table must avoid formatting of cells and tables. This is typically confusing to spreadsheet users, who might be used to merging cells, hiding columns, and adding bold, italic and color format to text. For data visualization purposes, a plain text format is required because visual attributes are a service of the software application. That means visual formatting is defined at the level of the XLS file format. The recommendation is to choose formats like CSV (comma-separated values), TSV (tab-delimited values), XML (extensible markup language), JSON (JavaScript Object Notation) or SQL (structured query language).

---

3 Popular tools for web scrapping today are https://www.import.io/, http://webscraper.io/ and integrated functions in Open Refine or Google Spreadsheets, such as =IMPORTHTML("url", "list/table").

4.2.2. *Visual descriptors*

In general, visual features refer to distinctive parts of objects (e.g. eyes are features of faces). They can also be seen as attributes derived from those objects (e.g. rectangularity and circularity). Furthermore, numerical features can be combined to form feature vectors, whose main characteristic is to be independent of geometrical transformations (scale, translation and rotation).

Visual descriptors are summary representations derived from an image. That means they create a formal structure of the image that will be mapped onto the data model. Hence, a data model may be composed of several kinds of visual information, typically:

– *Metadata independent of the content*: for example, name of author, date, location, format, etc. Formal models to describe this information are EXIF (Exchangeable Image File Format), XMP (Extensible Metadata Platform) and Dublin Core standards[4].

– *Content descriptors*: these include low-level (color, texture and shape) and intermediate-level (structure and spatial relationships) features.

- *Color*: from a physiological and psychological standpoint, color attributes are characterized by chromaticity, saturation and brightness. That means a color tonality is given by a combination of these three attributes. As we saw in section 2.2.2, there are various color models that can be used for a digital representation of color, namely HSL, HSB or RGB.

- *Texture*: also from a psychological standpoint, texture is perceived through granularity, directionality and repetitiveness. A texture descriptor is commonly a numerical vector that establishes if points in a region are lesser, greater or approximate to a central reference point.

- *Shape*: in section 2.2.4, we talked about algorithms for image analysis considering two entry points: image features and shape features. The first entry point considers the entire image plane, whereas the second is local (i.e. acts within a region of an image). Among the local shape features, we saw geometric features such as eccentricity, elongatedness, compactness, aspect ratio, rectangularity, circularity, solidity and convexity. Regarding image features, they take into account elements like corners, edges, interest points, curve vertices, edges, lines, curves or surfaces.

---

4 Recall from section 2.3.3 that this information can be included within the image file format.

- *Structure* is given by a "set of features that provide a gestalt impression of the shapes in the image" [DEL 99, p. 26]. The structure of an image can be approached by combining edges, corners and their location within the image. In retrieval systems, this is used to distinguish, for example, between photos and sketches.

- *Spatial relationships* can be of two kinds: directional and topological [DEL 99, p. 27]. On the one hand, once an orientation is established, directions can be described as "from left to right" or "from top to bottom". The metrics of directional relationships are typically the distance or angles between entities. On the other hand, topological relationships are described in terms of disjunction, adjacency, containment and overlapping. Usually, they are formalized in natural language but we can also use set operations as logical propositions.

– *Content semantics*: these are high-level human-namable entities. They describe real-world objects, temporal events, emotions, associated meanings and interpretations. Traditionally, we can use semantic primitives (object, role, action and event) and, more recently, with developments in machine learning, we talk about classifiers: holistic descriptors (e.g. furry, shiny, etc.) and localized parts (e.g. has-legs, has-wheels) [CHE 17, p. 50]. At a higher level, classifiers describe broader categories, like "human", "animal" or "vehicle".

As it can be imagined, a project might have virtually innumerable fields or dimensions that describe an image. If we take, for example, FeatureExtractor,[5] it had already defined 399 content descriptors. These dimensions can easily grow with EXIF and XMP metadata. Ultimately, we could define our own descriptors, based on mathematical and statistical functions that analyze visual content. Moreover, semantic categories can modulate between shared attributes, semantic groups, vocabularies and individual perceptions over time. The challenge now is how to manage and visualize large amounts of dimensions (columns in the data table), together with large amounts of images (the rows of the table). The latter case is commonly studied as *big data*, whereas the former has been proposed as "wide data" [MAN 16].

---

5 https://code.google.com/archive/p/softwarestudies/wikis/FeatureExtractor.wiki (retrieved May 2017). FeatureExtractor is a MATLAB script for automatically extracting visual features from images, created by members of the Software Studies Initiative in 2012.

4.2.3. *Exploratory data analysis*

In 1977, mathematician John Tukey inaugurated an approach to statistics called "exploratory data analysis" (EDA), which has largely influenced the way in which we interact with data today.

The originality of Tukey, who was already known in the computer science field for coining the terms "software" and "bit", was to embrace an investigative posture towards data analysis. For him, EDA was characterized by new or unfamiliar techniques based on procedures rather than on theories, an emphasis on graphical representations and the use of simple mathematics [TUK 93, p. 5]. Of course, Tukey did not disregard the EDA's counterpart, CDA (confirmatory data analysis), which was more interested in supporting or confirming hypotheses through data analysis. Indeed, the whole idea was to make them cooperate.

The influence of exploratory data analysis in modern data workflows can be seen in the following common techniques:

– *Data cleansing*: scaling data to comparable ranges, transposing (also known as swapping, rotating or pivoting) from rows to columns, filtering rows, handling missing elements and unifying formats (case, punctuation, etc.).

– *Data transformations*: these operations are applied to numerical data with the intention to create, summarize or generate new values. They include taking roots, reciprocals, logarithms and powers.

– *Statistics operations*: in descriptive statistics,[6] these include measures for central tendency (mean, median and mode) and dispersion (range and standard deviation).

Moreover, with the increase in data and descriptors (visual, but also social, economic, historical, geographical, etc.), one of the major issues to deal with has been: how should multiple columns of data be represented in a planar surface? In other words, how should many dimensions or descriptors

---

6 Descriptive statistics is concerned with the "use of statistical and graphic techniques to present information about the dataset being studied" in contrast to inferential statistics, which is "the practice of drawing conclusions about a population using statistics calculated on a sample considered to be representative of that population" [BOS 08, p. 54].

in our existing graphical supports be adjusted? To tackle these questions, statisticians have forged several techniques on "dimensionality reduction"[7].

4.2.4. Dimensionality reduction

Whenever we find ourselves dealing with data tables containing more than 15 columns with different data values, it is often recommended to use some method to reduce such dimensions for the sake of graphical analysis purposes, which means that instead of plotting few values, we could take advantage of the richness of the data and produce new data measures. Dimensionality reduction can be seen as "a mapping from the higher-dimensional space to a lower-dimensional one, while keeping information on all of the available variables" [MAR 11, p. 32]. From an applied perspective, this mapping can be linear or nonlinear depending on the data transformations. Table 4.2 summarizes linear and nonlinear methods, modified from [MAR 11].

Linear methods	Nonlinear methods
Principal component analysis (PCA)	Multidimensional scaling (MDS)
Singular value decomposition (SVD)	Local-linear embedding (LLE)
Linear discriminant analysis (LDA)	Isometric feature mapping (ISOMAP)
Nearest neighbor approach	Hessian locally linear embedding (HLLE)
Correlation dimension	Self-organizing maps (SOM)
Maximum likelihood approach	Generative topographic maps (GTM)
Intrinsic dimension estimation using packing numbers	Curvilinear component analysis (CCA)
	Stochastic Neighbor Embedding (t-SNE)

Table 4.2. *Dimensionality reduction methods*

From the last table, we highlight that PCA and MDS are among the most used; their algorithms and functions can be found integrated into various statistics software applications. On the one hand, the principle of PCA is to

---

7 It is obvious there have been many other issues and many more techniques have flourished. To mention some: factorial analysis (a kind of PCA), clustering, classification, regression, model selection, outlier detection and novelty detection among others have been explored within the machine learning community.

decompose a matrix of values in order to output a new matrix whose values correspond to maximizations of variations. The new values are linear combinations of the original, also called orthogonal components or factors. On the other hand, MDS is based on the dissimilarity of all data values in order to determine principal coordinates. As stated in [BOS 08, p. 312], the ordination process relies on a geometric representation of data to identify the principal components.

In this line, we would like to evoke other methods that rely on geometrical transformations of data to determine dimension reduction. That means they require, first, to represent graphically the properties of data and then to calculate distances, proximities and relations. Three of these methods are well summarized in [DON 03, p. 10]: LLE, ISOMAP and HLLE, in comparison to input data (top left in Figure 4.2).

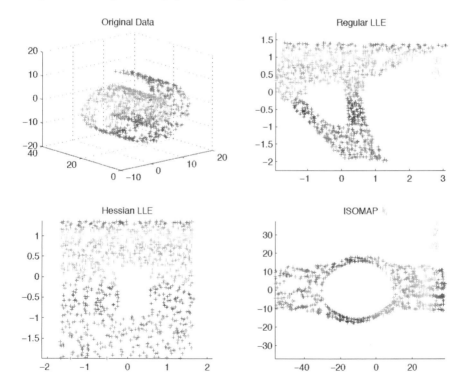

Figure 4.2. *Geometrical representations of dimensionality reduction [DON 03].*
For a color version of the figure, see www.iste.co.uk/reyes/image.zip

4.2.5. *Graphical methods for data visualization*

Graphical methods are concerned with the multiple ways to represent and organize data in space. Essentially, graphical methods are procedures and algorithms that work on visual data types to generate a graphical result on screen. This is also referred to as visualizing data, graph drawing, plotting or charting.

The main characteristic of graphical methods resides in the use of statistics and network science procedures. As we will see, all the basic visual data types that we studied in section 2.2.2 can be used: points, lines, polylines, polygons, fill areas, curves, solid geometry and surfaces. Hence, depending on the procedure and visualization kind, these data types vary in visual attributes: form (size, shape, rotation), color (hue, saturation, brightness), texture (granularity, pattern, orientation) and optics (blur, transparency)[8].

The data techniques we just mentioned in section 4.2.3 can be perceived in the visual space. This space is a coordinate system, mostly partitioned into regular bins and intervals, where visual elements are the subject of transformations, like axis orientation, polar coordinates, planar bending and projections. Furthermore, within a digital image context, graphical methods adapt exploratory techniques from interactive systems, most notably: labeling, navigation (zooming, panning, lensing, orbiting) and direct manipulation (selecting, hovering, dragging, clicking, reordering, linking, connecting, brushing, expanding, collapsing, fading).

We can identify six major types of graphics output: charts, plots, matrices, networks, geometrical sets and the various combinations that can be produced with them.

4.2.5.1. *Charts*

Charts are of course the most common graphical method at present. They are supported natively in applications like Microsoft Office, Google Docs and a variety of programming libraries. Figure 4.3 shows six simple examples: dot, line, bar, pie, Gantt and bubble. As we can see, charts can be

---

8 [WIL 05] adapted these visual attributes from the work of [BER 68].

traced back to the work of Nicolas Oresme (c. 1370) and, more recently, to engineer William Playfair, credited with the systematization of line, bar and pie charts.

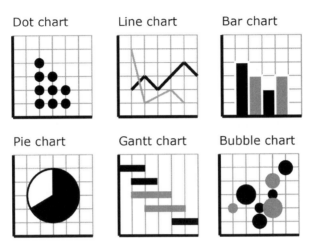

Figure 4.3. *Chart types*

4.2.5.2. *Plots*

In their most simple form, plots involve locating a point in space, at the intersection of two numerical values in two axes. When data have several dimensions, the point in space can be fashioned with visual attributes to convey more information. Besides 2D plots, it is also common to find 3D and 2.5D orthogonal views.

3D plots are known as surface plots when enough values are represented as dots but close enough to give the impression of succession. Another case is to calculate interpolations (or predictions between two dots) to generate the surface.

4.2.5.3. *Matrices*

Matrices, with respect to data visualization, are covariance approximations that show all the relationships in a set of fields. In other words, they show, at a glance, the shape of plots for any given intersection of columns. The idea is then to have a look at all possible combinations.

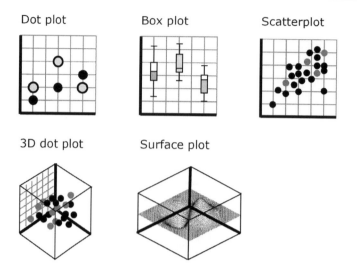

Figure 4.4. *Plot types*

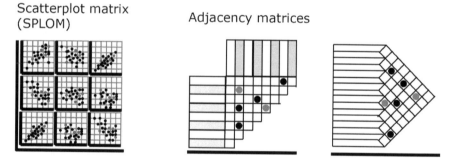

Figure 4.5. *Matrix types*

Among the many different types of matrices (e.g. simplex, band, circumflex, equi-correlation, block [WIL 05, p. 517] or the multi-thread method matrix (MTMM)), Figure 4.5 shows two: the scatter plot matrix (SPLOM) and the adjacency matrix.

4.2.5.4. *Trees and networks*

While graphs are invisible mathematical structures that connect nodes through links, graph drawing provides methods for laying out those elements in the visual space. These methods vary according to network science metrics and goals of analysis. Figure 4.6 shows large families of network visualizations that we observe in the literature as well as from current software packages (most notably d3 js, RAWGraphs and Gephi): hierarchical, clustering, force-atlas, sunbursts, radial (or layered), alluvial, parallel coordinates, arc diagram, circular layout, radial axis, hiveplot, isometric, concentric and event graph.

Without any intention of entering into details of network visualization or network science terminology, we should nevertheless evoke two main aesthetic criteria that are taken into account for graph drawing:

– Minimization of edge crossings, edge bends, uniform edge lengths and visible area surface;

– Maximization of angles (between two edges), symmetries (isomorphism with its physical counterpart) and node clustering into categories or families and layers (also called orbits or steps that separate levels of nodes).

These criteria come from different applications of networks, from integrated circuit design to social graphs. In general, they are promulgated to facilitate the readability and visibility of complex diagrams.

4.2.5.5. *Geometrical sets*

We call geometrical sets the different groupings of basic elements that introduce a figurative or symbolic interpretation. In this sense, while diagrams establish indexical relationships between parts, an iconical representation conveys a semantic identification of the figure it represents. This is the case with drawn faces, where simple elements such as two circles (eyes), a triangle (nose) and a line (mouth) can be organized to resemble a face. Furthermore, at a higher level, the combination of figures can be organized to signify structures only accessible through culture. This occurs when we can recognize the geographical shape of countries and other specific uses of images (tessellations, conex hull, treemaps, hexagon binnings). Figure 4.7 summarizes some of the most common geometrical sets.

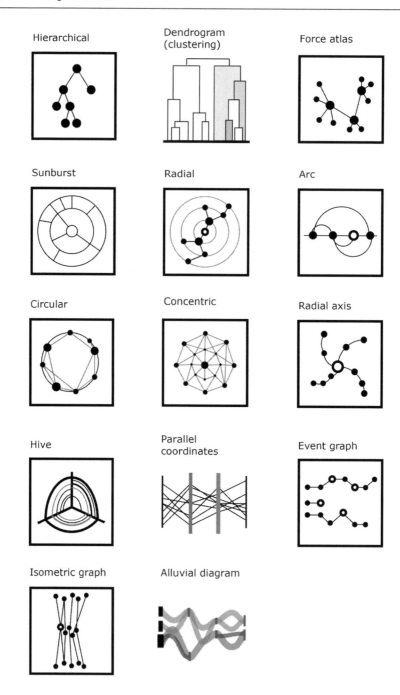

Figure 4.6. *Network layouts*

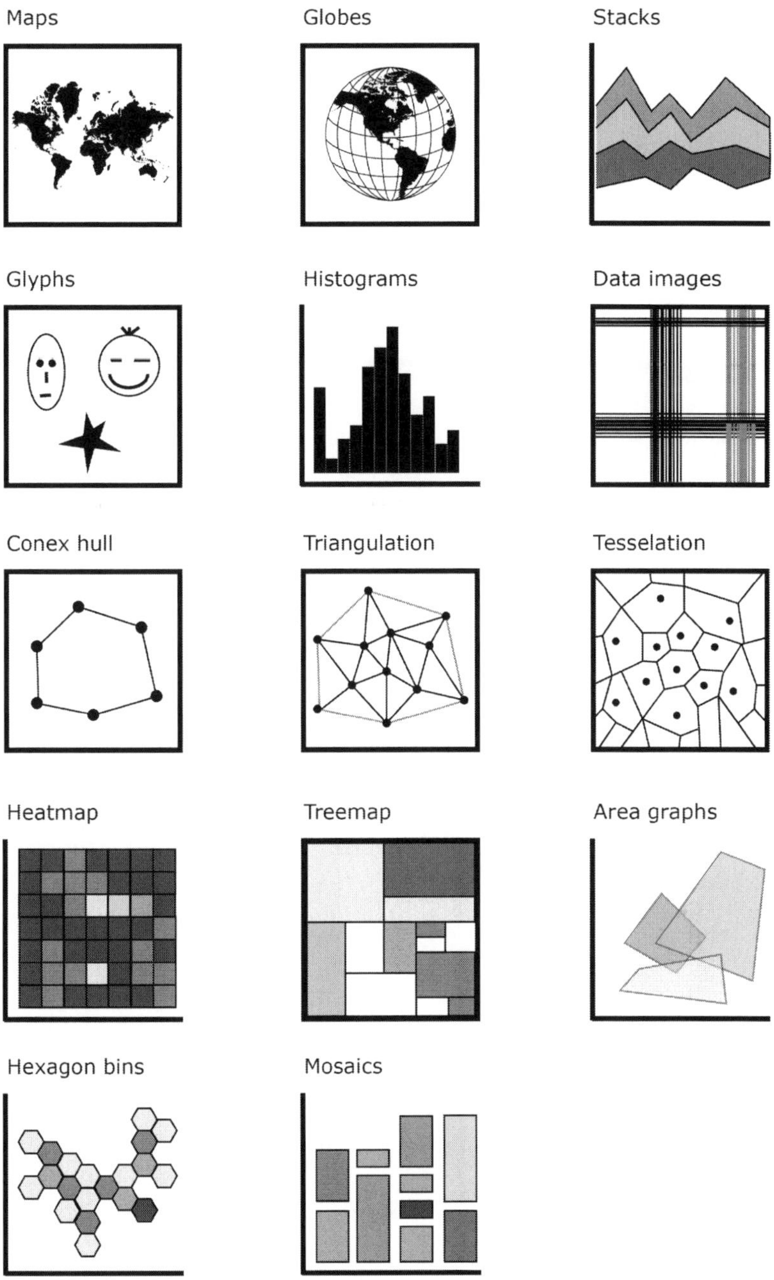

Maps

Globes

Stacks

Glyphs

Histograms

Data images

Conex hull

Triangulation

Tesselation

Heatmap

Treemap

Area graphs

Hexagon bins

Mosaics

Figure 4.7. *Geometrical sets*

4.2.5.6. *Variations and combinations*

The precedent models can be diversified into innumerable possibilities. By combining visual attributes as well as coordinate projections and navigation types (lensing, zooming, orbiting, etc.), we find juxtapositions and combinations of models. Figure 4.8 shows circular treemaps, circular dendrograms, circular heatmaps, map warpings and force-atlas variations (Fruchterman-Reingold, Yifan Hu) among other combinations of charts, plots and stacks.

4.2.6. **Data visualization as image-interface**

In practice, the design of image-interfaces for interactive environments implies assembling diagrammatical schemes from two domains: graphical user interfaces and graphical representations of data. In Chapter 3, we identified some interface logics from the evolution of software applications, especially those dedicated to handling graphical information. We also suggested the increasing importance of web-based applications due to the fact that web browsers provide improved support for graphics routines and ubiquitous cross-platform access.

We can study the exchange processes between platforms, domains and fields from a communicative perspective. The characterization made by semiotician Göran Sonesson of translation as a double act of communication is useful at this point [SON 12]. The idea is that communicative processes exist within similar cultures where we share similar codes and ideas. However, when we import and adopt elements from another culture, the translator is the actor in charge of bridging between two cultures. On the one hand, she has to understand the original message but she also has to use rhetorical figures to communicate it in terms of another culture. Thus, she has two strategies: either she adapts to the sender or she adapts to the receiver (or eventually a mix of both).

[SON 12] recalls that linguist Roman Jakobson stresses that translation not only occurs from one verbal language to another, but might also occur within a single language or extend to different sign systems. The typical case of translation is the *intralinguistic* (replacing one word by another from another language). However, when we depict a picture to represent a verbal story, we are dealing with *intersemiotic translation*. This theory applies well to images: replacing one image with another in the same discourse (poster, graphic design, etc.) could be called *intrapictorial*, whereas replacing a photograph by a drawing would be *interpictorial*.

Polar bar

Reflected polar bar

Polar bar divided

Radar plot

Polar plot

Bagplot

Spike charts

Interval charts

Box & dot plot

Stacked bars

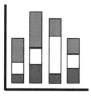

Bump chart

Triangular coordinates

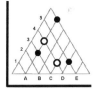

Vector plot

Jittered counts

Bivariate

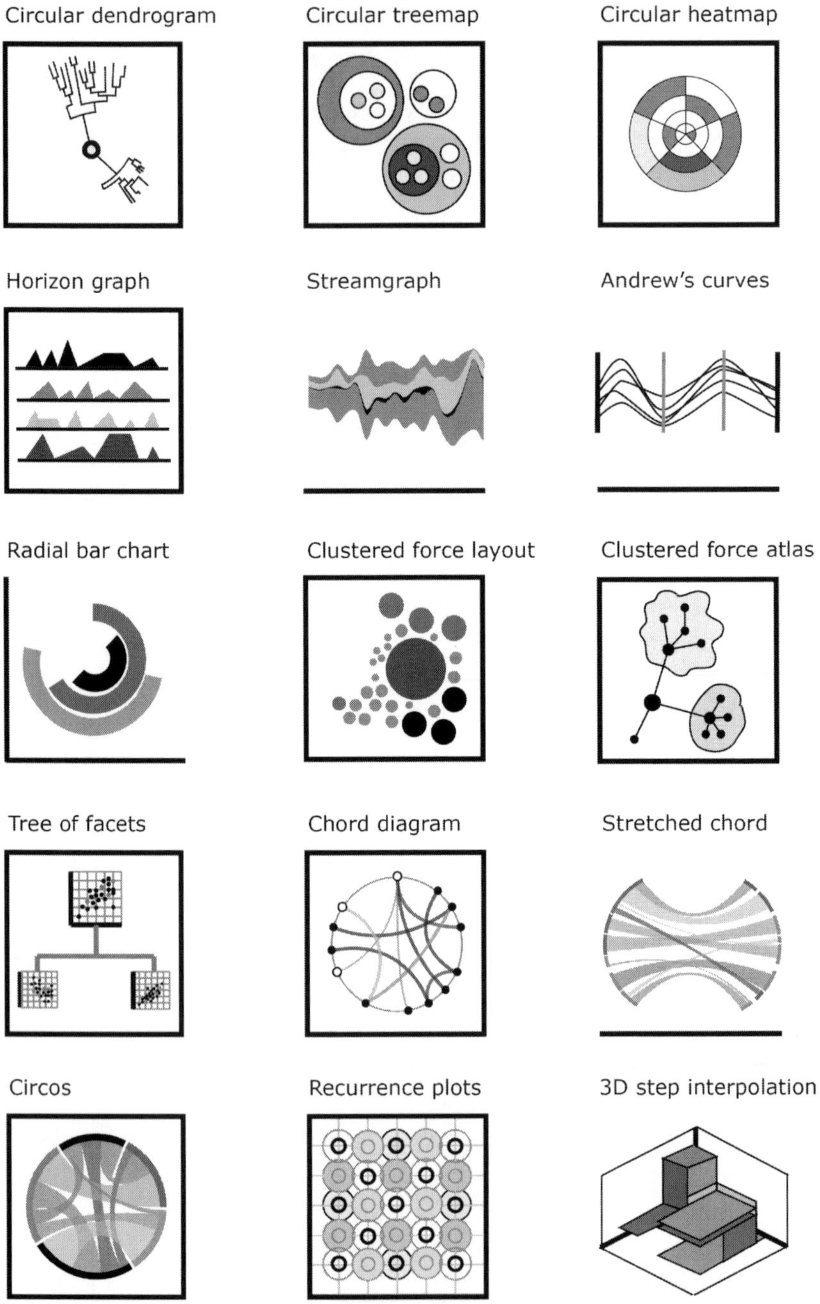

Circular dendrogram

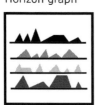

Circular treemap

Circular heatmap

Horizon graph

Streamgraph

Andrew's curves

Radial bar chart

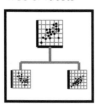

Clustered force layout

Clustered force atlas

Tree of facets

Chord diagram

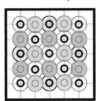

Stretched chord

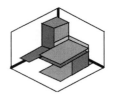

Circos

Recurrence plots

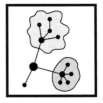

3D step interpolation

Figure 4.8. *Variations and combined types*

We believe the same schema applies to image-interfaces. Exchanging one controller by another of the same kind operates at an *intra-interfacial* level. A button might be relooked or stylized, but nonetheless remains a button. The same could be said when customizing keyboard short cuts. The other case is *inter-interfacial* exchanges. A designer could think that a slider is the best-suited solution for an interaction problem; however, the clever user might adapt a combo-box (or drop-down menu) or any other unit from the universe of GUI widgets to access the same commands (this process also applies to page layouts, grids, coordinate systems and all other factors that modify the graphical aspect of an image-interface).

Thus, the design of image-interfaces is a complex process because not only must designers construct for a given culture according to their own interpretations, but the visual properties of images can also be used as interactive triggers. At the same time, elements of interaction are depicted through visual attributes. In the following sections, we present examples derived from a small sample of domains where promising approaches to images-interfaces are constantly developed and prototyped.

4.2.6.1. *Infographics*

Infographics are popular in mass media such as blogs, newspapers, magazines, posters and advertising. They emphasize an appealing graphic design and visual style of data representations. Scholar Jay D. Bolter observed infographics as an example of visual metaphors, where it seems the symbolic structure of graphics does not suffice to convey meaning [BOL 01, p. 53]. For infographics, the strategy is to fuse visual elements from the domain depicted (let's say "colors of flags") with the visual attributes of the graphics (a chart colored with the colors of flags corresponding to the data country).

Most often, infographics include figurative images; in other words, they appear like pictures instead of symbolic network graphs, charts, plots or GUI. Moreover, it is common that visual attributes are modified in order to attract the eye (as they concur with many other kinds of images with the same media). We should also note that infographics are a fertile terrain for experimenting with modes of interaction, for example, using scroll events as action launchers, etc. The reader can find examples of infographics through a simple search on Pinterest[9], visiting specialized blogs[10] or websites of designer communities[11] or using online services for designing simple infographics[12]. Appendix C summarizes appealing infographics and data visualization projects with an accent on user interactivity and cultural data. Figure 4.9 offers a glance at interactive infographics, in this particular case working with data from Wikipedia.org.

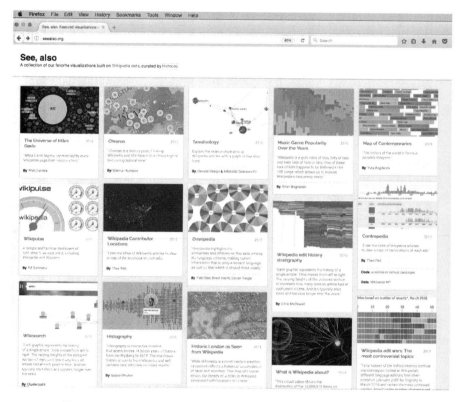

Figure 4.9. *seealso.org. A volunteer-run design studio created in 2012 that curates data visualizations made with Wikipedia data. For a color version of the figure, see www.iste.co.uk/reyes/image.zip*

9 https://pinterest.com/search/pins/?q=infographics

10 http://visualoop.com

11 https://dribbble.com/tags/infographic

12 https://infogr.am or https://piktochart.com

4.2.6.2. *Engineering graphics*

Engineering applications of data visualization have the purpose of optimizing and making efficient flows that will be applied at industry level. Throughout this book, we have already discussed some examples: representations of data structures, algorithms and signals. Another case of using images as interfaces is well illustrated with a couple of graphics standards: UML and VLSI diagrams.

– UML: the Unified Modeling Language appeared in 1997 and, maintained by the Object Management Group, proposes a graphical notation for describing and designing software systems, especially those based on object-oriented approaches. UML 2 includes 13 diagram types broadly grouped into two categories: structure diagrams (class, object, component, package, deployment) and behavior diagrams (activity, use case, state machine, interaction, sequence, communication, timing). Each diagram contains basic graphical elements (arrows, circles, boxes and a user glyph) that are connected by means of planar graphs. The interested reader might take a look at the official documentation[13] or check one among many different UML diagram examples[14] or use a software application to start creating her own[15].

– Integrated circuits layouts: in electric and electronic engineering, there are a series of symbols that represent circuit components such as transistors, inverters, gates, capacitors and inductors[16]. As we saw in section 2.4.2, CMOS (complementary metal oxide semiconductor) circuits are the most used in current electronic devices. The CMOS basic building block is the transistor, which is often represented as a logic gate and combined to form Boolean functions: OR, AND, NAND (not and), NOR (not or) and XOR (exclusive or). Figure 4.11 depicts three graphical representations of the same sample circuit. Graph theory is applied extensively to organize geometric layout. One example is the force-directed graph, which optimizes

---

13 http://www.omg.org/spec/UML/2.5/

14 http://holub.com/uml/

15 https://www.draw.io or https://www.gliffy.com/uses/uml-software

16 Simple reference available at: http://www.rapidtables.com/electric/electrical_symbols.htm

the wire length by calculating the position of cells at the equilibrium of forces (indeed, the force-atlas algorithm seen in section 4.2.5.4 is inspired by this technique) [KAH 11, p. 112].

OpenGL 4 general pipeline

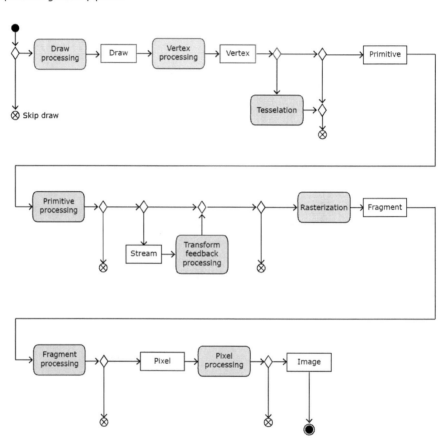

Figure 4.10. *UML activity diagram of OpenGL graphics*[17]

---

17 Sketched with Illustrator, a fragment of the bigger diagram in: http://www.seas.upenn. edu/~pcozzi/OpenGLInsights/OpenGL44PipelineMap.pdf

Digital standard cells

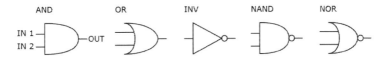

Example of circuit

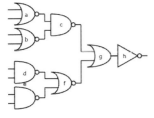

1D linear placement

Placement and routing on macro cell

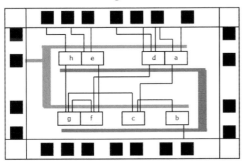

Figure 4.11. *Circuit layout*

The next level in the hierarchy of electronics concerns prototypes. Recently, with the introduction of free and open hardware such as Arduino micro-controllers, DIY printed circuit boards and low-cost electronic components (breadboards, LEDs, resistors, sensors, servo motors, etc.), software applications like Fritzing[18] help diagraming and documenting electronic prototypes.

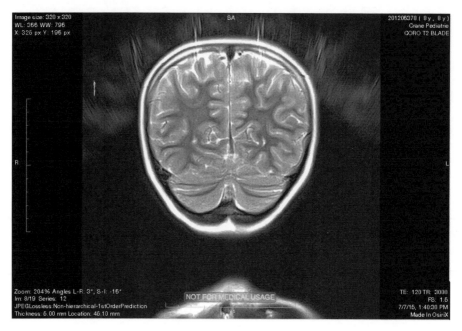

Figure 4.12. *Example of MRI visualization made with OsiriX*

4.2.6.3. *Scientific visualization*

We refer to scientific visualization in the sense of representation in science and technology studies (STS). It typically encompasses the use of images in disciplines like mathematics, physics, biology, chemistry, geology, oceanography, meteorology, astronomy and medicine. These areas have also revolved around the use of digital imaging techniques, from modeling to simulation and visualization. Researchers like [COO 14] address the complexities of visual artifacts (such as microscopic imaging, MRI scans, 3D-modeled organs, optical imaging) within the context of image

18 http://fritzing.org

distribution and publication. From a broad perspective, the study of the numerous transformations and manipulations of images in science is also a question of what is "scientific" in science after all [LAT 14, p. 347].

Visualization types and conventions in STS have been separated according to the kind of data they visualize[19]:

– *Scalar data*: slice planes, clipping regions, height-fields, isosurfaces, volume rendering and manifolds.

– *Vector data*: arrow glyphs, streamlines, streamtube, streamsurface, particle traces and flow texture.

4.2.6.4. *Digital humanities*

With the increasing growth of scholars interested in digital humanities, the types of data typically represented in these kinds of projects have diversified. While most efforts have been dedicated to digital text, current projects include images, 3D models, geo-location, and heritage data designed for different platforms. As a result, interface design has become paramount to digital humanities. Seminal examples such as "Mapping the republic of letters"[20], "Hypercities"[21] and, more recently, "AIME"[22] gained notoriety thanks to the functionality of representing multiple data types within an original interactive space.

Considered independently, text has always offered insights and inspirational approaches for designing image-interfaces. Raw text can be seen as unstructured data in the sense that text sequences of any kind (interview transcripts, speeches, novels, poems, essays, etc.) need data operations for their treatment and visualization. Some of these operations are: term frequency, term matrices (where columns represent words and rows represent documents), bigram proximity matrices [MAR 11, pp. 9–12], text encoding[23], syntax and semantic fields, topic modeling, lexicometric and

---

19 Readers can also refer to the taxonomy elaborated by [WRI 07, p. 65].

20 http://republicofletters.stanford.edu/

21 http://www.hypercities.com/

22 http://modesofexistence.org/

23 We evoke the TEI (Text Encoding Initiative), which defines recommendations for indexing semantic content: http://www.tei-c.org

stylometric analysis [ARN 15, pp. 157–175], and network plot analysis [MOR 13, pp. 211–240]. Among the diverse tools and graphical representations that have emerged from a text-oriented context, some of the well known are:

– *Text analyzers*: simple interfaces that count characters, words, sentences, unique words, paragraphs, ngrams, etc[24]. The typical outcome of this counter is numerical information.

– *Ngram viewers*: the celebrated website Ngram Viewer[25] that Google launched in 2010 allows searching among millions of digitized books and returns pairs of words, thirds, and up to 8 ngrams, depicted as line charts to locate publishing dates of books containing that words. Behind Ngram Viewer visualizations, data is structured as data tables and can be freely downloaded.

– *Word clouds*: in 2005, computer scientist Jonathan Feinberg created an algorithm to visualize corpora of words as "word clouds", inspired by his work on tag clouds in 2004, together with Bernard Kerr. In 2008, the famous website Wordle[26] popularized the use of word clouds by common users. Although Wordle is not easy to run nowadays (because of Java restrictions in web browsers), several alternatives, plugins and libraries exist on the web to create word clouds.

– *Word trees*: this kind of visualization was introduced by designers and computer scientists Martin Wattenberg and Fernanda Viégas in 2007[27]. The idea is to summarize recurrences of a word with respect to all other words that follow or precede it. Thus, the network draws a graph that links between words which can be expanded interactively. The first versions of word trees were designed for the visualization platform IBM Many Eyes; however, a free-to-use version is currently maintained by software developer Jason Davies[28].

---

24 http://textalyser.net/, https://www.online-utility.org/text/analyzer.jsp
25 https://books.google.com/ngrams/
26 http://www.wordle.net
27 http://hint.fm/projects/wordtree/
28 https://www.jasondavies.com/wordtree/

– *Phrase nets*: in 2009, Wattenberg & Viégas added phrase net visualizations to IBM Many Eyes[29]. Essentially, this type visualizes 2-grams in form of network graphs. An adaptation of these phrase nets can be seen as collocated graphs in Voyant Tools[30].

– *Voyant Tools*: humanities scholars Stéfan Sinclair and Geoffrey Rockwell have been the principal developers of Voyant Tools[31] since 2010. The project constitutes a robust environment that integrates different visualization tools that can be navigated at the same time. The standard organization is a rich space where word clouds, text analyzers and frequency charts can be explored. As with other windowed systems, they are synchronized and updated whenever a change is made in a different window tool. A major upgrade to Voyant was released in 2016 under a GNU/GPL license.

Besides the main interface in Voyant, it is possible to launch alternative text visualizations which are more creative and atypical[32]. The gallery of graphical models reinforces the perspective of continuing the exploration of text as a plastic element. Other creative productions inspired by texts describe the production process in [DRU 09, DRU 11, RUE 14, REY 17].

Word cloud

Word trees

Phrase nets

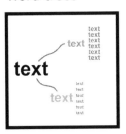
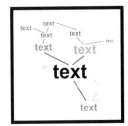

Figure 4.13. *Text visualization types*

---

29 http://hint.fm/projects/phrasenet/

30 https://voyant-tools.org/docs/#!/guide/collocatesgraph

31 https://voyant-tools.org

32 https://voyant-tools.org/docs/#!/guide/tools

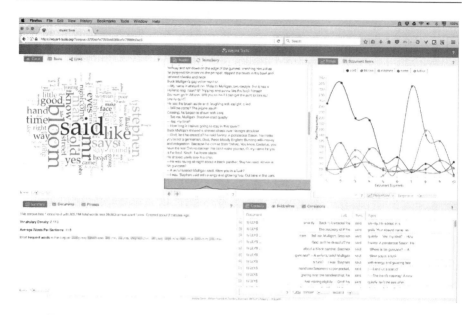

Figure 4.14. *Visualization of Ulysses by James Joyce using Voyant Tools*
For a color version of the figure, see www.iste.co.uk/reyes/image.zip

4.2.6.5. *Cultural analytics*

Media theorist Lev Manovich coined the term "cultural analytics" as an intellectual program in 2005 [MAN 16]. The main objective has been to analyze massive cultural data sets using computing and visualization techniques. For Manovich, the term culture is taken in a broader sense: it is about productions made by anybody and not only those created by specialists. This means that projects in cultural analytics cover not only scientific images, professional paintings, photographs and films, but also amateur photos, selfies, home videos, student designs, tweets, etc. Moreover, instead of focusing on social impacts and relationships between content and users, the accent is put on cultural transformations and forms. This last point implies adopting an elastic vision capable of adjusting to see large patterns and zooming into particular anomalies and singular events that may pass unnoticed otherwise.

Among the techniques elaborated within the context of cultural analytics (by members and collaborators of the Software Studies Initiative[33], later

---

33 http://lab.softwarestudies.com

renamed Cultural Analytics Lab[34]), we can now talk about some recognized models that have proven useful for the analysis of multiple images. These techniques are known as "media visualization" [MAN 13a]; they refer to the practice of analyzing visual media through visual media. In other words, it consists of making visualizations including the images being analyzed:

– *Image pixelation (color summarization)*: it basically involves obtaining the colors of an image and representing them according to a discreet sequence of mask shapes. The mask shape is often a square (it could also be another geometrical figure such as hexagons, triangles, circles or superimposed rings) and its color is sampled from the original image and organized along its relative position to the image. The size of a unitary shape determines the degree of pixelation. A bigger size of shape implies the summarization of more colors from the visual area where it gets its values.

– *Image averaging (z-visualization)*: this technique involves stacking a series of images on top of each other at the same spatial coordinates. It implies that all images are present in the same visual space but, in order to observe visual patterns, it is necessary to perform a statistical measure of visual features; otherwise, only the last image of the series would be visible. A single procedure for image averaging would be to reduce the opacity of each image by n-times its percentage. Another technique would be to output an image where each pixel depicts the calculated measure in all the series of images.

– *Image montage (image mosaicing)*: an image montage involves ordering the corpus of images one after another in a sequential manner. Similar to texts, images follow a consecutive order, reading orderly from left to right and top to bottom. The ordering rule could be obtained from measures of visual features (for instance, going from the brightest to the darkest), from metadata (for instance, by year) or by order of appearance in the sequence (from the first to the last frame). The resulting image mosaic shows a rhythm of variations and transformations that can be analyzed as a whole. In many cases, visual patterns appear clearer when there is no space between images (i.e. images are only divided by their own size) and when all the images of the corpus have the same width and height.

– *Image slicing (orthogonal views)*: this also presents the corpus of images one after another, but there is a fundamental difference in comparison to an image mosaic. We call a "slice" a thin region of an image

---

34 http://lab.culturalanalytics.info

cut all along the X- or Y-axis. A slice does not show or summarize the entire image, but only a delimited region. The size of the slice (how thin or thick it is) can be parameterized. For large collections of images, it seems thinner slices are the best option in order to depict variations and transformations of the entire corpus of analysis. The visual patterns then are observed by differences and variations in the regions generated.

– *Image plotting*: this is based on the general 2D plot chart type that uses dots and lines to represent data along the X- and Y-axis. An image plot places, at the crossing coordinate of two values, the image corresponding to those values. For example, we can decide to plot images by "year" on the X-axis, while the Y axis would be determined by the median brightness value. In this case, we can observe variations and evolution in time over the two scales. In the cases where more than 15 dimensions or columns describe an image, it might be interesting to use a dimension reduction technique such as PCA or MDS before plotting (see section 4.2.4).

– *Image and slice histogram*: this technique gives the distribution of a single dimension (or data column) by placing the corresponding image in the diagrammatic visualization [CRO 16, p. 180]. In the case of visualizing large collections of images, the histogram facilitates the identification of color and shape patterns. However, it is sometimes necessary to refine the variation in colors within a single image. For this purpose, media scientist Damon Crockett proposed to make slices at regions of interest in images. The result is a more homogeneous visualization of color fingerprints particularly useful for massive collections.

– *Growing entourage plot*: also discussed in [CRO 16, p. 190], the growing entourage plots tackle the issue of 2D representation of dimension reduction algorithms by creating clusters of images. Each cluster has a centroid and similar images entourage it by their ranking proximity, resulting in "islands of images".

One of the most interesting impacts of media visualization techniques has been their influence from an "info-aesthetic" point of view [MAN 14]. The exploration of graphical models for visual media has opened possibilities to think about visual spaces by considering the formal and material supports as plastic elements. In this line, we have introduced new media visualization methods that will be discussed in the following chapter: polar transformations and volumetric visualizations.

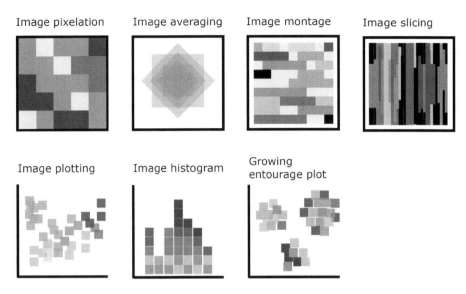

Figure 4.15. *Media visualization types*

4.2.6.6. *Data art*

To conclude this chapter, we shall provide other examples that deal more closely with the info-aesthetic perspective of data visualization. In this respect, some existing techniques can be approached as media art, whose community has been growing and attracted talented programmers and artists since the 1960s. Nowadays, several efforts have been made to classify and archive digital artworks in order to have an idea of the larger picture of themes, authors, materials and exhibitions (e.g. the "Art and Electronic Online Companion"[35] initiated by scholar Edward Shanken or the "Digital Art Archive"[36] maintained by scholar Oliver Grau).

Regarding text visualization, we can cite exemplary projects where text acquires image-interface features: "History words flow" by Santiago Ortiz[37], "The dumpster" by Golan Levin[38], "The preservation of favored traces" by

35 http://artelectronicmedia.com/

36 https://www.digitalartarchive.at/nc/home.html

37 http://moebio.com/research/historywordsflow/

38 http://www.flong.com/projects/dumpster/

Ben Fry[39] and "Gamer textually" by Jeremy Douglass[40], to mention only a few cases.

In addition, more related to media visualization, pixelation might evoke "pixel art", as it was introduced by artists Goldberg and Flegal in 1982 to describe the new kind of images being produced with Toolbox, a Smalltalk-80 drawing system designed for interactive image creation and editing [GOL 82]. Image averaging is related to the work of computer scientists Sirovich and Kirby on "Eigenfaces" in 1987 [SIR 87] and, more recently, to media artist Jason Salavon, who has produced a series of images by averaging 100 photos of special moments[41]. For image mosaics, media researcher Brendan Dawes presented "Cinema Redux"[42] in 2004, a project aimed at showing what he calls a visual fingerprint of an entire movie. His main idea was to decompose an entire film into frames and then to arrange them as rows and columns. Moreover, image slicing can also be seen as a remediation of slit-scan photography. Among other prominent slit-scan photographers, William Larson produced, from 1967 to 1970, a series of experiments on photography called "figures in motion". The trick was to mount a thin slit in front of the camera lens to avoid the pass of light into the film. Thus, the image is only a part of an ordinary 35 mm photograph. More recently, in 2010, artist Paul Magee has produced large print visualizations that reorder colors in photographs using C [MAG 16, p. 456].

39 http://benfry.com/traces/

40 http://jeremydouglass.com/gamertextually/

41 http://salavon.com/work/SpecialMoments/

42 http://brendandawes.com/projects/cinemaredux

Prototyping Image-Interfaces

This chapter presents my own productions and experiments created within the context of image-interface and data visualization. It covers a range of prototypes, screen shots and sample codes for scripting software applications, integrating data and media visualization, and extending the generated images beyond the screen to "data physicalization" via 3D printing. The accent is put on personal perspectives and ongoing procedures that have been assembled to produce image-interface prototypes.

5.1. Scripting software applications

One of the common practices to extend the standard functionalities of software applications is to create small programs that will process step-by-step operations that we would do repetitively by hand. In operating systems like macOS, the programming language that helps automatize routines is AppleScript, together with the graphical interface Automator. In other cases, software applications provide access to programmatic components via an API. We mentioned in section 2.3.1 that popular commercial packages like Adobe Photoshop can be scripted with JavaScript (among other languages such as Visual Basic, AppleScript and ExtendedScript).

Table 5.1 shows a basic script example written in JavaScript to be run with Photoshop. The idea is to generate 15 rectangles in different layers, each having different sizes, random colors and rotation angles. Figure 5.1 shows the resulting image.

```
/* ***************************
This scripts generates 15 random layers in Photoshop CS6.
1. Create new document.
2. File --> Scripts --> Browse...

Written by E. Reyes, 2017.
*************************** */


// Uncomment this line to run the script with no opened document
//app.documents.add();

app.preferences.rulerUnits = Units.PIXELS;
app.preferences.colorModel = ColorModel.RGB;

var message = confirm("Add new random layers?");

if(message){
        for(var i = 0; i < 15; i++){
                var layerRef = app.activeDocument.artLayers.add();
                layerRef.name = "Random Layer " + i;
                //layerRef.blendMode = BlendMode.NORMAL;

                app.activeDocument.selection.selectAll;
                var colorRef = new SolidColor();
                colorRef.rgb.red = Math.floor(Math.random()*255);
                colorRef.rgb.green = Math.floor(Math.random()*255);
                colorRef.rgb.blue = Math.floor(Math.random()*255);
                app.activeDocument.selection.fill(colorRef);

                var s = Math.floor(Math.random()*100);
                layerRef.resize(s,s);
                layerRef.translate(Math.random()*10, Math.random()*10);
                layerRef.rotate(Math.floor(Math.random()*360));
                layerRef.fillOpacity = 30;
        }
}
```

Table 5.1. *newLayers.js. JavaScript code to be run with Photoshop*

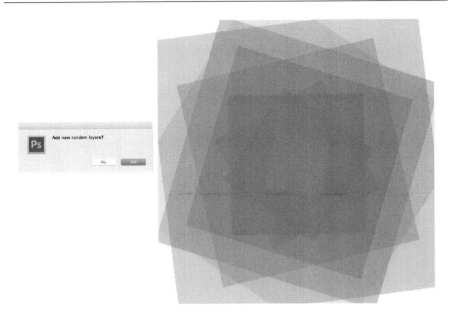

Figure 5.1. *Generated image with Photoshop using JavaScript. For a color version of the figure, see www.iste.co.uk/reyes/image.zip*

The way in which JavaScript "understands" Photoshop syntax and components is similar to that of HTML pages: through a Document Object Model (DOM). Adobe supports scripting via JS in almost 85 different objects, including the main application, documents, layers, actions, color management, save options, print options, metadata, etc. [ADO 12, pp. 3–31]. In our example, we have access to the "preferences" objects to set units to pixels and color model to RGB. We then call the method "confirm" which uses the standard GUI library in Photoshop to show a pop-up window. The rest of the script is nested inside a "for" loop in which we assign random values to layers, via the "artLayers" object.

We can imagine an orthogonal view of Figure 5.1. Recent versions of Photoshop include a 3D module which is handy at this point. Selecting all generated layers, we choose 3D → New Mesh From Layer → Volume… Figure 5.2 shows two orthogonal views of the same image.

Figure 5.2. *Orthogonal views of the generated layers. For a color version of the figure, see www.iste.co.uk/reyes/image.zip*

Another example is Autodesk Maya whose components can be manipulated with the Maya Embedded Language (MEL) and with Maya Python. While it is the native language used to communicate with Maya components, Python was introduced in version 8.5 as a solution to add object-oriented possibilities to MEL. Moreover, the popularity of Maya has attracted communities of developers and, in current practice, we use the set of tools PyMEL to instantiate the Command Engine, and in-house plug-ins can be developed with Qt [MEC 12, p. 234].

Figure 5.3 shows the basic GUI to generate procedural designs and the resulting image design (top right). Indeed, the interface offers two rule hints to help create two kinds of L-System: a Dragon Curve and a Gopser Curve (recall section 2.2.4). Just as we saw in the Photoshop examples, the generated image can be used as the basis for exploring further graphical interventions. The figure shows the same geometrical set with modified Phong shader values and a top perspective to observe the fractal iterated with 9 rewriting rules (bottom).

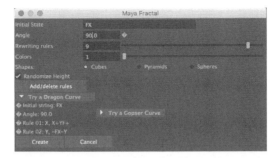

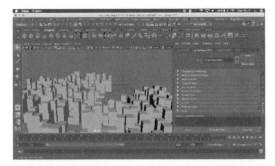

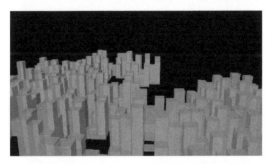

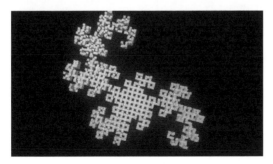

Figure 5.3. *Generated model using Python with Maya. For a color version of the figure, see www.iste.co.uk/reyes/image.zip*

```
####################################
# 1. Open the Script editor and select Python tab
# 2. Copy-paste the following code
# 3. Follow instructions in GUI
# 4. Save the script as plug-in : Save script to shelf
# Written by G. Miranda, J. Maya, E. Reyes. 2011-2017
# +info: brooom.org/mayaFractal
#####################################################

from pymel import *
import math
import maya.cmds as cmds
import random

global ANG,ang,x,y,Forma

class lSystem:
   def __init__(self):
      self.axioma = ''
      self.regla = ['']*256    #cadena que reemplaza
      for i in range (256):
         self.regla[i]=None
      self.noRe = 0
      self.axiom = ''
      self.angle=0
      self.forma=0
      self.random=None
      self.color=0
      self.lShader = ['']*30
      self.SG = ['']*30

   def setAxioma(self, a):
      self.axioma=a

   def setAngle(self,ang):
      self.angle=ang

   def addRegla(self,c,r):
      self.regla[ord(c)]=r
```

```
def delRegla(self,c):
    self.regla[ord(c)]=None

def setColor(self,col):
    self.color=col

    for i in range (int(self.color)):
        self.lShader[i]=None
        self.lShader[i] = cmds.shadingNode('blinn', name='LSys'+str(i), asShader=True)

def Cambio(self,nr):
    i=0
    j=0

    for i in range(nr):
        self.axiom = ''
        for j in range(len(self.axioma)):


            if self.regla[ord(self.axioma[j])]!= None:
                self.axiom = self.axiom + self.regla[ord(self.axioma[j])]

            else:
                self.axiom = self.axiom + self.axioma[j]

        self.axioma=self.axiom

def Dibujar(self):
    x = 0.0
    y = 0.0
    x1 = 0.0
    y1 = 0.0

    ANG = math.radians(self.angle)
    ang = 0

    self.grupo=cmds.group( em=True, name='LSystem' )
    self.random=setRandom()
```

```
f=0

for i in range(len(self.axioma)):
   if self.axioma[i]=='+':
      ang=ang-ANG

   else:
      if self.axioma[i]=='-':
         ang=ang+ANG

      else:
         if self.axioma[i]!='+' or self.axioma[i]!='-':
            x1=x
            y1=y
            x = x + math.cos(ang)
            y = y + math.sin(ang)
            f=f+1
            rando=random.random()

            if self.forma== 1:

               if self.random == False:
                  cmds.polyCube(height=.2,  depth=(x-x1), width=(y-y1))
                  cmds.move(x,0,y)

               else:
                  cmds.polyCube(height=rando*5,  depth=(x-x1), width=(y-y1))
                  cmds.move(x,(rando*5)/2,y)

               cmds.parent( 'pCube'+str(f), self.grupo )

               CUBO='pCube'+str(f)
               cmds.select(CUBO)
               SHADER=self.lShader[int(rando*int(self.color))]
               cmds.hyperShade( assign=SHADER)

            elif self.forma==2:
               if self.random == False:
                  cmds.polyPyramid(sideLength=1,numberOfSides=int(rando*3)+2)
```

```
                    cmds.move(x,0,y)

              else:
                  cmds.polyPyramid(sideLength=1,numberOfSides=int(rando*3)+2)
                  cmds.scale(1,rando*5,1)
                  cmds.move(x,0,y)

              cmds.parent( 'pPyramid'+str(f), self.grupo )

              CUBO='pPyramid'+str(f)
              cmds.select(CUBO)
              SHADER=self.lShader[int(rando*int(self.color))]
              cmds.hyperShade( assign=SHADER)

          elif self.forma==3:
              if self.random == False:
                  cmds.polySphere(r=.4)
                  cmds.move(x,0,y)

              else:
                  cmds.polySphere(r=.1)
                  cmds.scale(1,1+rando*5,1)
                  cmds.move(x,(rando*5)/2,y)

              cmds.parent( 'pSphere'+str(f), self.grupo )
              CUBO='pSphere'+str(f)
              cmds.select(CUBO)
              SHADER=self.lShader[int(rando*int(self.color))]
              cmds.hyperShade( assign=SHADER)

L=lSystem()

def CrearFra(*args):
    setAxioma()
    setAngle()
    setRepeticiones()
    setColor()
    L.forma=setForma()
    L.Dibujar()
```

```
   cerrarVentana(0)

def AddRule(*args):
   result = cmds.promptDialog(          title='Add Rule',    message='Change,Rule:',
button=['+', '-'])

   if result == '+':
      texto = cmds.promptDialog(query=True, text=True)
      texto2="

      for i in range(2,len(texto)):
         texto2=texto2+texto[i]

      print 'Rule added: ' + texto
            L.addRegla(texto[0],texto2)

   elif result == '-':
      texto = cmds.promptDialog(query=True, text=True)
      print 'Rule Deleted: ' + texto[0]
            L.delRegla(texto[0])

def setColor(*args):
   COL= cmds.textFieldGrp('Colores', q=True,text=1)
   L.setColor(COL)

def setAxioma(*args):
   AXM= cmds.textFieldGrp('Axioma', q=True,text=1)
   L.setAxioma(AXM)

def setAngle(*args):
   ANG= cmds.floatFieldGrp('Angulo', q=True, value=1)[0]
   L.setAngle(ANG)

def setRepeticiones(*args):
   REP= cmds.intSliderGrp('Repeticiones', q=True, value=1)
   L.Cambio(REP)


def setForma(*args):
```

```
       return cmds.radioButtonGrp( 'Formas', q=1, select=1)

def setRandom(*args):
    return cmds.checkBox('Random',q=1,value=1)

def cerrarVentana(arg):
   cmds.deleteUI('LSystem', window=True)

#### GUI ####
if cmds.window('LSystem', exists=True):
    cerrarVentana(0)
cmds.window('LSystem',title="Maya Fractal")

cmds.columnLayout(adjustableColumn=True)

#Fields
cmds.textFieldGrp( 'Axioma',label='Initial State', columnAlign=[1, 'left'])
cmds.floatFieldGrp( 'Angulo',label='Angle', extraLabel='°',columnAlign=[1, 'left'])
cmds.intSliderGrp( 'Repeticiones', field=True, label='Rewriting rules', minValue=0,
maxValue=10, fieldMinValue=0, fieldMaxValue=10,columnAlign=[1, 'left'])
cmds.intSliderGrp( 'Colores', field=True, label='Colors', minValue=1, maxValue=30,
fieldMinValue=1, fieldMaxValue=30,value=1,columnAlign=[1, 'left'])

cmds.radioButtonGrp('Formas', label='Shapes: ', labelArray3=['Cubes', 'Pyramids',
'Spheres'], numberOfRadioButtons=3, columnAlign=[1, 'left'] )

cmds.checkBox('Random', label='Randomize Height',align='right')

cmds.columnLayout(adjustableColumn=False,columnAlign='right')
cmds.button(label="Add/delete rules", width=150, align="center", command = AddRule )

cmds.rowLayout( numberOfColumns=2,columnAlign=(1, 'right'))
cmds.frameLayout( label='Try a Dragon Curve    ', collapsable=1,collapse=1 )
cmds.text( label="• Initial string: FX", align="left")
cmds.text( label="• Angle: 90.0", align="left")
cmds.text( label="• Rule 01: X, X+YF+      ", align="left")
cmds.text( label="• Rule 02: Y, -FX-Y"    , align="left")
cmds.setParent( '..' )
```

```
cmds.frameLayout( label='Try a Gopser Curve ', collapsable=1,collapse=1 )
cmds.text( label="• Initial string: FX", align="left")
cmds.text( label="• Angle: 60.0", align="left")
cmds.text( label="• Rule 01: X, X+YF++YF-FX--FXFX-YF+ ", align="left")
cmds.text( label="• Rule 02: Y, -FX+YFYF++YF+FX--FX-Y ", align="left")
cmds.setParent( '..' )
cmds.setParent( '..' )


cmds.columnLayout()
cmds.rowLayout( numberOfColumns=2,columnAlign=(1, 'right'))
cmds.button("Create", command= CrearFra, align="right", width=100)
cmds.button("Cancel", command=cerrarVentana,align="right", width=100)
cmds.setParent( '..' )
cmds.setParent( '..' )


cmds.showWindow()
```

Table 5.2. *mayaFractal.py. Python script to be run with Maya*

In our experience, when prototyping image-interfaces it is often necessary to customize functionalities of software applications. In fact, whenever we use macros in office software like Word and Excel, we are also scripting applications. This is an excellent way to understand the data types, data structures and actions supported by the environment. We might end up generating unexpected graphical results or perhaps we will have to solve a GUI readability problem. The ease of using a software API and the power to extend it is also a determining criteria that would encourage us to identify with it and continue its practice: designing workflows, new images and plugins.

5.2. Integrating data visualizations

I started working systematically on data and media visualization in 2007. At that time, one of the most popular development platforms was Adobe Flash, together with the scripting languages ActionScript 2 and 3 (although very different from each other). Among my first experiments was the idea to visualize interrelationships between media, arts and technology. The result was MediaViz, a standalone bubble chart interactive SWF application, which was exhibited at the University of Annecy in 2010 (Figure 5.4).

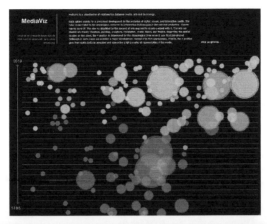

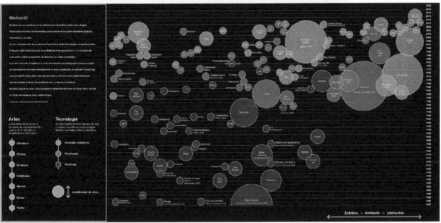

Figure 5.4. *MediaViz, 2010. Screenshot of Flash movie and static image. For a color version of the figure, see www.iste.co.uk/reyes/image.zip*

Among the traditional and recurrent issues encountered were: scale mapping (fitting a delimited range of years into a given width of pixels), interaction and objectivity of data. Answers to the first were solved with arithmetic calculations, the second depends on the software platform (handling mouse events, collision detection between cursor and object), and the third is more metaphysical. I arbitrarily selected 150 media from between 1895 and 2010, from cinema to DVD, from photograph to multimedia. When the latest version was finished, it was obvious that information could be rethought.

In 2012, I prototyped the "Map of digital arts", which was submitted to ACM SIGGRAPH as a poster co-authored with Paul Girard, technical head of the médialab at Science Po Paris[1]. For this experiment, I conducted an informal survey among students of the BA in Animation and Digital Art at Tecnológico de Monterrey at Toluca in Mexico. Students selected the 25 most representative arts, technologies and media. These were the entry points in Wikipedia to extract all the links pointing to further elements, using Open Refine. The result was a database of 5330 nodes and almost 6000 edges. For us, the most evident software application to visualize the network was Gephi, but the intention was to create a standalone interactive version. Paul Girard hard-coded the network exported from Gephi in gefx format to be loaded into Processing 1. Figure 5.5 shows one of the final versions, depicting the profile image in their Wikipedia page.

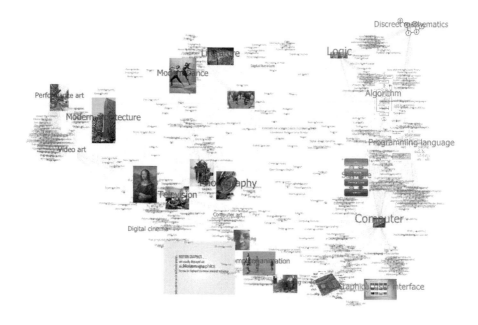

Figure 5.5. *Map of digital arts. 53330 nodes extracted from Wikipedia. For a color version of the figure, see www.iste.co.uk/reyes/image.zip*

1 Although the poster was not accepted due to a very small discrepancy between reviewers, the comments we received were highly valuable and appreciated.

5.3. Integrating media visualizations

In 2008, I was introduced to the concept of media visualization and other theoretical perspectives on software by media scientist Lev Manovich. The following year I had the opportunity to invite digital artist scholar Jeremy Douglass (then co-director of the Software Studies Initiative), to conduct hands-on workshops around a series of seminars and classes on cultural analytics I organized in Mexico.

Douglass demonstrated how to visualize visual media with Fiji[2] (a distribution of ImageJ which stands for Fiji Is Just Imagej). The kind of content we visualized was video and motion graphics: image generation steps with Context Free, video game sessions, videos of juggling, etc. This was appealing to students in 3D animation as they were used to thinking of videos as a sequence of images, as they render animated sequences frame-by-frame in Maya or 3ds Max.

In 2013, I assembled different visualizations of alternative rock group Nirvana for an invitation at the seminar "Social History of Rock" at the Institut Mahler in Paris. Figure 5.6 shows a poster placing together the complete videography of the group. I produced horizontal orthogonal views of each video. In my own workflow, I gathered videos from YouTube, then I used QuickTime 7 to export a video as an image sequence. Finally, in ImageJ, I imported that image sequence. The reader might also be interested to explore vertical orthogonal views. Both horizontal and vertical are created with Image→Stacks→ Orthogonal Views...

I called network media visualization a network graph where nodes were replaced with images being put in relation. In my work on Nirvana, I paid attention to cover designer Robert Fisher, who conceived the design layout of all Nirvana album and single covers, as well as many more designs for other groups while working at Geffen Records. Figure 5.7 depicts the network of Robert Fisher. Similar to the workflow in "Map of digital arts", I first obtained album credit information from the AllMusic website database. I then laid out the network using the force atlas algorithm in Gephi. I exported the network in gexf format and imported it into Processing, now using the Java library Gephi Toolkit[3].

---

2 https://fiji.sc
3 https://gephi.org/toolkit/

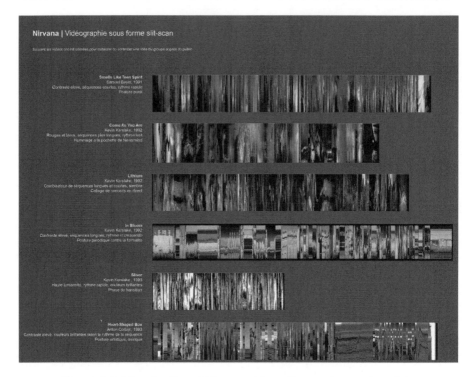

Figure 5.6. *Visualization of Nirvana videos. For a color version of the figure, see www.iste.co.uk/reyes/image.zip*

Another integration effort to reunite different visualization types into one discourse was a custom application made with Processing 1.5. NirViz synchronized audio playback, video, image slicing and most significant colors at each position in time. Figure 5.8 shows the interface, a standalone full screen Java app exported from Processing.

5.4. Explorations in media visualization

5.4.1. *Software visualization of Processing 2*

As mentioned earlier, choosing a software environment or a programming language greatly influences not only the kind of images obtained, but also how we think about the media they handle. In this study, the value of an environment such as Processing was essentially in the sense of "software esthetics".

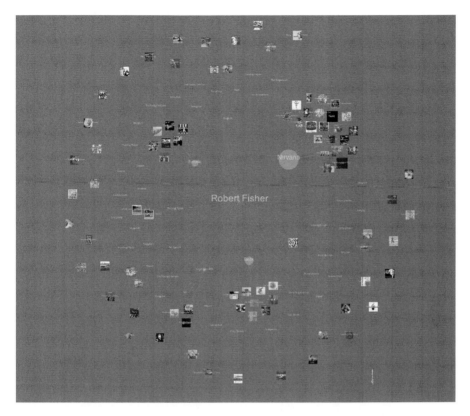

Figure 5.7. *Network media visualization of Robert Fisher. For a color version of the figure, see www.iste.co.uk/reyes/image.zip*

I have argued elsewhere that software art is important because it shows how software could behave differently, mainly through ruptures of function [REY 14]. Understanding such ruptures requires us also to understand how the software operates. Esthetics of software happens when we discover and use new software. Not only it is appealing to see and to interact with its elements, it also represents the vision of another designer or artist: how she thought the names, icons, functions and which algorithms were implemented.

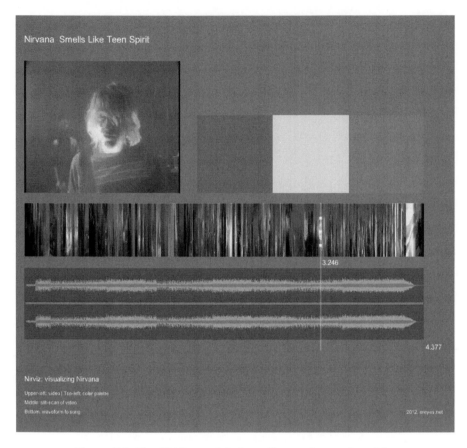

Figure 5.8. *The NirViz app interface. For a color version of the figure, see www.iste.co.uk/reyes/image.zip*

There is a deep and large effect underlying media art software. The more we use it, the deeper we go into its ecology and ideology. Fully adopted, software shapes us as media designers and media artists, but at the same time it also means challenging its paradigms and mode of existence. When we discover new software, it happens that the mere production of 'Hello World' is satisfying, but it is also of the most significant importance precisely because it embraces engagement and motivates us to continue experimenting.

Furthermore, software esthetics finds an echo in software criticism. For example, media theorist Matthew Fuller understands software as a form of digital subjectivity [FUL 03, p. 19]. The human–computer interface is seen as having a series of ideological, socio-historical and political values attached to it. Studying the HCI implies investigating power relations between the user and the way the software acts as a model of action. This idea resonates with Winograd and Flores: "We encounter the deep questions of design when we recognize that in designing tools we are designing ways of being" [WIN 86, p. ix].

Inspired by the notion of "object-oriented ontology" and their visual representation as ontographs [BOG 12, p. 51], I created views of the Processing 2 source code (Figure 5.9) using software visualization tools and techniques. The idea was to put in relation to the underlying components of the software classes and entities. I downloaded the source code from the Processing github repository, then I used inFusion for basic software metrics and to convert into Moose format, which is required by CodeCity and X-Ray applications to produce a more graphical representation.

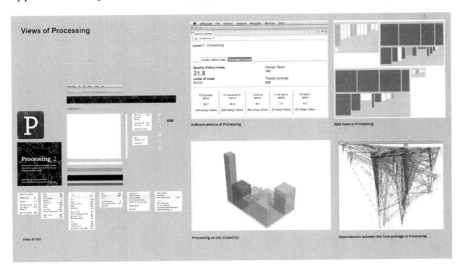

Figure 5.9. *Visualizations of Processing 2. For a color version of the figure, see www.iste.co.uk/reyes/image.zip*

5.4.2. *Graphical interventions on Stein poems*

While Processing 1.x was an exciting tool for experimenting with visual information, one of the main caveats was its support for web browser distribution. In 2008, the situation changed when computer engineer John

Resig, best known for creating jQuery, wrote the first version of Processing.js to be displayed on an HTML canvas. At that time, the graphical web was still in its early stages of development, thus Processing.js was only featured in WebKit-based browsers (Firefox, Safari, Opera).

Processing.js was inspiring to explore artistic hypertext as it does not ascribe specific forms of representation to data, but rather allows for the exploration of interrelationships between the system components. In collaboration with scholar Samuel Szoniecky and digital poetry pioneer Jean-Pierre Balpe, we worked together on "Stein Poems" with the artistic goal of experimenting and provoking unexpected behaviors of conventional computing in order to challenge cultural and perceptual habits [REY 16].

Stein poems are short fragments of text that refer to life in general. In early 2015, Jean-Pierre Balpe started creating such structures as part of his extensive research and development in automatic literary text processing since the 1980s. As the first text generators developed by Balpe were created on Hypercard, it was necessary to migrate the dictionaries and rules into more recent technologies. In late 2014, Samuel Szoniecky developed a complete authoring tool for generating texts using Flex and made it available through the web.

I used the generator API to produce graphical interventions in the web browser. The idea was to exploit plastic properties of text through recent graphical web technologies. As Stein poems are short fragments and combine vocabulary from multiple domains, they can be "experienced" and "touched" as visual images and user interfaces. Figure 5.10 shows two output interfaces, one is based on Processing.js and the other is rendered as SVG text using the library D3.js[4]. Both applications are interactive and use the same text API. While the first handles the web page as 2D matrix and applies rotation and translation transformations with a GUI, the second randomizes position and allows dragging/dropping each individual letter[5]. In the end, both tools create patterns and textures of text from the Stein poems.

---

4 https://d3js.org

5 These applications and others can be seen online at : http://brooom.org/poemesStein/

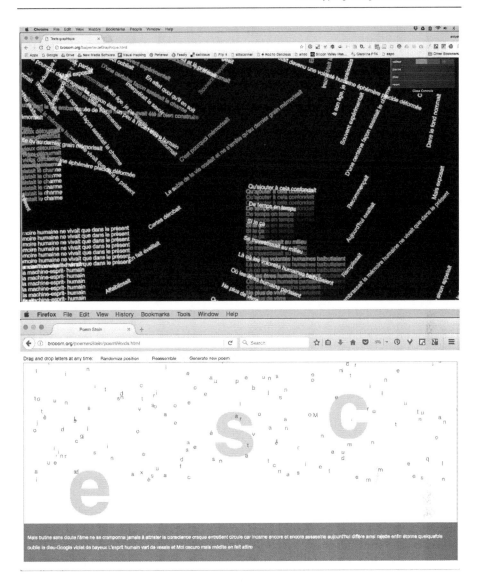

Figure 5.10. *Graphical interventions in digital poetry*

5.4.3. *Web-based visualization of rock album covers*

While text as plastic element allows exploring visual configurations, the main challenge of media visualization within a web environment is to load great amounts of images as individual elements. In 2014, I prototyped

"RockViz"[6] in an effort to design interactive web-based image plots and mosaics. For this production, I gathered the most representative albums of different rock genres according to editors of the platform AllMusic.com. I quickly obtained almost 2000 albums, from folk rock to progressive rock and heavy metal.

The metadata collected was about the artist/group name, album title, release date and album cover image. I then downloaded the album cover images and extracted their basic visual features with ImageJ. In this respect, members of the Cultural Analytics Lab have created macro scripts for ImageJ and MATLAB that help the extraction process: ImageMeasure.imj, ShapeMeasure.imj, ImageMontage.imj and ImagePlot.imj. As mentioned earlier, scripting applications are common when working in media visualization. I have contributed with a different version of ImageMontage that supports different compressed file formats (PNG and JPG) and another script to extract colors according to the RGB color model. The latter script, ImageMeasure-RGB.imj, is shown in Table 5.3.

When the database was completed, I used Open Refine to handle data, but more importantly to apply mathematical formulae to numerical visual attributes and dynamically calculate their Cartesian position. The result was a dynamically generated column in Refine that constructed a full line of CSS style for each individual image, for instance: <img style="left:70.5%; top:4.0%; visibility:visible;">

I adapted this method to create an image mosaic, ordered according to: 1) median of hue; 2) median saturation; 3) median brightness (Figure 5.11). In the image plot visualization, the horizontal axis represented years (from 1955 to 2014) and the vertical axis hue values (from 0 to 360, following the HSB color model) (Figure 5.12). In GREL scripting language, which is natively supported by Refine, my formula to calculate plot horizontal positions is $(((cells["year"].value/1.0) - 1950) * 1500) / 1000$ and vertical positions is $(((value/1.0) - 0) * 3500) / 10000$. As can be seen, the delimited space is no bigger than 1500 x 900 screen pixels.

---

6 http://ereyes.net/rockViz/

```
// This macro measures a number of statistics of every image in a directory:
// red median and stdev, green median and stdev, blue hue and stdev
// To run the macro: open ImageJ; select Plugins>Macros>Run... from the imageJ top
menu
// For information on how to use imageJ, see
// http://rsbweb.nih.gov/ij/
// Everardo Reyes, 2014
// ereyes.net
// www.softwarestudies.com


run("Clear Results");


dir = getDirectory("Choose images folder to be measured");
list = getFileList(dir);
print("directory contains " + list.length + " files");


savedir = getDirectory("Choose folder to save output file measurementsRGB.txt");
f = File.open(savedir +"measurementsRGB.txt");


// option: save measurementsRGB.txt inside images folder
// f = File.open(dir+"measurementsRGB.txt");


// option: to save measurements.txt inside to user-specified location
// uncomment next two lines and change the mydir path to the path on your computer
// mydir = "/Users/the_user/";
// f = File.open(mydir+"measurementsRGB.txt");


//write headers to the file
print(f, "filename" + "\t"  + "imageID" + "\t" + "red_median" + "\t" + "red_stdev" + "\t"
+"green_median" + "\t" +"green_stdev" +"\t" + "blue_median" + "\t" +"blue_stdev" +
"\n");


setBatchMode(true);


run("Set Measurements...", "  standard median display redirect=None decimal=2");


for (i=0; i<list.length; i++) {
        path = dir+list[i];
        open(path);
        id=getImageID;
```

```
            // if image format is 24-bit RGB, measure it
        if (bitDepth==24) {
                image_ID = i + 1;
                print(image_ID + "/" + list.length + "\t" + list[i]);

                run("RGB Stack");
                run("Convert Stack to Images");

                selectWindow("Red");
                //rename(list[i] + "/brightness");
                run("Measure");
                red_median = getResult("Median");
                red_stdev = getResult("StdDev");
                close(); // close the active image - "Brightness")

                selectWindow("Green");
                //rename(list[i] + "/saturation");
                run("Measure");
                green_median = getResult("Median");
                green_stdev = getResult("StdDev");
                close(); // close the active image - "Saturation")

                selectWindow("Blue");
                //rename(list[i] + "/hue");
                run("Measure");
                blue_median = getResult("Median");
                blue_stdev = getResult("StdDev");
                close(); // close the active image - "Hue")
        }
        // if image format is not 24-bit RGB, print the name of the file without saving
measurements
        else
                print("wrong format:" + "\t" + list[i]);
        // write image measurements to measurements.txt
        print(f, list[i] + "\t" + image_ID + "\t" + red_median + "\t" + red_stdev + "\t" +
green_median + "\t" + green_stdev + "\t" + blue_median + "\t" + blue_stdev + "\n");
}
// setBatchMode(false);
```

Table 5.3. *ImageMeasure-RGB. Macro script for extracting RGB colors*

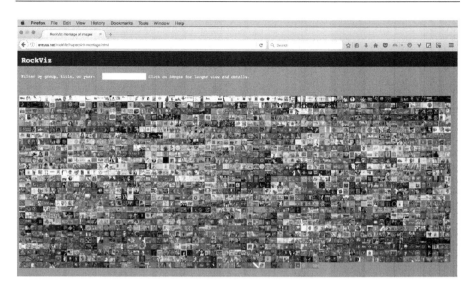

Figure 5.11. *Interactive image mosaic of 2000 rock album covers.*
For a color version of the figure, see www.iste.co.uk/reyes/image.zip

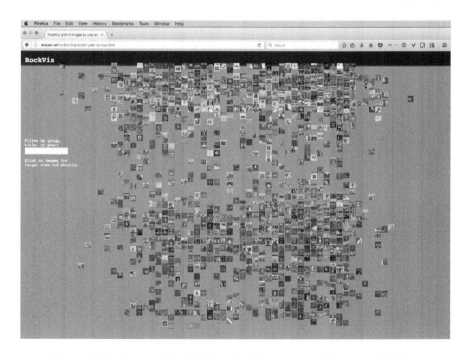

Figure 5.12. *Image plot of 2000 rock album covers. X = years; Y = hue.*
For a color version of the figure, see www.iste.co.uk/reyes/image.zip

An additional functionality I added was a text input filter. Given the amount of images, I found it useful to explore by typing a year, an artist name or an album title. To make the loading of images a little faster, I produced two versions of each image: one is scaled to 100 x 100 px. and the other to 500 x 500 px. The small version is used for visual representations and the larger appears when the user clicks on an image therefore allowing her to observe more details of a single cover. I originally used JQuery and the function getJSON to communicate with a JSON database, but the loading time is very slow for more than a few hundred images.

With the intention of producing different organizations of images and to eventually observe different patterns, I modified my original formulae. I explored some combinations of sine and cosine functions taking advantage of the fact that GREL supports trigonometric calculations. Figure 5.13 plots the formula $r2 = x2 + y2$; $x = r \cos(\theta)$; $y = r \sin(\theta)$ and Figure 5.14 plots the formula $r2 = x2 + y2$; $x = r \cos(\theta) * \cos(\iota)$; $y = r \sin(\theta) * \cos(\iota)$. Other variations are sketched in Figure 5.15.

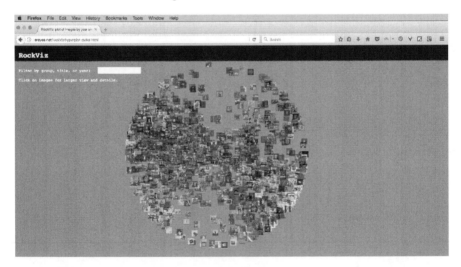

Figure 5.13. *Experimental radial plot of images. r2 = x2 + y2 ; x = r cos(θ); y = r sin(θ). For a color version of the figure, see www.iste.co.uk/reyes/image.zip*

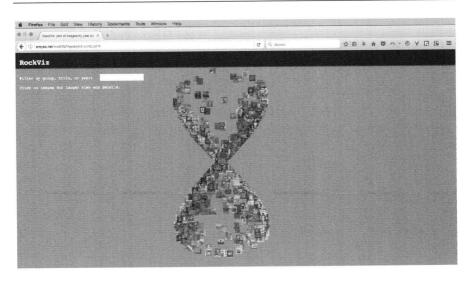

Figure 5.14. *Experimental radial plot of images.* $r2 = x2 + y2$; $x = r\cos(\theta)$ * $\cos(\iota)$; $y = r\sin(\theta)$ * $\cos(\iota)$. *For a color version of the figure, see www.iste.co.uk/reyes/image.zip*

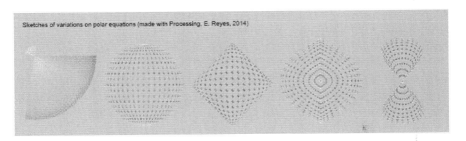

Figure 5.15. *Sketches of polar plot variations. For a color version of the figure, see www.iste.co.uk/reyes/image.zip*

5.4.4. *Esthetics and didactics of digital design*

With the more recent development of web graphics, the possibilities of HTML5, CSS3 and JavaScript facilitate the way in which we can approach data visualization. Within an educational context my endeavor has the intention to introduce digital humanities to undergraduate students. Indeed, it may be regarded from three angles: first, as the construction of tailored toolkits of digital methods for students; second, as a contribution to the analysis of material properties of cultural productions; and third, as a mid-term strategy to orient students towards design-based learning techniques.

The way in which the three perspectives connect is as follows: we consider the realm of cultural productions populated by music albums, films, comic books, TV series, video games, digital art, architecture, industrial design, etc. Now, with the emergence of various kinds of tools and scripts for analyzing media data (text, images, audio, etc.), we select and assemble several of them in a tailored toolkit for studying cultural productions. Then we use the toolkit as a teaching methodology in the classroom. In the mid/long-term, our intention is to move students from the use of tools (as it happens in undergraduate courses) to the creation and design of tools, services and processes (as it happens in postgraduate courses).

The analysis of cultural productions deals with tasks such as gathering, documenting, representing and exploring valuable data about forms, materials, contexts, techniques, themes and producers of these productions. The resulting visualizations are put together into what I call "analytical maps", which are helpful in the processes of identification of relationships, observation, comparison, evaluation, formulation of hypothesis, verification of intuitions, elaboration of conclusions and other humanities methods.

For example, a media visualization model might emerge from an abstraction of forms and layouts of web graphics, from simple HTML element positions to data and images. I coded an interactive version of the interface shown in Figure 5.16 (top), using exclusively HTML, CSS and jQuery. The GUI controller is implemented with the dat.GUI library[7], made available by the Google Data Arts Team. In the bottom picture, the same organization is generated from a data table saved in JSON format. This table contains 201 images of paintings by artist Paul Klee (http://ereyes.net/kleeviz/). We had previously extracted visual attributes with ImageJ: red, green, blue, hue, saturation, brightness, and some shape descriptors. Of course, I am conscious that Klee was a prolific artist whose entire production counts in the thousands; however, I limited myself to images available from the website wikiart.org.

---

7 https://workshop.chromeexperiments.com/examples/gui/

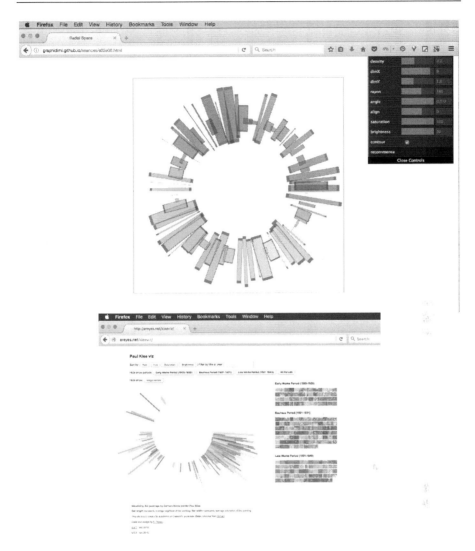

Figure 5.16. *Adapting HTML positions to media visualization. For a color version of the figure, see www.iste.co.uk/reyes/image.zip*

I present to students this and other examples in order to stimulate the exploration of different manners of using the same web technologies we employ in conventional websites. Among the original results, Figure 5.17

presents an experimental visualization made by three MA students in Interface Design. They chose to represent 609 comic magazine covers from Marvel in a vertical orthogonal view[8]. Each bar stands for a cover and its most prevalent color. Bars are positioned in a chronological order and clustered by season: spring, summer, autumn and winter. Other functionalities were proposed by students themselves: a color chart containing the 10 most common colors and hexadecimal color notations.

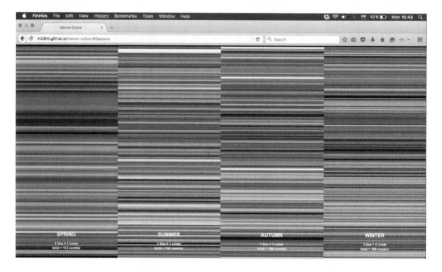

Figure 5.17. *609 Marvel comics covers by season, published between 2000 and 2015 (created by Blumenfeld, Mauchin and Lenoir). For a color version of the figure, see www.iste.co.uk/reyes/image.zip*

Other examples made with students are shown in Figure 5.18 and 5.19. The first one shows a simple implementation in CSS for an image slicing. Students of the MA Analysis of Digital Uses gathered pictures from actresses who won an Oscar between 2010 and 2016. With a simple right float position and shrinking the width value, the images are depicted in chronological order. When the user passes the mouse over an image, its size changes while showing a larger preview below the analytical map[9].

---

8 http://m2dimi.github.io/marvel-colors/#Home
9 http://ereyes.net/2017-london/oscars-dress-viz/

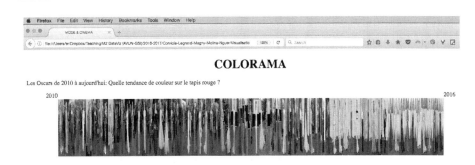

Figure 5.18. *120 dress photos from Oscar awards between 2010 and 2016 (created by Corviole, Legrand, Magny, Molina and Nguer). For a color version of the figure, see www.iste.co.uk/reyes/image.zip*

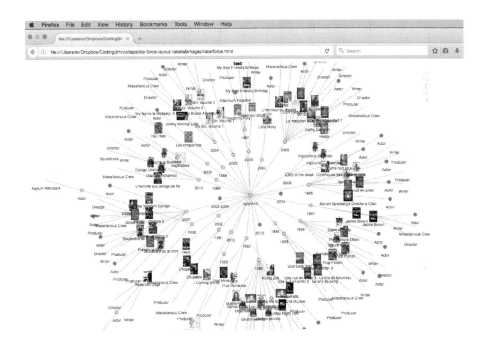

Figure 5.19. *D3.js force-directed graph with images. Created by J. Caignard. For a color version of the figure, see www.iste.co.uk/reyes/image.zip*

The third example presents a modification of a D3.js script. Similar to Figure 5.7, this visualization replaces nodes as circles with images themselves –in this particular case, movie posters from films by director Quentin Tarantino. My workflow to introduce and personalize D3.js examples relies on RAW Graphs[10], an open-source tool created by the DensityDesign Research Lab (Politecnico di Milano). Once students have constructed a database, RAW Graphs allows them to copy/paste the data to generate and personalize a static visualization. It is interesting to note that such visualizations can be downloaded as a compressed image (PNG), a vector image (SVG), and also as a data model in JSON format. Specifically regarding network graphical models, the output structure is an object containing two arrays: nodes and links. This data structure is the same employed in D3.js, hence students can easily personalize scripts from the examples by replacing the JSON file.

5.4.5. *Prototyping new graphical models for media visualization with images of paintings by Mark Rothko*

I have started working on media visualization with colleagues from other disciplines, most notably semiotics and information sciences. The Paul Klee visualization that I presented earlier was the subject of a communication at the congress of the International Association for Visual Semiotics held in Liège in 2014. Klee is a peculiar artist who has attracted semiotic analyses and thus my own visualization tried to put in perspective the different paintings analyzed within his complete production.

Another attractive artist for semioticians has been Mark Rothko. For this occasion, I prototype "Rothko Viz"[11]. I gathered 203 images of paintings from wikiart.org and followed the already discussed workflow for extracting visual attributes: shape measurements, RGB and HSB color modes together with a variety of statistical derivations (median, standard deviation, mean). The database quickly had 60 columns and I produced Principal Component Analyses (PCA) of those dimensions. Figure 5.20 shows a parallel coordinate visualization of the 60 data columns made with Mondrian, and Figure 5.21

---

10 http://rawgraphs.io/
11 http://ereyes.net/rothkoviz/

plots images according to the first two factors of the PCA, made with ImagePlot.imj. The main difference of plotting PCA values instead of, for example, years versus hue values as we did before is that images seem closer according to similarity. As we saw in section 4.2.4, PCA is a statistical method dedicated to dimension reduction and the numerical result derives from all the data columns.

Figure 5.20. *Parallel coordinate visualization of multiple dimensions*

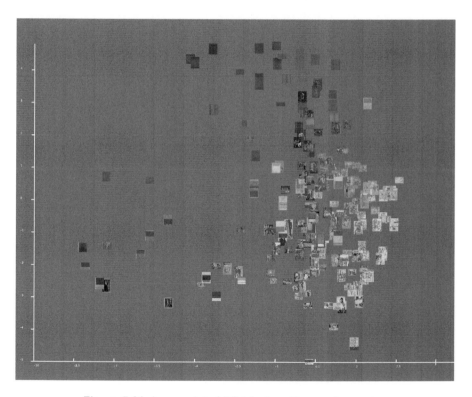

Figure 5.21. *Image plot of PCA factors. For a color version of the figure, see www.iste.co.uk/reyes/image.zip*

With the intention to produce new media visualization models, I explored plugins already available for ImageJ. Among such plugins, the Polar Transformer[12] (created by scholars E. Donnelly and F. Mothe in 2007) proves to be useful with our context. The idea is to apply a Cartesian 360 degree transform to an orthogonal view of a series of images. Figure 5.22 depicts an infographic in which I placed an image mosaic to situate a range of images within the polar plot.

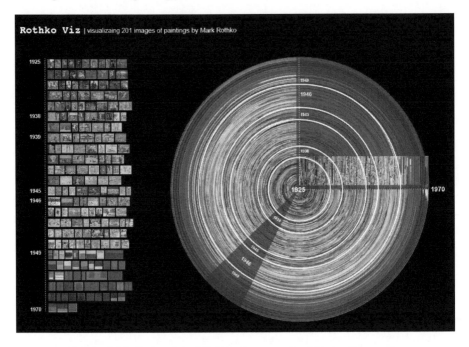

Figure 5.22. *Polar plot of Rothko images of paintings. For a color version of the figure, see www.iste.co.uk/reyes/image.zip*

Although it may seem rather abstract at first glance, above all because the image set does not contain an image sequence that would help to create a continuous discourse, the design of guides and labels might assist in completing the sense. To furnish one more example where radial plots can be pictured, let us come back to Figure 5.6 (visualization of Nirvana videos). If we apply our technique to both vertical and horizontal orthogonal views, we obtain the graphical patterns in Figure 5.23.

12 https://imagej.nih.gov/ij/plugins/polar-transformer.html

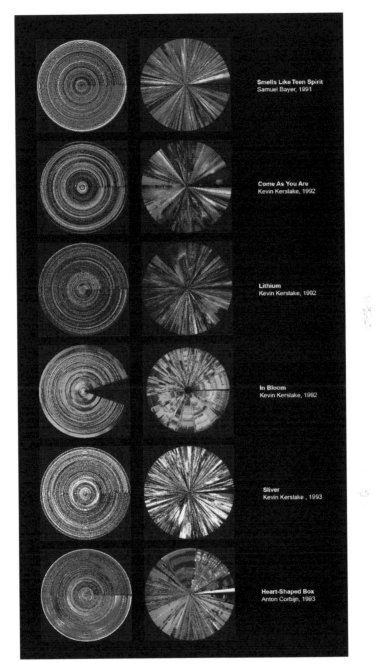

Figure 5.23. *Polar plots of Nirvana videography. For a color version of the figure, see www.iste.co.uk/reyes/image.zip*

One more model we introduced using Rothko images is the 3D image plot media visualization. In its first and foremost form, it is an extension of the 2D plot, but it now takes into account three different values for each of the three axes. The RGB model defines a cube, whose vertices map the relationships between red, green and blue: magenta, cyan, yellow, black and white. Another model that can be plotted in 3D is the HSB with a cylindrical form, where the top corresponds to the 360 degrees of the hue values, the height to the brightness and the distance from the centroid to the saturation. In ImageJ, it is possible to generate these visualizations with the 3D Color Inspector[13] plugin (developed by scholar K. Barthel in 2004). A simplified version only for RGB cubes is also available as a plugin for Firefox, the Color Inspector 3D[14] (developed by scholar David Fichtmueller in 2010). I developed a simple version of 3D color plots in Processing. Figure 5.24 shows these different versions.

The latest version of the prototype for 3D media visualization in web-based environments was an adaptation of the visualization engine by graduate student Mathias Bernhard [BER 16, pp. 95–116]. Although Bernhard's project has different research goals, I employed the basis of his engine using WebGL and three.js. For this prototype, I adapted algorithms and layouts to display 3D media visualization in three plot forms: the RGB color model, the HSV color model and the same algorithm I conceived for "Rock Viz" in Figure 5.14.

As a matter of fact, given that the algorithm has now been used in 2D and 3D graphical spaces, it can be formalized as follows:

Given the equation of sphere S as:

$\forall\, \theta \in [0, 2\pi],\ \forall\, \varphi \in [0, \pi]$

$x = x_0 + r \cos \theta \sin \varphi$

$y = y_0 + r \sin \theta \sin \varphi$

$z = z_0 + r \cos \varphi$

13 https://imagej.nih.gov/ij/plugins/color-inspector.html
14 https://addons.mozilla.org/en-US/firefox/addon/color-inspector-3d/

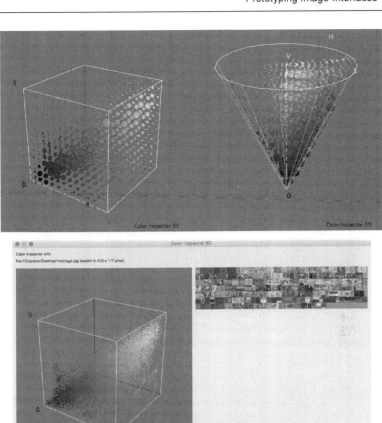

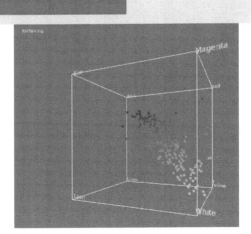

Figure 5.24. *3D plots of Rothko images. For a color version of the figure, see www.iste.co.uk/reyes/image.zip*

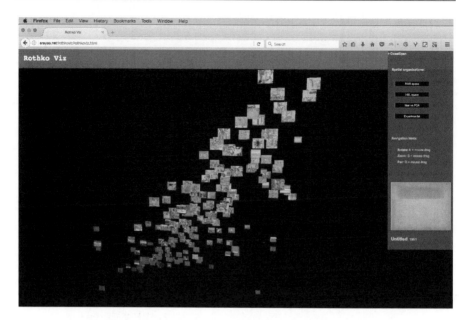

Figure 5.25. *Interactive web-based 3D media visualization. For a color version of the figure, see www.iste.co.uk/reyes/image.zip*

– *Algorithm Polar HSB*: Given a set values h = hue; s = saturation; b = brightness; where $0 \leq h \leq 360$; $0 \leq s \leq 100$; and $0 \leq b \leq 100$:

1) For each row in the database, get values representing h, s and b.

2) Plot values according to x, y and z in function SVn (Sphere Variation n).

3) Display source image file at point positions.

The variation SV1 being:

$x = x_1 + r \cos h\pi \cos s\pi$

$y = y_2 + r \sin h\pi \cos s\pi$

$z = z_3 b$

The graphical result is shown in Figure 5.26.

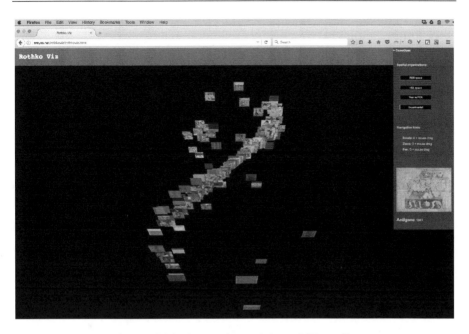

Figure 5.26. *Interactive web-based 3D media visualization of variation SV1 of algorithm Polar HSB*

To conclude this section about emerging web-based graphical models, I want to point to recent ideas on creating an image generator with iconic similarity to the late works by Rothko. Indeed, the idea is to employ the visual attributes existing in a determined painting style. Then, as the forms are basically abstract, we can describe basic spatial composition rules. Incorporating colors, combinations of tonalities and format (portrait or landscape), I wrote a simple generator of Rothko images. For me, the interesting aspect of this kind of visualization is that of synthesizing images proven to mislead the viewer or to evoke Rothko values; then, the descriptive rules are effective. Furthermore, it could be imagined that the generator might be useful in experimental tests and other cognitive and psychological applications. Figure 5.27 shows a screenshot of one of the Rothko generators.

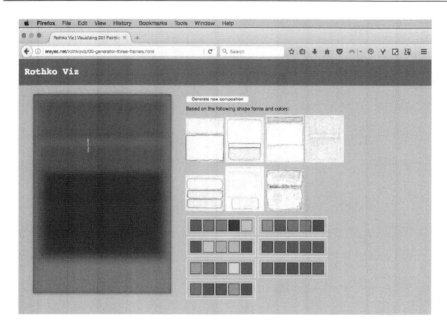

Figure 5.27. *Image generator based on visual attributes and composition rules. For a color version of the figure, see www.iste.co.uk/reyes/image.zip*

5.4.6. *Volumetric visualizations of images sequences*

In 2011, I used the term "motion structures" to describe my ongoing approach to exploring and interacting with motion media such as film, video and animations, as volumetric media visualization. My aim is based on the idea of representing spatial and temporal transformations of an animated sequence. For this kind of visualization, I am interested in representing the shape of spatial and temporal transformations that occur within the same visual space of the frame. The final outcome thus traces those transformations in the form of a 3D model. The mode of interaction with the 3D object allows for different ways of exploration: orbiting around, zooming in and out and even exploring the inside structure of the model.

Our process pays special attention to shapes above other visual features. From a technical point of view, to create volumetric media visualization, we use a script we wrote for ImageJ. Figure 5.28 depicts the overall workflow used to generate the 3D model that can be consulted in Table 5.4. Basically, an image sequence is manipulated as a stack and several operations are applied: converting to 8-bit format, subtracting background and transforming the stack as 3D shape in the 3D Viewer window. From the 3D Viewer, it is possible to save the result as a static image, as a 360° rotation movie and to export it as a mesh surface.

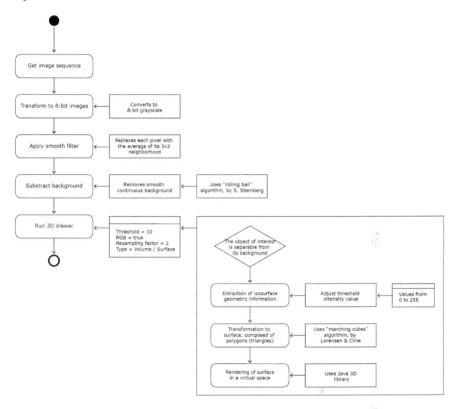

Figure 5.28. *Overall volumetric media visualization workflow*

The obtained 3D shape encodes the changes in the objects in a frame: the different positions, the movement traces and spatial and temporal relations. The way in which we can interact with an object is not limited to ImageJ. An exported 3D mesh can be manipulated in other 3D software applications such as Maya, Sculptris or MeshLab. Furthermore, it is also possible to export a motion structure for the web or to 3D print it; however, both techniques require destructive 3D model processing, i.e. reducing geometry by simplification, decimation or resampling. For technical records, a motion structure exported from ImageJ has an average of 500,000 vertices and more than 1 million faces, which is a very large amount compared with an optimized 2000-face model for the web, to be loaded with the library three.js.

```
// motionStructure-v2
// Description:
// This macro creates a digital 3D object from an image sequence
// It asks for a directory path, then impots all images, converts them to 8-bit, substracts
background, applies a smooth filter and runs the 3D viewer with some predefined
parameters
// To run the macro: open ImageJ, from the top menu Plugin, select Macros then Run...
choose the file from your local disk.
// For information on how to use imageJ, see
// http://rsbweb.nih.gov/ij/
// Created: October 29, 2015, in Paris.
// By: Everardo Reyes Garcia
// http://ereyes.net

dir = getDirectory("Choose image sequence");
list = getFileList(dir);

print("directory contains " + list.length + " files");

run("Image Sequence...", dir);

name = getTitle;
print(name);

run("8-bit");
run("Smooth", "stack");
run("Subtract Background...", "rolling=50 stack");

// Display as Volume (last parameter in 0). Goes faster if no immediate need to export as
OBJ
//run("3D Viewer");
//call("ij3d.ImageJ3DViewer.add", name, "None", name, "0", "true", "true", "true", "2",
"0");
//selectWindow(name);

// Display as Surface (last parameter in 2). 1 as threshold value... higher values mean less
shapes because only pixels above such threshold are taken into account.
// Description of parameters
// where 1 = threshold value, 2,3,4 = r,g,b, 2 = resampling factor, 2 = type
```

```
// Types: 0 = volume, 1 = Orthoslice, 2 = surface, 3 = surface plot 2D, 4 = Multiorthoslices
//run("3D Viewer");
//call("ij3d.ImageJ3DViewer.add", name, "None", name, "1", "true", "true", "true", "2",
"2");
//selectWindow(name);
// Display as Surface (last parameter in 2). 10 as threshold value... higher values handle
better large images sequences
run("3D Viewer");
call("ij3d.ImageJ3DViewer.add", name, "None", name, "50", "true", "true", "true", "2",
"2");
selectWindow(name);
```

Table 5.4. *MotionStructure-v2.imj script*

My first experiments with motion structures, initiated in late 2011 working on the shape of CGI visual effects sequences, started with the Paris fold-over sequence from the film "Inception" (Nolan, 2010). In November 2012, I produced a second motion structure: it came from the title sequence of the TV series Game of Thrones. I took a 5-second shot of a traveling pan of the fictional city of Qarth. The image sequence of the fragment has 143 images and they were staked and converted into a 3D model. For this project, I felt compelled to 3D print the model as a physical piece, a technique that can be called "data physicalization" (Figure 5.30). As it was required to reduce geometry for printing, the final object can be seen as a map of traces. We selected white plastic as printing material in order to convey the esthetics of rapid prototyping[15].

At the occasion of the re-new 2013 digital arts forum, I selected image sequences from seminal video artworks by Charles Csuri, Peter Weibel and Bill Viola. The importance of taking into account video as input media was its inherent characteristics in opposition to cinema. The introduction of video

---

15 These printed piece and process were included in the 3D Additivist Cookbook [REY 16, pp. 65–66], a call to push 3D printer technologies to their limits and into the realm of the speculative, the provocative and the weird and recently part of the exhibition "*Imprimer le monde*" at Centre Pompidou in Paris (March-June 2017).

and animation technologies for recording, processing and playing back moving pictures opened a wide range of possibilities for artists to explore and experiment with the esthetics of space and time. Contrary to cinema, video was more accessible, malleable and portable for artists. It was also easier and faster to watch and project the recorded movie. Finally, the look and size of the technological image was based on lines, reproduced at a different pace than film. While video art has been in itself a rhetorical movement against the traditional representation of moving images, motion structures of video artworks are at a second degree; an esthetization of the shape of time and space. Figure 5.29 shows a volumetric visualization of Bill Viola's "Acceptance" (2008), 02:03 minutes, equivalent to 1231 frames; Figure 5.30 of Charles Csuri's "Hummingbird" (1967), 02:10 minutes, 1295 frames; and Figure 5.31 of Peter Weibel's "Endless Sandwich" (1969), 00:38 seconds, 378 frames.

Figure 5.29. *Motion structure from the title sequence of Game of Thrones*

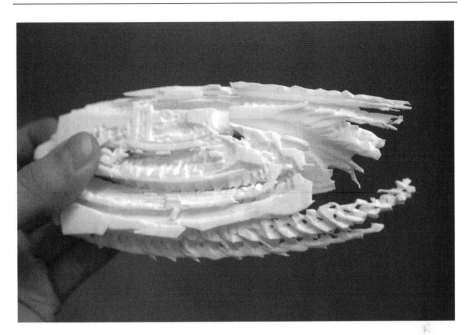

Figure 5.30. *3D print motion structure from the title sequence of Game of Thrones*

Figure 5.31. *Volumetric visualization of Bill Viola's "Acceptance"*

Finally, in a more recent prototype, I have applied the same technique to a series of image sequences from web page design. "Google Viz" contains almost 200 screen shots from the Google home page, from 1998 to 2015, obtained with the Internet Archive Wayback Machine[16] (Figure 5.32).

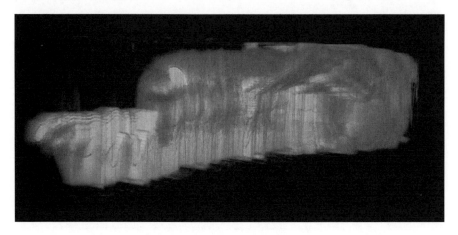

Figure 5.32. *Volumetric visualization of Charles Csuri's "Hummingbird"*

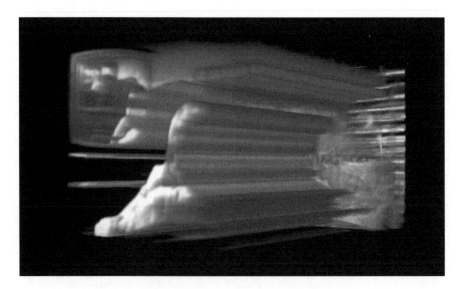

Figure 5.33. *Volumetric visualization of Peter Wibel's "Endless Sandwich"*

---

16 https://web.archive.org/web/*/google.com

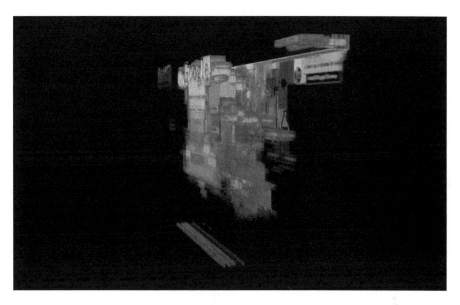

Figure 5.34. *Goggle Viz*

Conclusion

Into Visual Hacking

This book studies interfaces as images and images as interfaces. On the one hand, it considers the graphical properties of user interfaces as they appear on electronic screen. On the other hand, it also takes into account the image and graphical representations of symbolic data as a mechanism to interact and produce knowledge. As we have seen, this double perspective has become a prominent paradigm in sciences and humanities, which constantly allow their field to be assisted by software and computers. Moreover, with the growing interest in "data culture" and associated terms ("big data", "open data", "data visualization", "datification", etc.), the use of graphical methods to present and analyze data has grown exponentially.

The purpose of the book has been to unfold, or rather to have a brief glance at the layers underlying digital imagery. The intention of this endeavor has been to understand how and where graphical supports come from, and to question and make design interventions on them. This pragmatic approach exhorts not only to understand but also to produce new methods and graphical configurations.

The methodology chosen to uncover the intricate layers of digital imagery complexity has followed a rather linear model of semiotic inspiration that goes from signs to texts to objects to practices and then to strategies. At the bottom layer, the most basic and abstract entities are situated, which create meaning: signs. For digital images, the main signs are similar to other digital media: data types, data structures and algorithms. Then, the text level is determined by programming languages, graphical interfaces and file formats. At the object level, the most concrete materiality of digital image is seized: screens, cameras and printing devices.

In the last two chapters, the book offers examples of how the layers of elements are practiced. First, in Chapter 4, a historical review of media software is given to locate how interfacial arrangements and interfacial logics appear. Second, in Chapter 5, I document and discuss my own productions and graphical interventions within a scientific and educational context.

It is clear that more work needs to be done. Some levels demand to be unfolded more deeply and appreciated in full detail. This task became too large for the scope of the present book because of issues of time and length. Nonetheless, I hope in its actual form, this study serves as an overall guide to identify entry points and potential connections between levels.

At the current state, I want to conclude by pointing to some exciting developments and clues for future projects, a series of practices that cover what I call "visual hacking", allowing movement and flowing from one level to another, to use and re-use techniques from one visual domain into another, to construct or intervene on optical devices and to gain awareness that images are delimited by greater layers of technical, social and political complexities that have to be considered.

Non-visible wave visualization

In section 1.1.1, the electromagnetic spectrum helped us to situate visible light among other types of wave radiation: (in decreasing magnitude order) gamma, X-ray, ultraviolet, infrared, T-ray, microwave and radio waves.

Regarding gamma rays, image examples can be found in astrophysics. For example, the popular images captured with the Energetic Gamma Ray Experiment Telescope (EGRET), specially the gamma-ray sky maps, are well known[1]. For X-ray, UV and infrared, museums and professional institutions have produced techniques based on such waves that allow for

---

1 https://heasarc.nasa.gov/docs/cgro/images/epo/gallery/skymaps/index.html

analyzing a painting differently. For example, X-radiography penetrates the paint layers and might uncover previous sketches by an artist[2]. Finally, for radio wave and Wi-Fi range waves, artist Nickolay Lamm, for example, produced in 2013 a series of photographs where the viewer can imagine the size, color and shape of signals[3].

Nanoscale

It was discussed in section 2.2.1 that the passage from binary code to data types is the departing point in our study. It was mentioned that we could go deeper into electronic operations if we place our interest in circuits and how signals behave among digital components. In section 4.2.6.2, we explored graphical representations of circuit components. Continuing the reduction of scale several steps further, we could also go into the details of electrons and other subatomic particles (recall section 1.1.1): properties of quantum information (qubit systems) such as parallelism, entanglement, interference or superposition, or nanophotonics and its applications (plasmonic nanolasers, nanostructure light-emitting diodes, photonic crystal nanowires, nanostructured waveguides, thin films with a negative refractive index, anti-reflection with nanostructures for solar cells, high-sensitivity plasmonic biosensors, etc. [LEE 15, p. vii]), to mention some examples. At this level, we could find new representation models of probably new electronic components that go beyond binary oppositions.

Exotic data structures, esoteric languages and obfuscated code

In section 2.3.2, we saw different data structures that prove efficient at handling and storing visual information. If we take, for example, a series of objects within a digital world, we typically have a scene graph containing the objects. However, it is common to store the same data scene in several different structures, for example, "a list of characters in the world for

---

2 The Art Institute of Chicago has elaborated examination techniques applied to the work of painter Pablo Picasso: UV light, X-rays and infrared reflectography. More info at: http://www.artic.edu/collections/conservation/revealing-picasso-conservation-project/examination-techniques

3 http://nickolaylamm.com/art-for-clients/what-if-you-could-see-wifi/

efficient iteration during Artificial Intelligence simulation, a hash grid for collision detection, and a BSP tree for rendering them" [HUG 14, p. 1102]. As graphics programs evolve and differ in their needs, new structures can also be designed. Sometimes called *exotic data structures*, because they combine simpler data structures or data types in different manners required for very particular tasks. An example, applicable to visual information, would be the left-leaning red–black (LLRB) tree, as it might provide "a fast priority queue for a large data set" [HUG 14, p. 1102], others could be the smushed list, the unlinked list and search-bush[4]. The manner in which we can design and implement new data structures depends on the programming language we use.

While the customization of data structures to achieve a specific goal might seem exotic to some users, programming languages may also be created as means of political, artistic and individual expression. Esoteric languages like Piet, Haifu, Chef, among many other languages, algorithms and operating systems emphasize the expressive aspect of enunciation. For example, in Piet, the code is considered itself a piece of modern art inspired by painter Piet Mondrian; in Haifu, the language is based on Eastern philosophy; and, in Chef, programs produce kitchen recipes[5].

But we do not have to use an esoteric language to intentionally signify the difficult of understanding code (or at least the expected ease championed by commercial discourses). The practice of obfuscated code suggests that "coding can resist clarity and elegance to strive instead for complexity... making the familiar unfamiliar" [MON 08, p. 198]. Thus, examples of such code can be found in the work of beginners who misspelled or wrote erroneous yet executable lines of code. Indeed, for some experimented programmers, the way in which JavaScript handles data types and structures has led to thinking of fragments of code as incomprehensible or unpredictable.

---

4 As proposed by blogger Leigh Simpson in https://blog.simpleigh.com/2012/10/exotic-data-structures/. A larger list of data structures can be found at: https://en.wikipedia.org/wiki/List_of_data_structures

5 A list is available online: http://www.dangermouse.net/esoteric/

Speculative and critical software

Following media theorist Matthew Fuller, in terms of "speculative software" software simulates ideology. In this respect, all software components, from the most abstract to the most concrete, figure as simulations that can be interrogated and questioned. Speculative software would be software that reveals its processes as it enacts them: "What characterizes speculative work in software is, first, the ability to operate reflexively upon itself and the condition of being software (...) to make visible the dynamics, structures, regimes, and drives of each of the little events which it connects to. Second, (...) to make the ready ordering of data, categories, and subjects spasm out of control. Third, it is to subject the consequences of these first two stages to the havoc of invention" [FUL 03, p. 32]. For any speculative effort on software, it is, once again, necessary to go further down the GUI.

As we mentioned, one of the main departing point of thinking differently about our graphical interfaces and interactive systems is to keep considering them as fulfilling a need of some imaginary user. Users may not have needs. Users may not have a determined goal or information to obtain from a system. What happens if we think about users as "wanderers", or as "specialized researchers", or as tourists in a new city, trying to understand differences and culture. Speculative software would then satisfy more fuzzy and general objectives. Which lessons can we learn from here? How can we formalize an interface with this scenario in mind?

The relationship between art, design and technology can be observed from the standpoint of disruption and esthetic provocations. The importance of fostering such practices is to challenge traditional movements toward standardization and sustainable perfection of society. Computers and code, however, hold a human imprint, which is charged with questions that art and philosophy can speculate on. For example, my project "Disrupting 3D models" is a small application made with processing with the intention of opening an external 3D model (STL format) and rendering its geometry in three different modes: quads, triangles and points. The application proposes three parameters to disrupt the geometric composition following semi-stochastic procedures. The results are chaotic 3D meshes of the original model; it is a non-figurative approach to 3D models that drives attention to the unstable and material part of digital media.

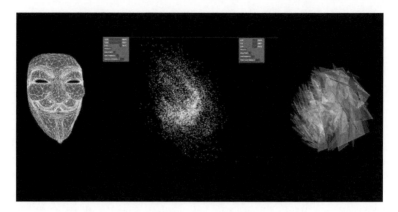

Figure 1. *Disrupting 3D models. Three geometric configurations of the same 3D object. For a color version of the figure, see www.iste.co.uk/reyes/image.zip*

New directions for graphical supports

At the moment of writing these words, machine and deep learning are trying to consolidate themselves as prominent contemporary fields of research, not only in visual computing (via machine vision, for example) but also in experimental psychology (to test supervised and unsupervised learning algorithms) and next-gen user interfaces.

Perhaps Google is the enterprise that has made the most of publicity from their research advances. They have made publicly available programming libraries such as TensorFlow[6], and datasets generated with their own social doodling projects such as Quick Draw[7].Moreover, machine intelligence has been applied to automatically detect similarities among tens of thousands of art images in the form of artistic experiments[8].

At different stages and moments, the emergence of new interface paradigms has been advocated for some time now: natural, ambient, conversational and intelligent, to mention a few examples. While it is clearly promising to fusion developments in speech recognition and machine learning, we also believe information will always be ultimately displayed on graphical supports. Voice commands and body gestures might be replicated

6 https://www.tensorflow.org/

7 https://quickdraw.withgoogle.com/

8 https://artsexperiments.withgoogle.com

by graphical navigational functionalities while returning visual feedback. In ambient intelligence and hypercities, the graphical supports might be projected onto physical objects or perhaps simulated into VR devices. For those scenarios to become widespread, we also believe more research is still required in 3D interfaces[9] and in higher spatial dimensions (using non-Euclidean geometry or 4D).

Anyone who is interested in taking charge in the upcoming challenges and producing new visual methods and graphical supports, let's not be discouraged by the complexity of levels studied in this book. Hand-drawn designs and self-made sculptures have proven versatile and powerful aids to thinking outside the box of delimited software functionalities. As we saw with data visualization precursors, this is also valid for post-digital comers[10]. All fields are invited to collaborate (anthropology, literature, archaeology, documentation and archival, game studies, religious studies, chemistry, biology, cognitive science, etc.) and, as it often occurs elsewhere, the most important step is the first one, as long as we have an idea of the surface support and the direction we might take. Let us then try to continue hacking digital visual information.

---

9 3D is used in the sense of the Experimental Visualization Lab at UCSB, USA: http://vislab.mat.ucsb.edu/

10 Check architect François Blanciak's catalog on 1001 building forms, all sketched by hand with the intention to go beyond computational possibilities [BLA 08].

Appendices

Appendix 1

Name	Latest version	License	Scope
After Effects	CC 2017.2 (Apr. 2017)	Adobe	VFX, motion graphics
AutoCAD	2018 (Mar. 2017)	Autodesk	Architecture
CMI	CMI-30AX	Fairlight	Audio synthesis, audio viz.
Dreamweaver	2017.1 (Apr. 2017)	Adobe	Code editor, web design
Grasshopper	1.0 (Apr. 2014)	McNeel	Procedural design
Illustrator	CC 2017.1 (Apr. 2017)	Adobe	Vector graphics
MadMapper	2.5.1	GarageCUBE	Video mapping
Mathematica	11.1 (Mar. 2017)	Wolfram	2D & 3D graphics
MATLAB	R2017a (6.10) (Mar. 2017)	Mathworks	2D & 3D graphics, data viz.
Max/MSP	7.2.5 (2016)	Cycling'74	Visual programming
Maya	2017 (Jul. 2016)	Autodesk	3D entertainment
Media Composer	8.5 (Jan. 2016)	Avid	Video editing
Modul8	2.9.2	GarageCUBE	VJ
NUKE	10.5v3 (Apr. 2017)	The Foundry	Compositing, tracking
Photoshop	CC 2017.0.1 (Dec. 2016)	Adobe	Image editing
Rhinoceros	5 (Feb. 2015)	McNeel	3D design
Storyspace	3.2 (Aug. 2016)	Eastgate	Creative writing
Substance Painter	2.6 (Apr. 2017)	Allegorithmic	3D painting

Tinderbox	7.0.3 (Apr 2017)	Eastgate	Spatial hypertext, Text viz.
Visual Studio	2017 (Mar. 2017)	Microsoft	IDE
Word	16.0.7967 (Apr. 2017)	Microsoft	Text processing
Unity	5.6 (Mar. 2017)	Unity Tech.	Game engine
ZBrush	4R7 (2015)	Pixologic	3D sculpting

Table A1.1. *Summary of commercial software applications*

Name	Latest version	License	Scope
Atom	1.16 (Apr. 2017)	MIT	Code editor
Blender	2.78c (Feb. 2017)	GPL	3D
CodeCity	1.4.3 (Dec. 2009)	Non-commercial	Software viz.
Context Free	3.0.10 (v42) (Jan. 2017)	GPL	Procedural design
Eclipse	4.6.3 (Mar. 2017)	Eclipse Public	IDE
Firefox	53 (Apr. 2017)	Mozilla PL	Web browser
Fritzing	0.9.3b (Jun. 2016)	GPL	Circuit design
Gephi	0.9.1 (Feb. 2016)	GPL/CDDL	Network viz.
ImageJ	1.51k (Mar. 2017)	Public domain	Scientific viz.
MeshLab	2016 (Dec 2016)	GPL	3D
NodeBox	3.0.45 (May 2016)	GPL	Procedural design
Open Refine	2.7-rc2 (Mar. 2017)	BSD	Data
Processing	3.3.2 (Apr. 2017)	GPL	Creative coding
Pure Data	0.47.1 (Jul. 2016)	BSD	Sound, graphics, visual prog.
QGIS	2.18.7 (Apr. 2017)	GPL	GIS
Rekall	1.0 (Nov. 2015)	GPL	Documentation
RStudio	1.0.136 (Dec. 2016)	AGPL and commercial	Data viz.
Sonic Visualizer	3.0 (Mar. 2017)	GPL	Audio viz.
Structure Synth	1.5 (2010)	LPGL	Procedural design
SuperCollider	3.8 (2016)	GPL	Audio synthesis
Twine	2.1.1 (Mar. 2017)	GPL	Creative writing

Table A1.2. *Summary of open-source software applications*

Name	Latest version	License	Scope
Sculptris	Alpha 6 (2009)	Pixologic	Digital sculpture
Tableau Public	10.2 (Mar. 2017)	Tableau	Data viz.
Web Designer	1.7.2.0222 (Feb. 2017)	Google	Web design

Table A1.3. *Summary of free commercial software*

Appendix 2

Name	URL	Scope
ColorBrewer	http://colorbrewer2.org/	Colors
contextFree.js	http://azarask.in/projects/algorithm-ink/	Context Free
CSS Filters	http://www.cssfilters.co/	css, filter, photo,
GLSL Sandbox	http://glslsandbox.com/	shader, graphics
I Want Hue	http://tools.medialab.sciences-po.fr/iwanthue/	color, generator, palette
IMJ	http://www.zachwhalen.net/pg/imj/	image plot, image slice
Nodebox port to JS	http://billmill.org/static/viewji/viewji.html	nodebox, generative, 2d
PhotoFrac	http://www.skeezix6.com/	fractals, filters, photo
RAW Graphs	http://rawgraphs.io/	Graphs, data viz.
SculptGL	http://stephaneginier.com/sculptgl/	sculpting, graphics, webgl,
Shadertoy	https://www.shadertoy.com/	glsl, shader, cgi
Stereogram Maker	http://www.easystereogrambuilder.com/3d-stereogram-maker.aspx	stereogram, images, upload, generator, 3d
Tridiv	http://tridiv.com/	css, 3d, figures
Voyant	http://voyant-tools.org/	text analysis, java
VVVV.js	http://lab.vvvvjs.com/index.php	visual programming, generative, creative
Web Colour Data	http://webcolourdata.com/	color, web, analysis, extraction

Table A2.1. *Summary of web-based tools*

Name	URL	Scope
Devotter Tools	http://devotter.com/	Data
jQuery Rain	http://www.jqueryrain.com/	jQuery libraries
Text Mechanic	http://textmechanic.com/	text, algorithms
Unheap	http://www.unheap.com/	jQuery plugins
Use Your Interface	http://useyourinterface.com/	GUI plugins

Table A2.2. *Summary of directories for web tools*

Name	URL	Scope
box2dweb.js	https://github.com/hecht-software/box2dweb	physics engine
chroma.js	https://gka.github.io/chroma.js/	colors
Colorify	http://colorify.rocks/	colors
ConvNetJS	http://cs.stanford.edu/people/karpathy/convnetjs/	deep learning, Neural Networks
Cubism.js	https://square.github.io/cubism/	real time viz.
Cytoscape JS	http://js.cytoscape.org/	graph, network
D3.js	http://d3js.org/	Data viz., svg
D3plus	http://d3plus.org/	data, data viz., d3, svg, charts
Easel JS	http://www.createjs.com/easeljs	2d, engine
HeatMap JS	http://www.patrick-wied.at/static/heatmapjs/	heatmap, web
Highlight.js	https://highlightjs.org/	text, highlight, code
HTML widgets for R	http://hafen.github.io/htmlwidgetsgallery/	R, data viz., graphs, d3
Impress Js	https://github.com/impress/impress.js	slides, presentation, demo
JQuery	http://jquery.com/	js, effects, data
JQuery UI	https://jqueryui.com/	ui
JSDOCed	http://jsdocedjs.org/	js, documentation
Matter.js	http://brm.io/matter-js/	physics, engine, 2d
Modest Maps.js	http://modestmaps.com/	maps
p5.js	http://p5js.org/	processing, canvas, graphics, creative
Paper.js	http://paperjs.org/	vectors graphics
Pex	http://vorg.github.io/pex/	3d, engine, plask

PhiloGL	http://www.senchalabs.org/philogl/	3d, webgl, graphics, games, creative, data
Pixi.js	http://www.pixijs.com/	2d, web, graphics, renderer
Plotly.js	https://plot.ly/javascript/	data viz.
Plumin.js	http://www.pluminjs.com/	font, text, typo
Polymaps	http://polymaps.org/	dynamic maps
Popcorn.js	http://popcornjs.org/	audio, video synch
Raphael.js	http://raphaeljs.com/	svg
Scene JS	http://scenejs.org/	3d, engine
Sigma.js	http://sigmajs.org/	Gephi
Sprite3D	http://minimal.be/lab/Sprite3D/	colors, css, 3d
SVG JS	http://svgjs.com/	2d, svg
TensorFlow	https://www.tensorflow.org/	neural network, data flow, machine intelligence
Three.js	http://threejs.org/	3D graphics
Toxiclibs.js	http://haptic-data.com/toxiclibsjs	geometry, generative, processing
Two.js	https://jonobr1.github.io/two.js/	2D canvas, svg
Vega.js	https://trifacta.github.io/vega/	Canvas, HTML5, JSON
Visjs	http://visjs.org/	data viz., 3d, plot,
Visual sedimentation	http://www.visualsedimentation.org/	real time viz.
ViziCities	https://github.com/UDST/vizicities	maps, geo, location
XeoGL	http://xeogl.org/	3d, engine

Table A2.3. *Summary of JavaScript, CSS and HTML libraries*

Name	Creator	URL
A Visual Introduction to Machine Learning	T. Chu	http://www.r2d3.us/visual-intro-to-machine-learning-part-1/
Arclight	Arclight Software Development Team	http://projectarclight.org/
Baltigram	Cerrone, Manovich, Kalvo, Giovannini	http://www.baltigram.eu/
California's Getting Fracked	Faces of Fracking	http://www.facesoffracking.org/data-visualization/
Carta Histórica	Museo de Historia de Barcelona	http://cartahistorica.muhba.cat/
Charting culture	Schich, Martino	https://www.youtube.com/watch?v=4gIhRkCcD4U
Cinemetrics	F. Brodbeck	http://cinemetrics.fredericbrodbeck.de/
Close The Gap	Studio Metric	http://closethegap.studiometric.co/
Clues. Anomalies. Understanding	B. Latour	http://modesofexistence.org/anomalies/
Computers Watching Movies	B. Grosser	https://bengrosser.com/projects/computers-watching-movies/
Culturegraphy	Albrecht, Müller, Dörk	http://kimalbrecht.com/project/culturegraphy/

Every Noise at Once	G. McDonald	http://everynoise.com/engenremap.html
Forma Fluens	Martino, Strobelt, Cornec	http://formafluens.io/index.html
Good City Life	Quercia, Schifanella, Aiello	http://www.goodcitylife.org/#
Google Arts & Culture Experiments	Google	https://artsexperiments.withgoogle.com/#/introduction
Google Cultural Institute	Google	https://www.google.com/culturalinstitute/beta/u/0/
Graphics	The Wall Street Journal	http://graphics.wsj.com/
Graphics	Bloomberg Business	http://www.bloomberg.com/graphics
Gugelmann Collection	M. Bernhard	http://www.mathiasbernhard.ch/gugelmann/
Historiography	M. Stauber	http://histography.io/
Interaktiv	Berliner Morgenpost	http://www.morgenpost.de/interaktiv/
Life and death of data	Y. Loukissas	http://lifeanddeathofdata.org/
Marvel colors	Wall Street Journal	http://graphics.wsj.com/avengers/
Migration in the Census and in the News	Clever & Franke	http://seeingdata.cleverfranke.com/
Money Wins Elections	T. Chu	http://letsfreecongress.org/
Object:Photo	Moma NY	http://www.moma.org/interactives/objectphoto/#home
On Broadway	Goddemeyer, Stefaner, Baur, Manovich	http://on-broadway.nyc/
Pantheon dataset	MIT	http://pantheon.media.mit.edu/treemap/country_exports/IQ/all/-4000/2010/H15/pantheon
Personal website	B. Foo	http://brianfoo.com/
Personal website	J. Salavon	http://www.salavon.com/
Photogrammar	Yale	http://photogrammar.yale.edu/

Projects	G. Legrady	http://www.georgelegrady.com/
QuickDraw	Google	https://quickdraw.withgoogle.com/
See Also	Hatnote	http://seealso.org/
Selfiecity	Manovich, Stefaner, Tazdani, Baur, et. al.	http://selfiecity.net
Stadtbilder	M. Stefaner	http://stadt-bilder.com
The Exceptional and the Everyday: 144 hours in Kyiv	Manovich, Yazdani, Tifentale, Chow	http://www.the-everyday.net
The Origin of Species	B. Fry	http://benfry.com/traces/
Trump Twitter Insults	NY Times	http://www.nytimes.com/interactive/2016/01/28/upshot/donald-trump-twitter-insults.html
VideoVortex	R. Ochshorn	http://rmozone.com/videovortex9//#
Visualize the Public Domain	NYPL	http://publicdomain.nypl.org/pd-visualization/
World's Int. Trade	C. Hidalgo	http://atlas.media.mit.edu/en/

Table A3.1. *Summary of online exploratory data visualization projects*

Bibliography

[ADO 12] ADOBE, "Photoshop CS 6: JavaScript Scripting Reference", Adobe, San Jose, 2012.

[ALE 77] ALEXANDER C., ISHIKAWA S., SILVERNSTEIN M., *A Pattern Language*, Oxford University Press, New York, 1977.

[AND 97] ANDERSEN P., *A Theory of Computer Semiotics*, Cambridge University Press, New York, 1997.

[AND 04] ANDLER D., *Introduction aux Sciences Cognitives*, Gallimard, Paris, 2004.

[APP 85a] APPLE INC., *Inside Macintosh*, vol. I, Addison-Wesley, Reading, 1985.

[APP 85b] APPLE INC., *Inside Macintosh*, vol. III, Addison-Wesley, Reading, 1985.

[ARN 15] ARNOLD T., TILTON L., *Humanities Data in R*, Springer, New York, 2015.

[BER 98] BERNSTEIN M., "Patterns of hypertext", *Proceedings of the 9th ACM Conference on Hypertext and Hypermedia (HT'98)*, ACM Press, New York, pp. 21–29, 1998.

[BER 12a] BERGEN B., *Louder Than Words*, Basic, New York, 2012.

[BER 12b] BERNSTEIN M., *The Tinderbox Way*, Eastgate Systems, Watertown, 2012.

[BER 16] BERNHARD M., "Gugelmann Galaxy: an unexpected journey through a collection of Schweizer Kleinmeister", *International Journal for Digital Art History*, no. 2, pp. 95–116, Graphentis/Verlag, Munich, available at: http://journals.ub.uni-heidelberg.de/index.php/dah/article/viewFile/23250/27208, 2016.

[BOG 12] BOGOST I., *Alien Phenomenology*, University of Minnesota Press, Minneapolis, 2012.

[BOL 99] BOLTER J., GRUSIN R., *Remediation*, MIT Press, Cambridge, 1999.

[BOL 01] BOLTER J., *Writing Space*, Lawrence Erlbaum, Mahwah, 2001.

[BOS 08] BOSLAUGH S., WATTERS P., *Statistics in a Nutshell*, O'Reilly, Sebastopol, 2008.

[BOU 17] BOUHAÏ N., SALEH I., *Internet of Things: Evolutions and Innovations*, ISTE, London and John Wiley & Sons, New York, 2017.

[BUR 09] BURGER W., BURGE M., *Principles of Digital Image Processing: Core Algorithms*, Springer, London, 2009.

[BUS 07] BUSBEA L., *Topologies*, MIT Press, Cambridge, 2007.

[CHE 17] CHEN C., JAYARAMAN D., SHA F. *et al.*, "Divide, share, and conquer: multi-task attribute learning with selective sharing", in FERIS R., LAMPERT C., Parikh D. (eds), *Visual Attributes*, Springer, Cham, 2017.

[CHU 11] CHUN W., *Programmed Visions: Software and Memory*, MIT Press, Cambridge, 2011.

[COO 14] COOPMANS C., VERTESI J., LYNCH M. *et al.*, *Representation in Scientific Practice Revisited*, MIT Press, Cambridge, 2014.

[CRO 16] CROCKETT D., "Direct visualization techniques for the analysis of image data: the slice histogram and the growing entourage plot", *International Journal for Digital Art History*, no. 2, pp. 179–196, available at: http://journals.ub.uni-heidelberg.de/index.php/dah/article/view/33529/27217, 2016.

[DAN 02] DANDAMUDI S., *Fundamentals of Computer Organization Design*, Springer, New York, 2002.

[DE 05] DE SOUZA C., *The Semiotic Engineering of Human-computer Interaction*, MIT Press, Cambridge, 2005.

[DE 08] DE BERG M., CHEONG O., VAN KREVELD M. *et al.*, *Computational Geometry: Algorithms and Applications*, Springer-Verlag, Berlin, 2008.

[DEL 68] DELEUZE G., *Différence et répétition*, PUF, Paris, 1968.

[DEL 86] DELEUZE G., *Foucault*, Editions de Minuit, Paris, 1986.

[DEL 99] DEL BIMBO A., *Visual Information Retrieval*, Morgan Kaufmann, San Francisco, 1999.

[DON 03] DONOHO D., GRIMES C., "Hessian Eigenmaps: new locally linear embedding techniques for high-dimensional data", *Proceedings of the National Academy of Science*, vol. 100, pp. 5591–5596, 2003.

[DRU 09] DRUCKER J., *Speclab*, University of Chicago Press, Chicago, 2009.

[DRU 11] DRUCKER J., "Humanities approaches to graphical display", *Digital Humanities Quarterly*, vol. 5, no. 1, available at: http://www.digitalhumanities.org/dhq/vol/ 5/1/ 000091/000091.html, 2011.

[DRU 14] DRUCKER J., *Graphesis*, Harvard University Press, Cambridge, 2014.

[DUN 08] DUNNE A., *Hertzian Tales*, MIT Press, Cambridge, 2008.

[ECO 61] ECO U., ZORZOLI G., *Histoire illustrée des inventions*, Pont Royal, Paris, 1961.

[ELK 08] ELKINS J., *Six Stories from the End of Representation*, Stanford University Press, Stanford, 2008.

[EVA 15] EVANS B., FLANAGAN D., *Java in a Nutshell*, O'Reilly, Sebastopol, 2015.

[FER 13] FERSTER B., *Interactive Visualization*, MIT Press, Cambridge, 2013.

[FON 08] FONTANILLE J., *Pratiques sémiotiques*, PUF, Paris, 2008.

[FRA 15] FRABETTI F., *Software Theory: A Cultural and Philosophical Study*, Rowman & Littlefield, London, 2015.

[FRY 08] FRY B., *Visualizing Data*, O'Reilly, Sebastopol, 2008.

[FUL 03] FULLER M., *Behind the Blip: Essays on the Culture of Software*, Autonomedia, New York, 2003.

[FUL 08] FULLER M., *Software Studies: A Lexicon*, MIT Press, Cambridge, 2008.

[GAL 12a] GALLOWAY A., *The Interface Effect*, Polity, Cambridge, 2012.

[GAL 12b] GALLOWAY A., *Les nouveaux réalistes*, Léo Sheer, Paris, 2012.

[GAR 58] GARDNER M., *Logic Machines and Diagrams*, McGraw-Hill, New York, 1958.

[GIB 86] GIBSON J., *The Ecological Approach to Visual Perception*, Psychology Press, New York, 1986.

[GIE 13] GIEDION S., *Mechanization Takes Command*, University of Minnesota Press, Minneapolis, 2013.

[GLE 17] GLEIZES D., REYNAUD D., *Machines à voir*, PUL, Lyon, 2017.

[GOL 82] GOLDBERG A., FLEGAL R., "Pixel Art", *Communications of the ACM*, vol. 25, no. 12, ACM Press, New York, pp. 861–862, 1982.

[GON 08] GONZALEZ R., WOODS R., *Digital Image Processing*, Pearson, Upper Saddle River, NJ, 2008.

[GRA 07] GRAU O., *MediaArtHistories*, MIT Press, Cambridge, 2007.

[GRO 16] GROYS B., *In the Flow*, Verso, London, 2016.

[HEA 04] HEARN D., BAKER P., *Computer Graphics with OpenGL*, Pearson, Upper Saddle River, 2004.

[HEC 05] HECHT E., *Optique*, Pearson, Paris, 2005.

[HOF 85] HOFSTADTER D., *Gödel, Escher, Bach*, InterÉditions, Paris, 1985.

[HOO 14] HOOKWAY B., *Interface*, MIT Press, Cambridge, 2014.

[HUG 14] HUGHES J., VAN DAM A., MCGUIRE M. *et. al.*, *Computer Graphics: Principles and Practice*, Addison-Wesley, Upper Saddle River, 2014.

[KAH 11] KAHNG A., MARKOV I., HU J., *VLSI Physical Design: From Graph Partitioning to Timing Closure*, Springer, New York, 2011.

[KIT 10] KITTLER F., *Optical Media*, Polity, Cambridge, 2010.

[KNU 68] KNUTH D., *The Art Computer Programming. Volume 1: Fundamental Algorithms*, Addison-Wesley, Reading, 1968.

[KNU 73] KNUTH D., *The Art Computer Programming. Volume 3: Sorting and Searching*, Addison-Wesley, Reading, 1973.

[LAT 14] LATOUR B. "The more manipulations, the better", in COOPMANS C., VERTESI J., LYNCH M. *et al.* (eds), *Representation in Scientific Practice Revisited*, MIT Press, Cambridge, 2014.

[LEE 15] LEE C., *The Current Trends of Optics and Photonics*, Springer-Verlag, Heidelberg, 2015.

[LER 73] LEROI-GOURHAN A., *Milieu et technique*, Albin Michel, Paris, 1973.

[LÉV 98] LÉVY P., *Qu'est-ce que le virtuel?*, La découverte, Paris, 1998.

[LIM 11] LIMA M., *Visual Complexity*, Princeton Architectural Press, New York, 2011.

[LIP 13] LIPSON H., KURMAN M., *Fabricated*, Wiley, Indianapolis, 2013.

[LIS 03] LISCHNER R., *C++ in a Nutshell*, O'Reilly, Sebastopol, 2003.

[MAG 16] MAGEE P., "Metropolis", in REYES E., ZREIK K., CHATEL P. (eds), *Archiving and Questioning Immateriality: Proceedings of the 5th Computer Art Congress*, Europia, Paris, 2016.

[MAN 01] MANOVICH L., *The Language of New Media*, MIT Press, Cambridge, 2001.

[MAN 13a] MANOVICH L., "Media visualization: visual techniques for exploring large media collections", in GATES K. (ed.), *The International Encyclopedia of Media Studies. Vol. 6: Media Studies Futures*, Blackwell, Malden, available at: http://manovich.net/index.php/projects/media-visualization-visual-techniques-for-exploring-large-media-collections, 2013.

[MAN 13b] MANOVICH L., *Software Takes Command*, Bloomsbury, London, 2013.

[MAN 14] MANOVICH L., REYES E., "Info-aesthetics", in VEYRAT M. (ed.), *100 Notions for Digital Art*, Les Editions de l'Immatériel, Paris, 2014.

[MAN 16] MANOVICH L., "The science of culture? Social computing, digital humanities and cultural analytics", *Journal of Cultural Analytics*, available at: http://culturalanalytics.org/2016/05/the-science-of-culture-social-computing-digital-humanities-and-cultural-analytics/, May 2016.

[MAR 06] MARTELLI A., *Python in a Nutshell*, O'Reilly, Sebastopol, 2006.

[MAR 10] MARR D., *Vision*, MIT Press, Cambridge, 2010.

[MAR 11] MARTINEZ W., MARTINEZ A., SOLKA J., *Exploratory Data Analysis with MATLAB*, CRC Press, Boca Raton, 2011.

[MCL 03] MCLUHAN M., *Understanding Media*, Gingko Press, Corte Madera, 2003.

[MEI 13] MEIRELLES I., *Design for Information*, Rockport, Beverly, 2013.

[MIN 85] MINSKY M., *The Society of Mind*, Simon and Schuster, New York, 1985.

[MON 08] MONTFORT N., "Obfuscated code", in FULLER M. (ed.), *Software Studies: A Lexicon*, MIT Press, Cambridge, 2008.

[MON 16] MONTFORT N., *Exploratory Programming for the Arts and Humanities*, MIT Press, Cambridge, 2016.

[MOR 13] MORETTI F., *Distant Reading*, Verso, London, 2013.

[NAK 08] NAKE F., GRABOWSKI S., "The interface as sign and as aesthetic event", in FISHWICK P. (ed.), *Aesthetic Computing*, MIT Press, Cambridge, 2008.

[O'RE 05] O'REILLY T., "What is web 2.0: design patterns and business models for the next generation of software", available at: http://www.oreilly.com/pub/a/web2/archive/what-is-web-20.html, 2005.

[PAR 11] PARKER J., *Algorithms for Image Processing and Computer Vision*, Wiley, Indianapolis, 2011.

[PEI 98] PEIRCE EDITION PROJECT, *The Essential Peirce. Volume 2*, Indiana University Press, Bloomington, 1998.

[PET 13] PETERS B., PETERS T., *Inside Smartgeometry: Expanding the Architectural Possibilities of Computational Design*, Wiley, Chichester, 2013.

[PRE 12] PRESNER T., BURDICK A., DRUCKER J. *et al.*, *Digital Humanities*, MIT Press, Cambridge, 2012.

[PRE 15] PREECE J., SHARP H., ROGERS I., *Interaction Design: Beyond Human-computer Interaction*, Wiley, New York, 2015.

[RAS 00] RASKIN J., *The Humane Interface: New Directions for Designing Interactive Systems*, ACM Press, New York, 2000.

[REY 14] REYES E., "On media art software", *Proceedings of the 4th Computer Art Congress*, RIO Books, Rio de Janeiro, pp. 39–47, 2014.

[REY 16] REYES E., "Design by disruption", in MOREHSHIN A., ROURKE D. (eds), *The 3D Additivist Cookbook*, The Institute of Network Cultures, Amsterdam, available at: http://additivism.org/cookbook, 2016.

[REY 17] REYES E., BOUHAI N., *Designing Interactive Hypermedia Systems*, ISTE, London and John Wiley & Sons, New York, 2017.

[RUE 12] RUECKER S., RADZIKOWSKA M., *Sinclair, Visual Interface Design for Digital Cultural Heritage*, Ashgate, Surrey, 2012.

[RUS 11] RUSS J., *The Image Processing Handbook*, CRC, Boca Raton, 2011.

[SAC 06] SACK W., "Aesthetics of information visualization", in PAUL C., VESNA V., LOVEJOY M. (eds), *Context Providers*, MIT Press, Cambridge, 2006.

[SAC 14a] SACK W., "Image, nombre, programme, langage", in STIEGLER B. (ed.), *Digital Studies*, FYP Editions, Limoges, 2014.

[SAC 14b] SACK W., "Code and critical theory", *Les Entretiens du Nouveau Monde Industriel*, Centre Georges Pompidou, available at: http://danm.ucsc.edu/~wsack/ENMI2014/dec6.pdf, 2014.

[SCH 08] SCHREIBMAN S., SIEMENS R., UNSWORTH J., *A Companion to Digital Humanities*, Wiley-Blackwell, New York, 2008.

[SER 07] SERRES M., "Les nouvelles technologies: révolution culturelle et cognitive", *Les 40 ans de l'INRIA*, Lille, 2007.

[SHI 12] SHIFFMAN D., *The Nature of Code*, available at: http://natureofcode.com/, 2012.

[SHN 03] SHNEIDERMAN B., "Direct manipulation: a step beyond programming langues", in WARDRIP-FRUIN N., MONTFORT N. (ed.), *The New Media Reader*, MIT Press, Cambridge, 2003.

[SHR 13] SHREINER D., SELLERS G., KESSENICH J. *et al.*, *OpenGL Programming Guide*, Addison-Wesley, Upper Saddle River, 2013.

[SIM 69] SIMONDON G., *Du mode d'existence des objets techniques*, Aubier, Paris, 1969.

[SIR 87] SIROVICH L., KIRBY M., "Low-dimensional procedure for the characterization of human faces", *Journal of the Optical Society of America*, vol. 4, no. 3, pp. 519–524, 1987.

[SON 89] SONNESON G., *Pictorial Concepts*, Lund University Press, Lund, 1989.

[SON 94] SONNESON G., "Les rondeurs secrètes de la ligne droite", *Nouveaux actes sémiotiques: approches sémiotiques sur Rothko*, PULIM, Limoges, pp. 41–75, 1994.

[SON 08] SONKA M., HLAVAC V., BOYLE R., *Image Processing*, Thomson, Toronto, 2008.

[SON 12] SONNESON G., "Translation as a double act of communication", *Proceedings of the 11th World Congress of Semiotics of IASS*, Chinese Semiotic Studies, Nanjing, pp. 1–18, 2012.

[SPU 16] SPUYBROEK L., *The Sympathy of Things*, 2nd ed., Bloomsbury, London, 2016.

[STJ 07] STJERNFELT F., *Diagrammatology*, Springer, Dordrecht, 2007.

[SUT 03] SUTHERLAND I., "Sketchpad; a man-machine graphical communication system", in WARDRIP-FRUIN N., MONTFORT N. (eds), *The New Media Reader*, MIT Press, Cambridge, 2003.

[SZE 10] SZELISKI R., *Computer Vision*, Springer, Berlin, 2010.

[SZO 17] SZONIECKY S., BOUHAI N., *Collective Intelligence and Digital Archives: Towards Knowledge Ecosystems*, ISTE, London and John Wiley & Sons, New York, 2017.

[TAI 13] TAILLET R., VILLAIN L., FEBVRE P., *Dictionnaire de physique*, De Boeck, Brussels, 2013.

[TAN 10] TANAKA-ISHII K., *Semiotics of Programming*, Cambridge University Press, New York, 2010.

[TER 06] TERZIDIS K., *Algorithmic Architecture*, Architectural Press, Oxford, 2006.

[THO 05] THOMAS J., COOK K., Illuminating *the Path: The Research and Development Agenda for Visual Analytics*, IEEE Press, available at: http://vis.pnnl.gov/pdf/RD_Agenda_VisualAnalytics.pdf, 2005.

[TID 11] TIDWELL J., *Designing Interfaces*, O'Reilly, Sebastopol, 2011.

[TRE 94] TREU S., *User Interface Evaluation: A Structured Approach*, Plenum, New York, 1994.

[TUF 97] TUFTE E., *Visual Explanations*, Graphics Press, Cheshire, 1997.

[TUK 93] TUKEY J., *Exploratory Data Analysis; Past, Present, and Future (Technical Report)*, Princeton University, Princeton, 1993.

[TUR 08] TURBAK F., GIFFORD D., *Design Concepts in Programming Languages*, MIT Press, Cambridge, 2008.

[WAR 09] WARDRIP-FRUIN N., *Expressing Processing*, MIT Press, Cambridge, 2009.

[WIL 05] WILKINSON L., *The Grammar of Graphics*, Springer, New York, 2005.

[WIN 86] WINOGRAD T., FLORES F., *Understanding Computers and Cognition: A New Foundation for Design*, Addison-Wesley, Reading, 1986.

[WIN 96] WINOGRAD T., *Bringing Design to Software*, Addison-Wesley, New York, 1996.

[WIR 04] WIRTH N., *Algorithms and Data Structures*, ETH, Zurich, 2004.

[WRI 07] WRIGHT H., *Introduction to Scientific Visualization*, Springer, New York, 2007.

[ZEM 66] ZEMANEK H., "Semiotics and programming languages", *Communications of the ACM*, ACM Press, New York, 1966.

Index

N, O, P

R, S, V

Other titles from

in

Information Systems, Web and Pervasive Computing

2017

DUONG Véronique
Baidu SEO: Challenges and Intricacies of Marketing in China

LESAS Anne-Marie, MIRANDA Serge
The Art and Science of NFC Programming
(Intellectual Technologies Set – Volume 3)

REYES-GARCIA Everardo, BOUHAÏ Nasreddine
Designing Interactive Hypermedia Systems
(Digital Tools and Uses Set – Volume 2)

SAÏD Karim
Asymmetric Alliances and Information Systems:Issues and Prospects
(Advances in Information Systems Set – Volume 7)

SZONIECKY Samuel, BOUHAÏ Nasreddine
Collective Intelligence and Digital Archives: Towards Knowledge Ecosystems
(Digital Tools and Uses Set – Volume 1)

2016

BEN CHOUIKHA Mona
Organizational Design for Knowledge Management

BERTOLO David
Interactions on Digital Tablets in the Context of 3D Geometry Learning
(Human-Machine Interaction Set – Volume 2)

BOUVARD Patricia, SUZANNE Hervé
Collective Intelligence Development in Business

DAUPHINÉ André
Geographical Models in Mathematica

EL FALLAH SEGHROUCHNI Amal, ISHIKAWA Fuyuki, HÉRAULT Laurent,
TOKUDA Hideyuki
Enablers for Smart Cities

FABRE Renaud, in collaboration with MESSERSCHMIDT-MARIET Quentin,
HOLVOET Margot
New Challenges for Knowledge

GAUDIELLO Ilaria, ZIBETTI Elisabetta
Learning Robotics, with Robotics, by Robotics
(Human-Machine Interaction Set – Volume 3)

HENROTIN Joseph
The Art of War in the Network Age
(Intellectual Technologies Set – Volume 1)

KITAJIMA Munéo
Memory and Action Selection in Human–Machine Interaction
(Human–Machine Interaction Set – Volume 1)

LAGRAÑA Fernando
*E-mail and Behavioral Changes: Uses and Misuses of Electronic
Communications*

LEIGNEL Jean-Louis, UNGARO Thierry, STAAR Adrien
Digital Transformation
(Advances in Information Systems Set – Volume 6)

NOYER Jean-Max
Transformation of Collective Intelligences
(Intellectual Technologies Set – Volume 2)

VENTRE Daniel
Information Warfare – 2nd edition

VITALIS André
The Uncertain Digital Revolution

2015

ARDUIN Pierre-Emmanuel, GRUNDSTEIN Michel, ROSENTHAL-SABROUX Camille
Information and Knowledge System
(Advances in Information Systems Set – Volume 2)

BÉRANGER Jérôme
Medical Information Systems Ethics

BRONNER Gérald
Belief and Misbelief Asymmetry on the Internet

IAFRATE Fernando
From Big Data to Smart Data
(Advances in Information Systems Set – Volume 1)

KRICHEN Saoussen, BEN JOUIDA Sihem
Supply Chain Management and its Applications in Computer Science

NEGRE Elsa
Information and Recommender Systems
(Advances in Information Systems Set – Volume 4)

POMEROL Jean-Charles, EPELBOIN Yves, THOURY Claire
MOOCs

SALLES Maryse
Decision-Making and the Information System
(Advances in Information Systems Set – Volume 3)

SAMARA Tarek
ERP and Information Systems: Integration or Disintegration
(Advances in Information Systems Set – Volume 5)

2014

DINET Jérôme
Information Retrieval in Digital Environments

HÉNO Raphaële, CHANDELIER Laure
3D Modeling of Buildings: Outstanding Sites

KEMBELLEC Gérald, CHARTRON Ghislaine, SALEH Imad
Recommender Systems

MATHIAN Hélène, SANDERS Lena
Spatio-temporal Approaches: Geographic Objects and Change Process

PLANTIN Jean-Christophe
Participatory Mapping

VENTRE Daniel
Chinese Cybersecurity and Defense

2013

BERNIK Igor
Cybercrime and Cyberwarfare

CAPET Philippe, DELAVALLADE Thomas
Information Evaluation

LEBRATY Jean-Fabrice, LOBRE-LEBRATY Katia
Crowdsourcing: One Step Beyond

SALLABERRY Christian
Geographical Information Retrieval in Textual Corpora

2012

BUCHER Bénédicte, LE BER Florence
Innovative Software Development in GIS

GAUSSIER Eric, YVON François
Textual Information Access

LANGLOIS Patrice
Simulation of Complex Systems in GIS

MATHIS Philippe
Graphs and Networks – 2nd edition

THERIAULT Marius, DES ROSIERS François
Modeling Urban Dynamics

2009

BONNET Pierre, DETAVERNIER Jean-Michel, VAUQUIER Dominique
Sustainable IT Architecture: the Progressive Way of Overhauling Information Systems with SOA

PAPY Fabrice
Information Science

RIVARD François, ABOU HARB Georges, MERET Philippe
The Transverse Information System

ROCHE Stéphane, CARON Claude
Organizational Facets of GIS

2008

BRUGNOT Gérard
Spatial Management of Risks

FINKE Gerd
Operations Research and Networks

GUERMOND Yves
Modeling Process in Geography

KANEVSKI Michael
Advanced Mapping of Environmental Data

MANOUVRIER Bernard, LAURENT Ménard
Application Integration: EAI, B2B, BPM and SOA

PAPY Fabrice
Digital Libraries

Printed and bound by CPI Group (UK) Ltd, Croydon, CR0 4YY